DUNKIRK

DIE WEHRMACHT IM KAMPF

DUNKIRK

German Operations in France 1940

HANS-ADOLF JACOBSEN

With text by
DR. K. J. MÜLLER

Series editor:
MATTHIAS STROHN

CASEMATE
Philadelphia & Oxford

AN AUSA BOOK
Association of the United States Army
2425 Wilson Boulevard, Arlington, Virginia, 22201, USA

Published in the United States of America and Great Britain in 2019 by
CASEMATE PUBLISHERS
1950 Lawrence Road, Havertown, PA 19083, USA
and
The Old Music Hall, 106–108 Cowley Road, Oxford OX4 1JE, UK

Hardcover Edition: ISBN 978-1-61200-659-8
Digital Edition: ISBN 978-1-61200-660-4

A CIP record for this book is available from the British Library

Printed and bound in the United States of America

For a complete list of Casemate titles, please contact:

CASEMATE PUBLISHERS (US)
Telephone (610) 853-9131
Fax (610) 853-9146
Email: casemate@casematepublishers.com
www.casematepublishers.com

CASEMATE PUBLISHERS (UK)
Telephone (01865) 241249
Email: casemate-uk@casematepublishers.co.uk
www.casematepublishers.co.uk

Cover image: Propaganda companies of the Wehrmacht – the Heer and Luftwaffe. (Bundesarchiv,
Bild 101I-126-0310-08)

Contents

Translator's Note

The German Wehrmacht was composed of the three branches of service: Kriegsmarine, Luftwaffe and Heer. *Heer* is the German word for 'Army' in the sense of the national Army. 'Army Group A' for example is the translation into English of 'Heeresgruppe A'.

Lesser than Heer and Heeresgruppe in the military structure were the many army corps – 'XIV Armeekorps', 'V Armeekorps' and the numbered armies, '4. Armee', '6. Armee'.

The difficulty can be seen particularly in the translation of OKH (Oberkommando des Heeres = Army High Command) and AOK (Armee Oberkommando = Armee High Command), both of which occur frequently throughout the book. To avoid confusion therefore both will be referred to exclusively in acronym form.

Preface

In late May and early June 1940 a battle took place in northeastern France that had been, for many, unthinkable only a few weeks earlier: on 20 May armored formations of the German Wehrmacht reached the English Channel at Abbeville. This meant that the entire Allied Army Group 1, comprising 29 French, 22 Belgian, and 12 British divisions, with approximately 1.2m men, was encircled in arguably the biggest encirclement operation in the history of warfare. The Germans reduced the pocket step by step and this operation reached its climax in the battle of Dunkirk which raged until early June. When the weapons fell silent on the beaches of Dunkirk, the Wehrmacht had achieved an operational and even strategic victory: Belgium was defeated, and France was practically defenceless; she would not be able to hold out much longer and would surrender on 22 June. Finally, the British Army had been thrown back into the Channel and would not play a role on the continent for several years. The outcome of the entire campaign in the West had practically been decided on the beaches of the English Channel. And yet, the battle of Dunkirk has gone down in history – especially in Britain – as what can nearly be described as a British victory. How can this discrepancy be explained? The British succeeded in evacuating the bulk of their expeditionary force back to England – although they lost all of their equipment – and so the British Army did not vanish on the shores of the Channel. The Belgians and the French were less lucky and most of them fell into German captivity. But why did the Germans let the British escape? This question has been debated ever since the last British boats left the beaches of Dunkirk. Over the years, several views and arguments have been put forward; for instance, that Hitler did not want to humiliate the British, or that Hermann Göring had promised that the German Luftwaffe could give the British Army the coup de grâce.

The academic debate surrounding this topic was opened in Germany with the book that you, the reader, are currently holding in your hands in the English translation. It was published in 1958 in a series that covered many important battles of the war. Most of these volumes were written by former senior officers. This book on Dunkirk was not. It was written by a rising star on the German academic firmament, Dr (later Professor) Hans-Adolf Jacobsen. After his military service in World War II and five years in Soviet captivity as a prisoner of war, he went to university and gained his PhD with a thesis on the German plans for the invasion of the West in 1940. In 1969, he became a full professor at the University of Bonn and, for many years, he was one of the most prominent historians in Germany. The same can be said of his *adlatus*, who wrote the sections of this book on the Allied actions and reactions. Dr (later Professor) Klaus-Jürgen Müller in his later life became a doyen of the academic study of the period of National Socialism.

The fact that they approached the topic through their academic lens gives it a different perspective to that of many other books in this series. And yet they did not regard their arguments as finite. For the historian, sources are the spring of life and, in 1958, the authors did not have access to all the files required to write an all-encompassing history of the battle of Dunkirk. Many of the relevant sources had been requisitioned by the Allied powers in 1945 and, at the time of writing, were still being held overseas. It would be the task of future generations of historians to analyse these sources once they had been returned to Germany.

This means that there are gaps in the analysis and the authors were the first to acknowledge these – they do so in the foreword to the book. This begs the question: why is this book still relevant? It is relevant for a number of reasons: first, it shows the understanding of the battle of Dunkirk from a predominately German perspective as it was understood in the late 1950s. This in itself makes it a significant source. The most important aspect is, however, that the authors were able to utilise the knowledge and understanding of former German senior generals who had held important positions in 1940 – the names are listed at the end of the authors' foreword. So, albeit indirectly, the book offers a path into the mindset of the German military leadership in 1940 and the views and ideas that these officers had held in 1940. It is this fact in particular which makes the book relevant even today.

Dr Matthias Strohn, M.St., FRHistS
Head Historical Analysis,
Centre for Historical Analysis and Conflict Research Camberley

Senior Lecturer,
Royal Military Academy Sandhurst

Reader in Modern War Studies,
University of Buckingham

Foreword

'The correct historical account provides the harshest criticism.'

MOLTKE

The miracle of Dunkirk in 1940 will probably always be one of the most significant and fascinating research problems of World War II. The achievement of the Allies in retrieving 360,000 men of their expeditionary force from the Flanders Pocket was almost as brilliant as the planning and execution of the German offensive in the West itself.

National Socialist propaganda spoke of the 'greatest battle of destruction of all time' when proclaiming the first, undoubtedly astounding, victory on 4 June 1940, but after concluding the evacuation of their troops the British could claim with pride and satisfaction that despite the military defeat they had pulled off a success of unexpected enormity. This gave them not least that mental power of resistance which they maintained throughout the war to its victorious conclusion.

How could Dunkirk happen? Since 1945 many military men and historians have applied themselves to this question. The majority have come to the conclusion, based on their own first-hand experiences or insight gained from the existing sources, that this 'miracle' was primarily the result of the famous 'Halt Order' to the German panzers approaching Dunkirk (25 May 1940). As British historians have also demonstrated with justification, the importance of this order has been exaggerated up until now and a false conclusion drawn. In the light of more recent sources, very careful studies are being undertaken to determine the validity of the various hypothesesin this matter. German research is only now embarking on its attempts to place World War II on a scientific footing.

It has not been able to deal with Dunkirk 1940, the culmination and at the same time the conclusion of the first phase of the Western campaign, the consequences of which would lead Germany swiftly into diminishing political and military heights, in the framework of a large investigation.

At one point the research had only a limited selection of documents available to it (the Army and Luftwaffe archives are still to be found today – thirteen years after the war ended – in the United States and Great Britain!) and also lacked a detailed study of the antecedents of the campaign. As will be shown, these documents are an important pre-condition to understanding the whole problem of Dunkirk. We thank H. Meier-Welcker, the first German author to have dug deep below the surface with his research on the 'Halt-Order', and to whose pioneering preliminary studies the author feels indebted.

What has been particularly noticeable in the research on this subject hitherto is how most writers begin with an investigation of one area only, namely who gave the order to halt the panzers and motorized units, and what reasons played a role in the decision. Undoubtedly that is right provided that the investigation does not simply stop there. It is equally important to study what the order of 24 May 1940 actually said. What in it remains uncertain? Who decided when the fast troops should continue their advance; Hitler, the OKH, or Rundstedt, the then Commander-in-Chief of Army Group A? Furthermore, what occurred in the decisive days from 24 to 26 May 1940 on the Allied side, and why could the German leadership not close off the encirclement after 26 May in time to prevent the withdrawal of the enemy force which did not get fully under way until 27 May? And finally, what was the true significance of the Dunkirk incident for the future course of World War II?

The historical investigation which follows, and which is supplemented by comprehensive documentation on the 1940 campaign in the West – published by this author – (also appearing simultaneously from Musterschmidt Verlag, Göttingen) – is considered to be a *contribution* to the foregoing questions. It will throw light principally upon the most important decisions and policy measures of the senior commanders, on the Allied but especially on the German side – to a certain extent synchronous – and depict the general course of the first phase, rather than attempt to offer an operational study. For the latter purpose adequate sources are lacking and it will have to be put on hold until a more propitious time.

The fighting from 10 May to 22 May therefore appears only as a resumé based on the various war diaries. If the operations of the Luftwaffe seem to have been left on the sidelines, it is due mainly to the inadequate situation as regards the sources.

On the whole we believe we can provide the reader with a research result which, though undoubtedly still requiring many individual corrections, does give an approximately accurate picture of the true events surrounding Dunkirk in 1940. Moreover, in contrast to numerous postwar representations, it is based on a careful weighing of all currently available sources.

We show how many details in the existing literature have been presented incorrectly (though maybe honestly from the subjective point of view) or coloured, so that many legends remain to be discarded. It is no wonder, therefore, that most judgements are false, not to mention dictated by wounded vanity or personal motives. The majority of the works on Dunkirk, we maintain, can no longer hold their ground today when subjected to a critical examination by the historian.

As regards his own representation the author has made clear the basic principle: 'how very much the judgement afterwards, in contrast to the military commanders actually engaged in the fighting, can see behind the curtain between the two Fronts', giving objectivity, impartiality and unpretentiousness pride of place over those who had to act, 'in the uncertainty and friction of the fighting.' No lesser a personality than Moltke pointed to that when he wrote in 1861: '…it is endlessly more difficult to act than to judge in retrospect.'

For their reading through of the manuscript and offering advice and pointers I am especially grateful to:

Col-General* F. Halder
Col-General* H. Hoth
Col-General* H. Reinhardt
General of Infantry* G. Blumentritt
Luftwaffe General* Deichmann
General of Artillery* W. Warlimont

Lt-General* G. Engel
Colonel* Greffrath
Colonel Dr H. Meier-Welcker
Professor Dr H. Gackenholz.

My co-worker Dr K. J. Müller (Hamburg) who authored all chapters relating to the Allied operational measures expresses his thanks above all for their valuable suggestions to:

Colonel* Goutard (Paris)
J. Venwelkenhuyzen (Brussels)
(The asterisk* following the rank in the lists above indicates retired status.)

Hans-Adolf Jacobsen
Koblenz-Pfaffendorf, August 1958

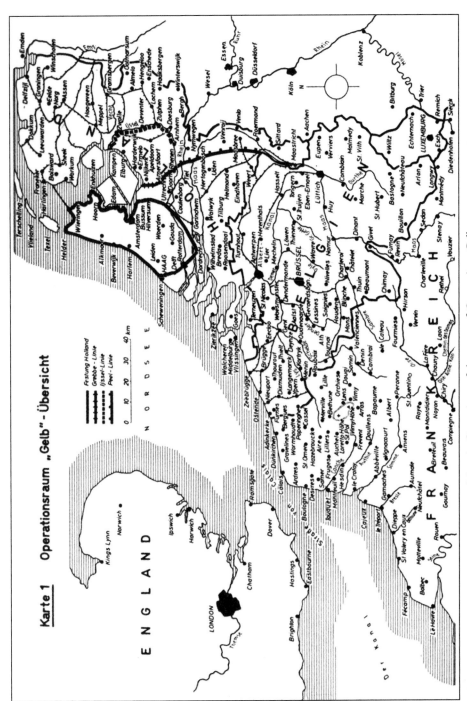

Map 1: Overview of the area of Operation *Gelb*

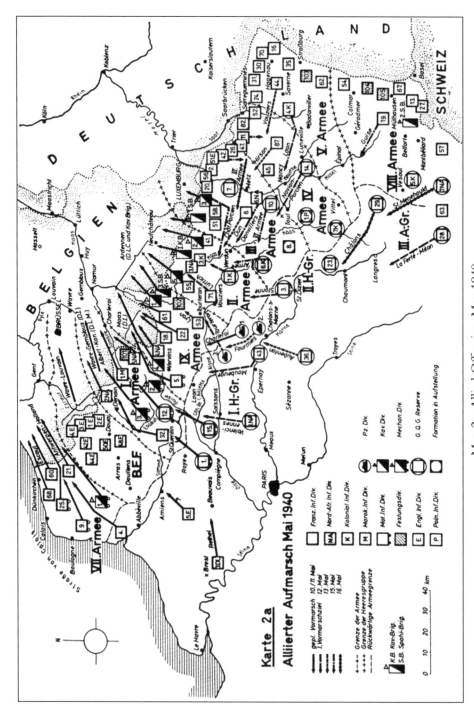

Map 2a: Allied Offensive, May 1940

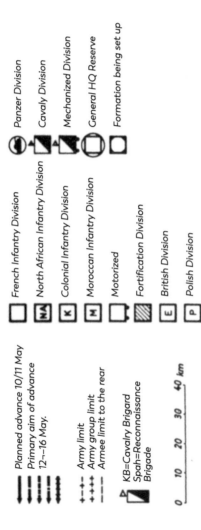

Planned advance 10/11 May

Primary aim of advance 12–16 May.

Army limit

Army group limit

Armee limit to the rear

KB=Cavalry Brigard
Spah=Reconnaissance Brigade

0   10   20   30   40 km

French Infantry Division

North African Infantry Division

Colonial Infantry Division

Moroccan Infantry Division

Motorized

Fortification Division

British Division

Polish Division

Panzer Division

Cavaly Division

Mechanized Division

General HQ Reserve

Formation being set up

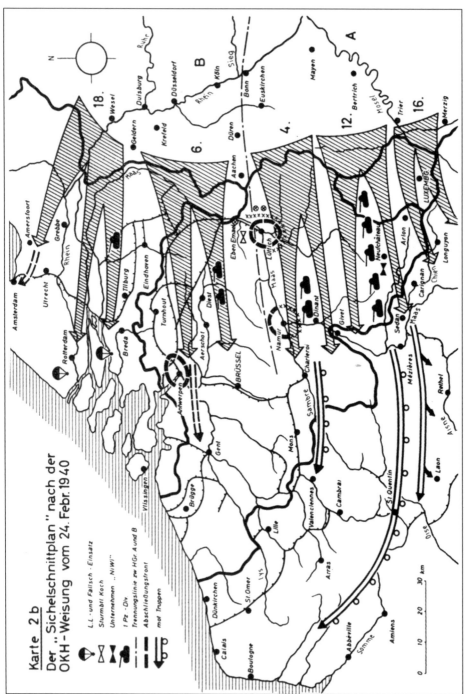

Map 2b: 'Fall Gelb'/Sichelschnittplan according to the orders of OKH of 24 February 1940

Airborne Infantry & Paratroop Operations

Assault Batallion Koch

Operation "Niwi"

1.Panzer Div.

Dividing Line between Army Groups A and B

Encirclement Front

Motorized troops

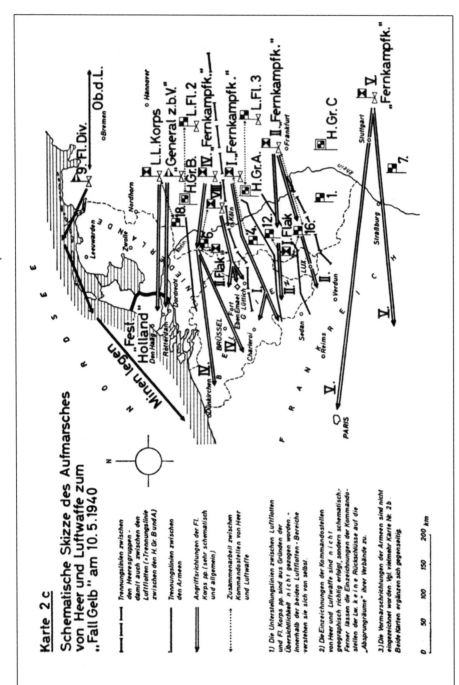

Map 2c: Schematic sketch of the Heer and Luftwaffe Advance for 'Fall Gelb', 10 May 1940

Dividing line between Army Groups A and B and also between the Air Fleets

Dividing line between the (German) Armees.

Direction of attack by Flying Korps (very schematic and general)

Cooperation between Army and Luftwaffe command centres

(1) The lines of assignment between Air Fleets and Flying Korps are not included for lack of clarity, within the two Air Fleet regions they are self-evident.

(2) The locations of the Army and Luftwaffe command centres are not geographically exact but schematic; no conclusions should be drawn from them regarding "drop zones" of Luftwaffe units.

(3) The directions of advance of the Armees have not been included, see instead map 2b. Maps 2b and 2c are complementary.

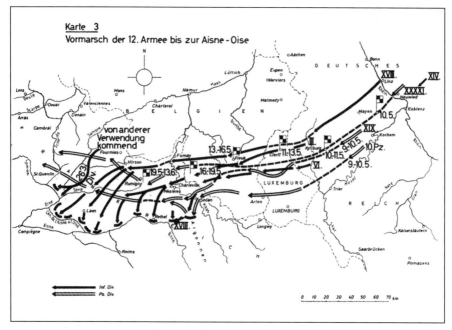

Map 3: Gains of 12. Armee up to Aisne–Oise

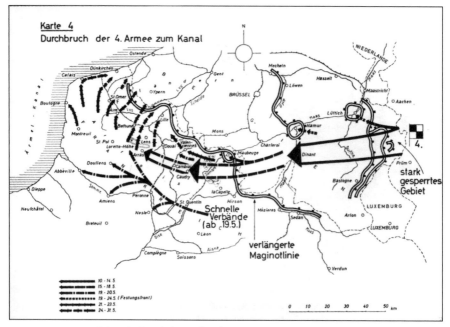

Map 4: Breakthrough of 4. Armee to the Channel

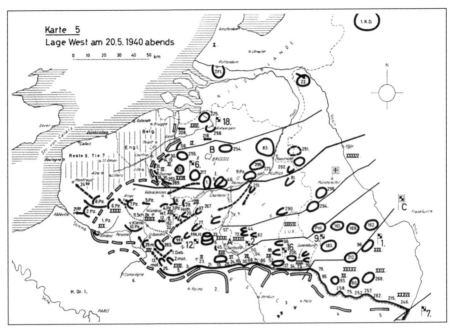

Map 5: Situation on the evening of 20 May 1940

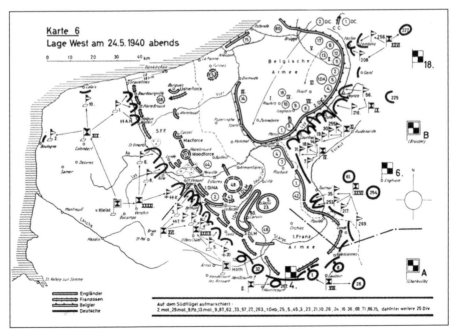

Map 6: Situation on the evening of 24 May 1940
*Moving up on the southern flank/wing … another 25 divisions behind

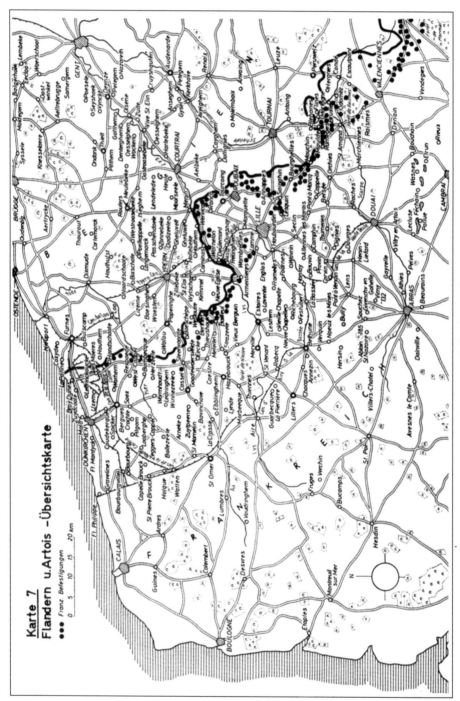

Map 7: Overview of Flanders and Artois

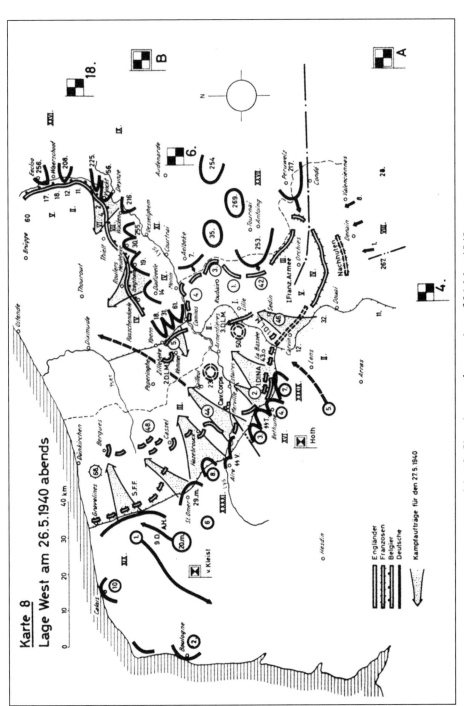

Map 8: Situation on the evening of 26 May 1940
★Battle missions for 27 May 1940

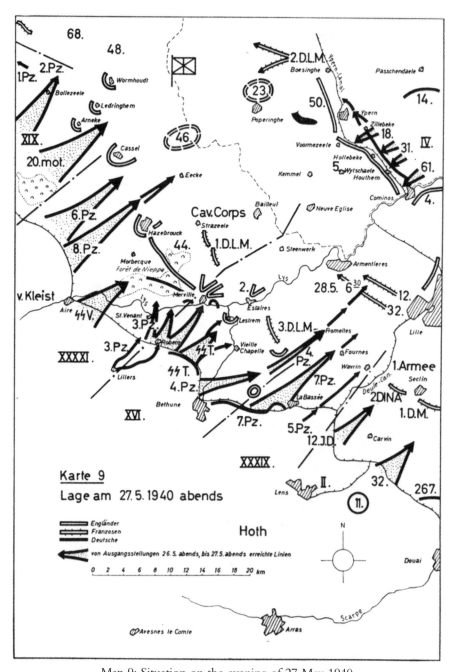

Map 9: Situation on the evening of 27 May 1940
*Exit positions from lines reached from evening of 26 May to evening of 27 May

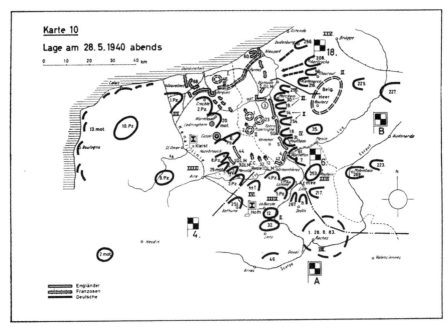

Map 10: Situation on the evening of 28 May 1940

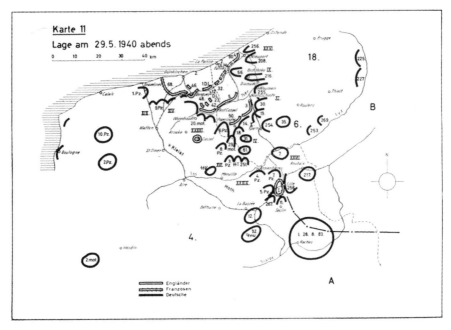

Map 11: Situation on the evening of 29 May 1940

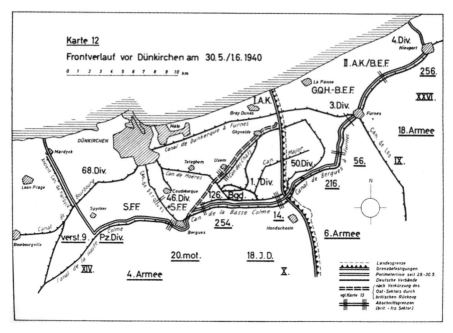

Map 12: Fronts around Dunkirk, 30 May–1 June 1940

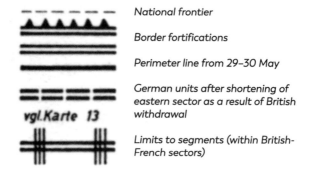

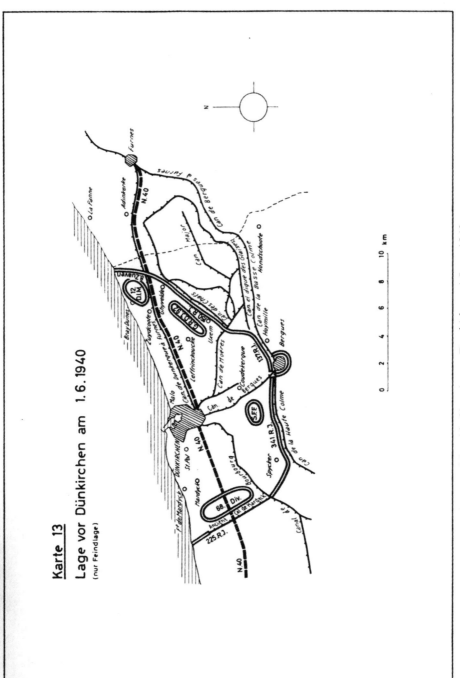

Map 13: Situation at Dunkirk on 1 June 1940

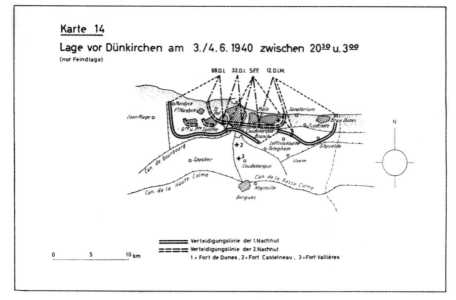

Map 14: Situation at Dunkirk on 3/4 June 1940 between 2030 and 0300

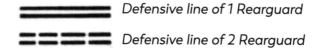

Defensive line of 1 Rearguard

Defensive line of 2 Rearguard

Operational objectives and deployment

On 1 September 1939 Hitler unleashed military conflict with Poland and set in train World War II.[1] When the Western Powers involved themselves in this conflict as a result of their pact of mutual assistance, his initial hope was that the declarations of war were made for the sake of appearances and he would not be opposed seriously.

Clearly it was during the Polish campaign that there ripened within him the plan for the 'final reckoning' with the Allies, which seemed to him unavoidable. At the end of September he communicated his intention to the surprised commanders-in-chief of the three Wehrmacht services and ordered that immediate preparations be made for an offensive in the West and that the first operational plan be formulated.[2] Only reluctantly and opposing it with all means within their province of responsibility did the OKH resign itself, for on the one hand it doubted it could meet the requirements in men and materials for such an objective and on the other had hopes that a political understanding could be reached to prevent the situation developing into a new world conflagration.

By the middle of October 1939 Hitler's decision was irrevocable: at the earliest possible point in time (the first target date he mentioned being 12 November 1939) he wanted to destroy the Western Powers militarily in a campaign which would sweep through Holland, Belgium, and Luxemburg. The breach of neutrality had no importance for him; as he revealed to his generals on 23 November 1939, nobody would enquire into it if Germany emerged victorious. The tangible opposition to his attack plans in the winter, the uncertain weather, the invasion of Norway, and the unsatisfactory operational planning forced him to postpone unleashing the offensive until May 1940.[3]

On 24 February 1940 the concept of 'Fall Gelb' came about. This has gone down in modern history as the 'Sichelschnittplan' (Sichelschnitt = cut of the scythe) and was based primarily on achieving victory in the West in 1940.[4]

As the *strategic aim of the offensive* this proposed: '...Attack "Yellow" has as its purpose a swift occupation of Holland so as to withdraw Dutch sovereign territory from Britain's grasp: and an attack through the territories of Belgium and Luxemburg to destroy strong elements of the Anglo-French army, *thereby laying the foundations for the destruction of the enemy's military might.*'

At a conference of commanders on 13 March 1940, the Army Commander-in-Chief, Col-General von Brauchitsch, specified the objective precisely as having the primary aim of *separating the British from the French and inflicting a decisive blow against the former!*[5]

In contrast to the military assessment of 1939, the concentrated effort now lay along the southern wing of the German armies preparing to attack. The basic thinking behind the operation was for Army Group A (Col-General von Rundstedt) to use a powerful force of motorized and panzer units *to tear apart the enemy front between Liège and Sedan,* in order to encircle to the south everything which the enemy threw into Belgium and wipe it out in combination with Army Group B (Col-General von Bock) north of Liège.

It was the job of Army Group B to swiftly occupy Holland, drawing as many enemy forces as possible towards itself in central Belgium and so tie them down there. The rapid attack of this Army Group would leave the enemy uncertain for some time as to where the German concentration of effort (*Schwerpunkt*) was focussed and prevent an enemy action against the inner flank of the encircling wing. The success of this bold operational plan depended upon it.[6]

In this respect OKH ordered individually:

'*Objective of Army Group B* is to quickly occupy Holland using rapid forces and so prevent the establishment of a link between Dutch and Anglo-Belgian forces. By a quick and powerful attack, the Belgian frontier defences will be broken down and the enemy forced back across the Antwerp-Namur Line. Fortress Antwerp is to be closed down in the north and east, Fortress Liège from the north-east and north of the Meuse.

'*18. Armee* will, by rapid occupation of all Holland (including Fortress Holland), prevent enemy forces becoming established along the Dutch coastal region.

'Simultaneous with the advance of forces north of the Waal against the eastern front of Fortress Holland, the coast between Holländisch Diep and Westerschelde is to be captured by means of rapid forces thrusting south of the Waal, thus frustrating the attempt of Anglo-Belgian forces to link up with Dutch forces. This will create the conditions for a surprise penetration into the southern front of "Fortress Holland" in cooperation with German airborne troops.

'The Scheldt Estuary is to be blocked off towards Antwerp and secured. At the same time the province of Groningen is to be occupied by weaker forces using platoons of panzers. The surprise occupation of the northern dam of the Ijssel is to be aimed for.

'The early occupation of the West Frisian islands is important for the purposes of the German Luftwaffe.

'*6. Armee* will move out from the Venlo–Aachen Line (inclusive of these towns) in such a way that it quickly crosses the Meuse and penetrates the Belgian frontier defences with the least consumption of time. It will then advance farther north to the Liège–Namur Line in a generally westerly direction.

'Orders concerning the sealing off of Antwerp and Liège will come through Army Group B.

'*Objective of Army Group A* is, covered by the left flank of the full attack against enemy action from the protected region around Metz and Verdun, to force the crossing of the Meuse between Dinant and Sedan (including both towns) as quickly as possible, in order then to proceed under protection of the flanks as quickly and as strongly as possible into the rear of the Northern French border fortified zone in the direction of the Somme Estuary. For this purpose AOK 2 will be available in addition to AOK.

'Ahead of the Army Group A front, strong rapid forces are to drive ahead in deep formation against the Meuse sector Dinant-Sedan. Their objective is to break up advanced enemy forces in southern Belgium and Luxemburg, to capture the west bank of the Meuse in a surprise attack and create favourable conditions for the continuation of the advance in a westerly direction.

'*4. Armee* will break through the fortified border zone between Liège and Houffalize and after closer disposition of Army Group A close off

Fortress Liège to the south-east and south and – rapid forces to Dinant and Givet taking precedence – with cover facing Namur, force the crossing of the Meuse between Yvoire and Fumay (towns not included) for further advance in a westerly direction via Beaumont and Chimay.

'12. *Armee* will break through the Belgian border fortifications either side of Bastogne and, closely pursuing the advancing rapid forces ahead of its front, force a crossing of the Meuse between Fumay and Sedan (both towns included) in such a way that as quickly as possible strong forces linked to 4. Armee can continue the advance across the Signy le Petit–Signy l'Abbaye line westwards.

'16. *Armee*, advancing fast from the Wallendorf-Mettlach Line close behind the right wing, will capture first the general Mouzon–Longwy–Sierck Line, covering along this line the southern flank of the entire advance and keeping contact with the fortified Saar Line south of Mettlach after agreement with 1. Armee. After reaching the line ordered, attachment to Army Group C is foreseen. After meeting up, close contact is to be maintained with the Army Group.

'*Army Group C* will by means of feints and threatening movements combined with a powerful attack tie down the opposing forces – point of concentration of effort in the area west of the Pfalz Woods – and hold itself ready to support a rapid build-up of a strong defensive front in the area of 16. Armee. It is aimed to absorb 16. Armee into the area of the Army Group later.'[7]

To support and aid the rapid advance of Army Group B, for the first time airborne infantry (Luftlande=LL) and paratroopers were deployed in the Dutch-Belgian area. These had basically three objectives:

1. 7. Fl. Div. (Student) was to break up the so-called 'Fortress Holland' (see Map 1) in vertical encirclement and keep open the most important bridges at Moerdijk, Dordrecht and Rotterdam until the arrival of 18. Armee.
2. 22. Airborne (LL) Div. had to occupy The Hague and unseat the Dutch Government.
3. The paratroopers of Sturmabteilung Koch, 7. Fl. Div., received a dual task: to capture intact the three bridges Canne, Vroenhofen and Veldvezelt over the Albert Canal (Belgium) and to keep them open for the advance of 6. Armee, and also neutralize the heavily fortified Belgian Fort Eben-Emael in cooperation with Infantry Regiment 151.[8]

DEPLOYMENT*
(Units, large scale)[9]

Germany:			Western Powers		
I.	*Army Group B* (Bock) with:		1.	*Dutch Army*:	
	18. Armee =	1 panzer div. 1 airborne div., 1⅓ mot. div. 5 ID (including Cav. div.)			10 ID (including 1. and Peel Div.), 3 Inf. Brig.+ numerous border btl. (46)
	6. Armee =	2 panzer div. 13 Inf. divisions	2.	*Belgian Army*:	23 Inf. Div.
	Army Group Reserve =	1 mot. div. 5 ID	3.	*Army Group 1* of the Allies (Billotte) with:	
	Total:	29⅓ units ←		Seventh Army =	1 LMD 2 mot. div. 4 ID
	In cooperation with:			BEF =	9 infantry divisions (partially motorized)
	Air Fleet 2 (Kesselring) (IV, III Flying Korps: II Flak Korps, 7. Fl. Div., Fl. Korps for special purposes 2 *Putzier*)			First Army =	2 LM div. 3 mot. div. 5 Inf. div.s
II.	*Army Group A* (Rundstedt) with:			Total:	60 units**
	Panzer Group Kleist =				
	=	5 panzer div. 3⅓ mot.div.		Ninth Army =	2 L C divisions 1 mot. div. 6½ ID
	4. Armee =	2 panzer div. 9 Inf.divisions		Second Army =	2 LC div. 5½ ID
	12. Armee =	12 Inf.Div.		Army Group Reserve:	1 armoured division
	16. Armee =	12 Inf.Div.		Total:	18 units**
	Army Group Reserve =	3 Inf.Div.			
	Total:	46⅓ units[10] ←			

---

* See hereto: *Fall Gelb, op. cit.* p.244ff: Mueller-Hillebrand *op.cit* Vol II, p.39ff,
43ff, 122ff (with further details)

** These units correspond approximately to the divisions of Army Group B
brought up and Army Group A. The distribution of forces makes clear that the
Allies had the mass of their divisions in the central-Belgian region (opposite
Army Group B.)

Germany:

Army Group A and C in cooperation with:

Air Fleet 3 (Sperrle)

(I, II, V Flying Korps; I Flak Korps)

III. *Army Group C* (Leeb) with:

1. Armee =	11 Inf. div.
7. Armee =	4 Inf. div.
Army Group Reserve =	4 Inf. div.
Total:	19 Inf. Div.

OKH (Army High Command) Reserves:

	1⅓ mot. div.
	41 Inf. div.

Western Powers

Army Group 1 altogether: 44 units

Army Group 2 (Prételat) with:

Third Army =	1 LC div., 12½ Inf. div.
Fourth Army =	5 Inf. div.
Fifth Army =	9 Inf. div.
Army Group Reserve =	2 infantry divisions
Total:	29½ units (of which 1 armoured division)

Army Group 3 (Besson) with:

Eighth Army =	7½ Inf. Div.
Reserve =	2 Inf. Div.

GQG Army Reserves:

	2 armoured div.,
	1 mot. div.,
	17 Inf. div.

Comparative Totals:

Germany:

10	panzer divisions
7	motorized divisions
117	infantry divisions
1	airborne division
1	cavalry division (1 flying div.)

Total: 136 plus 1 divisions

(Additionally: Oberost and Wehrkreis I, B.d.E and Gen.Qu. Norway/Denmark = 21 divisions)

Western Powers:

11	armoured and partially armoured divisions
7	motorized divisions
119	infantry divisions

Total: 137 divisions

CHAPTER II

The German operations, 10–21 May 1940 (Maps 1–5)

1. The capitulation of the Netherlands and the advance to the Dyle (northern flank) 10–15 May 1940 (Maps 1, 2a, 2b, 2c)

In the morning hours of 10 May heavy air attacks against neutral and enemy airfields, traffic facilities and transport installations, barracks, HQ staffs and industrial centres began the German campaign in the West. The mass of the operationally ready Dutch and Belgian military aviation, and elements of the French Air Force, were wiped out (see Map 1) and enemy signals centres heavily damaged.[1]

Without a declaration of war, German troops marched into the Netherlands, Belgium, and Luxemburg in order to pave the way for 'the destruction of the military instruments of power'.[2] The 18., 6., 4., 12. and 16. Armees invaded from the North Sea to the Moselle (from right to left).

The borders were crossed at 0535 hrs. 1. Cavalry Division on the right flank of 18. Armee reached the general line Adorp–Assen–Havelte–Meppel[3] by 1800 hrs against weak resistance, mainly roadblocks and other obstacles. At the same time X Armee Korps advanced to the Ijssel, brushing aside enemy border protection troops. Arnhem, Zwolle, and Deventer were taken in the course of the afternoon.

The concentration of effort of 18. Armee lay with XXVI Armee Korps whose objective was to capture the Meuse bridges between Ravenstein and Gennep by surprise attack or powerful thrust.

Probably the korps succeeded – after the crossings at Gennep (iron railway bridge) and Mook were captured intact – during the course of the first day in penetrating the Peel defensive line, although despite air support they were unable to make the breakthrough. As was noted by the 18. Armee War Diary, the attack 'proceeded generally as had been calculated previously by AOK.'[4]

Towards midday General Putzier reported on the situation of the airborne and parachute troops: 'The operational goal of seizing the bridges at Moerdijk and Rotterdam intact and so create access to Fortress Holland' had been achieved and secured. On the other hand, the attempt to 'neutralize the Dutch Government by surprise attack and take the capital' had failed.[5]

It was necessary, therefore, that for 11 May the Army's top priority was to restore contact with the airborne troops in 'Fortress Holland'. Col-General von Bock, Commander-in-Chief of Army Group B ordered at 2130 hrs: '… The most important thing for 18 Armee is to break into the Peel defensive line immediately and throw forward strong fast units against Breda.'[6] For this purpose 9. Panzer Division was to be ready to set off next morning from Mook and Gennep, and SS-V. Division to cross the Rhine between Rees and Wesel.

Although the Dutch military commanders were prepared for the German attack, they were surprised and confused by its violence. From the outset they lost the initiative. On 10 May Commander-in-Chief General Winkelmann ordered III Army Corps to withdraw from the area east of Hertogenbusch to behind the Waal Line (south-west of Culembourg) while the Light Division was to move back to the northern bank of the Merwede (between Dordrecht and Gorinheim). On the night of 10 May the Peel Division took avoiding action behind the Zuid-Willems Canal. At the same time I Army Corps, the Dutch Army's operational reserve, was tied down between Rotterdam and The Hague by German 22. Airborne Division.[7]

For a fast advance by 6. Armee on 10 May, everything depended upon capturing several more bridges intact.

At midday, the following picture had developed ahead of the German Army's front sector:

At Maastricht, the main centre of effort of IV Armee Korps (i.e. the first operational breakthrough location for Army Group B, while Gennep was the second), despite the deployment of Special Commando Unit Hokke, the Dutch blew up all three bridges over the Meuse, delaying by almost 24 hours the motorized advance of XVI Armee Korps.[8] IV Armee Korps pioneer units began building temporary bridges at once after occupying the town. On the other hand paratroopers captured the important bridges at Vroenhoven and Veldvezelt over the Albert Canal (0600 hrs) which they then held until the arrival of 4. Panzer Division spearhead at midday. Even the airborne landings on Fort Eben Emael were completely successful.[9] However, numerous bridges were down or had been seriously damaged by explosives ahead of the other Armee Korps.

Supported throughout by ground-attack aircraft of VIII Flying Korps, on the afternoon of 10 May, 6. Armee (right flank from Roermond to Turnhout–Bechelen, left flank from Aachen to Liège–Namur) reached:

IX Armee Korps:	The line Horst–Sevenu–Roggel destroyed bridges 6 km east of Weert
XI Armee Korps:	Horn–Kinroy–Eelen
IV Armee Korps:	Meuse–Scheldt-Canal and set up bridgeheads at Eysden–Boorsheim–Neerhaven and on Albert Canal at Vroenhoven and Veldvezelt
XXVII Armee Korps:	Bridgeheads west of Eysden–Fouron St Pierre–Limbourg–Henri Chapelle

On 11 May, 6. Armee continued its advance, concentrating its effort around and west of Maastricht. While XXVII Armee Korps covered deeply staggered left side towards Liège, the bridgeheads at Maastricht had to be extended, primarily for strong, fast forces (XVI Armee Korps) crossing the Albert Canal and heading south-west.[10]

At 0930 hrs on 11 May, Air Fleet 2 air reconnaissance reported the first motorized transport movements on the Antwerp–Roosendaal road. Two hours later they confirmed units of all branches heading for Tilburg and Breda. These were advanced elements of Seventh French Army (1st Light Mechanized Division) hurrying to support the Dutch. The big question was: would they succeed in restoring communication with Fortress Holland before 18. Armee had joined the airborne and parachute troops? Flying Korps Putzier was directed to intercept this enemy group immediately. Their attack was apparently effective, for the French vanguard was broken up to the extent that the French commander decided to stay where he was and await reinforcements.

At the same time, XXVI Armee Korps broke through the Peel defensive line. The decisive obstacle for the motorized advance had therefore fallen. At 0630 hrs the leading elements of 9. Panzer Division crossed the Meuse by the bridge at Gennep; its spearheads were sighted at Volkel at 1000 hrs, and at Uden at 1045 hrs. This speedy advance enabled the Division to reach the Zuid Willems Kanal at Vechel by late afternoon. The SS-V. Division joined them shortly after.

On the Ijssel Front, X Armee Korps was approaching the general line Ede–Wageningen on the Grebbe Line, while 1. Infantry Division captured the banks of the Zuider Zee between Herlingen and Lemmer and prepared for the crossing into Fortress Holland.[11] The advance of 6. Armee, meanwhile, had also made good progress.

On the morning of 11 May, pioneers completed the first temporary bridge at Maastricht. XVI Armee Korps, to which 4. Panzer Division (already heading for Tongern), 3. Panzer Division and 20. Motorized Division were attached. The objective of this Korps was to strike deep into the flank of the enemy at Gembloux in order to prevent French forces reaching the Dyle defensive line, and also to cut off the enemy retreating from Liège. This would also confirm the enemy in his belief that the centre of effort of the German offensive was here.

At the same time, the battle for the Belgian Fort Eben Emael was reaching its climax. At 0700 hrs the first assault troops of Pioneer Battalion 51 had made contact with the assault group Witzig of 7. Flying Division. In cooperation with reinforced Infantry Regiment 151, towards 1300 hrs German paratroopers obtained the capitulation of this modern fortified installation (radio signal to AOK 6, 1535 hrs).[12]

During the evening, IV Armee Korps proceeded from Lengerloo on the Albert Canal to Bilsen for Gellick. The operations of XXVIII Armee Korps ran into the stubborn resistance of III Belgian Army Corps at Eysden–Wonck–Visé denying them twice over a crossing of the Meuse: additionally they had no bridging equipment. In the northern sector, IX and XI Armee Korps drove advanced Dutch and Belgian forces back to the Albert Canal (Heeze–west of Venlo–Hechtel–Houthalen–north of Hasselt).[13]

Col-General von Bock reported to the Army Commander-in-Chief (Col-General von Brauchitsch) the intentions of 6. Armee for 12 May as being: 'Forced forward drive of the south flank of the … Army in order to penetrate the Namur–Leuven Line as quickly as possible and fight through. The Army Group reserves have been distributed accordingly.'[14]

The AOK had expected the first decisive encounter for 18. Armee to be against strong enemy forces in the Breda area on 12 May, and it was important to establish contact with the paratroopers around the Moerdijk Bridge dropping zone. 7. Flying Division had radioed repeatedly: 'All bridges safely in our hands.'[15]

Air reconnaissance had confirmed the Roosendaal–Wuestwezel Westmalle–Breda area free of enemy and around 1155 hrs enemy troops were even retreating towards Antwerp. The expected fighting on the left flank of 18. Armee therefore did not materialize. 9. Panzer Division pushed forward unopposed via Loon op Zand to Gertruidenberg (northeast of Breda) and at 1825 hrs, assisted by reconnaissance detachment Lüttwitz, made contact with the paratroopers on the bridge at Moerdijk. The commander of Army Group B, Col-General von Bock could therefore make the observation in his notes: '… Having regard to the enormous difficulties of terrain, an outstanding achievement.'[16] 18. Armee had carried out its first important objective: the Dutch field army, which had begun to disengage into 'Fortress Holland', was isolated.

Meanwhile on the southern flank of the advance, XXVI Armee Korps had quickly taken Best and Merle (16 km south of Breda) and now went forward towards Antwerp shielded by advanced elements. On the way, sections of the beaten Peel Division, worn down by air attacks, fell into its hands.[17]

The attempts of X Armee Korps to penetrate the Grebbe Line had come to grief twice as a result of extremely stubborn and skilful enemy resistance but shortly before 1800 hrs it achieved the first breakthrough at Grebbe-Berg (north of Rhenen).[18]

On the same day, ground-attack aircraft of Flying Korps zbV 2 battered various important points of enemy resistance. Over Holland and northern

Belgium there were almost no air defences, while anti–aircraft fire was becoming noticeably weaker.[19]

OKH (Army High Command) assessed the enemy situation in general as follows: Apparently the enemy had the intention to defend 'in Fortress Holland, in Antwerp, in the Dyle Line and along the Meuse from Namur to the seam with the front of French forts.' Previous reports had probably not confirmed what British forces were expected to support the Dutch, although the evening report of Foreign Armies West (OKH) at 2345 hrs emphasized the landings of French troops on the island of Walcheren.[20]

The intentions of 18. Armee for 13 May remained unchanged. In the Army Order the objective was to begin the attack on Fortress Holland from south and east while covering towards Antwerp.[21]

The same day, XVI Armee Korps of 6. Armee, with the constant support of VIII Flying Korps on the wings and flanks (also covered by the advance of 269. Infantry Division to Noville), advanced as ordered in the direction of Nivelles to prevent at all costs the enemy force, which had retreated from the Albert Canal positions, settling behind the Dyle. At 0845 hrs the spearhead of 4. Panzer Division reported its location as Waremme, south of which was a Luftwaffe drop zone for fuel.

Concurrently 20. Motorized Division closed up around Heerlen while 3. Panzer Division had reached Looze, its advanced elements having detached to head for Engelmanshoven. At 1015 hrs 4. Panzer Division had taken Hannut with an advanced group at Burdinne (18 km north-east of Namur). Here for the first time they ran across French armour of 2. and 3. Mechanized Divisions (First Army) which apparently had orders to cover the retreat of the Belgians to Gette and Dyle and give their own motorized forces time to set up in the Dyle Line. General Hoepner (Commanding-General XVI Armee Korps) therefore considered himself forced to halt the advance and allow 3. Panzer Division to catch up.[22]

Meanwhile on the northern wing, IX Armee Korps – which had wiped out the remnants of the Dutch Peel Division at Widerweerten – XI and IV Armee Korps were making westwards with all the forces at their disposal, and in the evening they reached the line Reul (Holland)–south of Moll–south-east of Diest–St. Trond. At the same time XXVII Armee Korps was proceeding towards the north-eastern and eastern fronts of Fortress Liège. It was the objective of AOK 6 that the powerful southern wing would enclose and roll up the Allied positions in the south by an enforced and ruthless advance, but they encountered bitter resistance in the Hannut-Pervez sector from the French mechanized units. Repeated air attacks by VIII Flying Korps were necessary to provide XVI Armee Korps the chance to draw breath.[23,24] (see Map 2)

On the morning of 13 May, the enemy situation in front of 18. Armee was at first uncertain. At 1020 hrs 'long enemy motorized columns' were reported 'travelling from Antwerp to Breda heading towards the left wing of 9. Panzer Division'. It was assumed from the warships and other craft at Den Helder and the Hook of Holland that British land forces might be marching into Fortress Holland. The OKH situation report of 11,45 hrs spoke of French landings on the island of Walcheren. Amongst other things mention was also made that on the morning of 13 May 'fifteen transporter ships had been observed at Flushing.' All this provided a clue that the purpose of the landings might serve 'to protect the seaway to Antwerp' although it was conceivable that 'a naval operation using light forces against the bridges at Rotterdam or Moerdijk' might be intended.[25]

Undoubtedly these reports and the situation along the whole front created for OKH an atmosphere of constant 'high tension'. Would the objectives of the war policy be fulfilled before Allied units set foot in Holland?

After 9. Panzer Division had joined the paratroopers at Moerdijk, AOK regrouped its forces. For the attack on Fortress Holland it was now prepared to throw in the newly arrived XXXIX Armee Korps, 7. Flieger Division, 22. Airborne Division, the 254th, 9. Panzer Division, and the SS-Leibstandarte Adolf Hitler. This finally guaranteed a uniform command structure to embrace all units proceeding from the south to attack 'Fortress Holland'. The purpose of this Armee Korps was to launch the attack with its centre of effort based on Rotterdam–Dordrecht and relieve 22. Airborne Division. The mass of the Army artillery was also distributed here.[26]

At 0700 hrs the motorized units of 9. Panzer Division began their advance in a single column across the Moerdijk bridge, passed through Dordrecht during the day, arriving towards 1800 hrs in the southern suburbs of Rotterdam, which had been occupied since 10 May by airborne troops (Infantry Regiment 16) who had held it against a superior enemy.

A second column together with XXVI Armee Korps covered the line Rijsbergen (south of Breda)–Baarle–Nassau facing Antwerp.

Here weak attacks by the French 1e. Mechanized Division were warded off with the help of the Luftwaffe, resulting in the enemy withdrawing to the Antwerp fortifications, this was also a consequence of the unexpected German crossing of the Meuse in the Army Group A sector.[27]

Meanwhile X Armee Korps was finding it tougher going. In the Grebbe Line the Dutch offered stubborn resistance. When the korps attacked with Stuka support at 1500 hrs, they reached the western and eastern sides of Scherpenzeel but were then bogged down. There were no indications that the enemy would weaken. Probably they were attempting to hold out in the expanded defensive positions for as long as they could until their allies brought up fresh forces in support.

AOK therefore issued orders at 1630 hrs to begin the combined attack against 'Fortress Holland' from the north, east, and south on 14 May 1940. XXXIX Armee Korps was to push forward with its main effort across the Dordrecht–Rotterdam Line to Utrecht, resume contact with the encircled elements of 22. Airborne Division, and secure the area from Breda to Roosendaal facing Antwerp until XXVI Armee Korps could take over.[28]

On the left wing of Army Group B (6. Armee), Panzer Korps Hoepner (XVI Armee Korps) had meanwhile reached the railway line Huppaye-Eghezée against stubborn opposition and joined up with 20. Motorized Division in the area south-west of Tongern. While IV Armee Korps was mopping up the sector between greater and smaller Gette (west of St. Trond) that afternoon, XI Armee Korps was split between the northern edge of Diest and 'deeply stretched out' advancing towards Hall. That morning, French armoured units had attacked IX Armee Korps (right wing of 6. Armee) at Moll. From a captured French divisional order it transpired that this armour had the task of providing cover for strong units being brought up before and during their transportation.

During the course of the day, the korps forced the crossing of the Canal d'Embranchement east of Moll and Meerhout but was not able to effectively prevent enemy action against the outer flank of 18. Armee. The main problem arose in that Army Group B had had to release VIII Flying Korps to Army Group A (crossing of the Meuse) that afternoon.

For 14 May, the objective for 6. Armee was to advance towards Nivelles and penetrate the Dyle Line between Wavre and Namur.[29]

Meanwhile *Foreign Armies West* (OKH) had made the following assessment of the enemy situation: Endless transport movements were occurring on railways and roads in the Brussels-Antwerp area originating from the Lille-Maubeuge region. This indicated that from now on the BEF and First French Army were being brought into Belgium under cover of Seventh Army, operating since 10 May on the left side of the Allied northern wing. According to German calculations, by 14 May north of the Sambre Line – therefore opposite 6. and 18. Armees – the enemy could throw into the struggle more or less the following divisions: 12–13 of Seventh French Army, 7– 9 of the British Army, 6–8 of First French Army and in addition 15 Belgian divisions, though in the opinion of OKH these were barely 'capable of attacking.' Nevertheless, these 40–45 divisions were opposed by 21 divisions of Army Group B (including Army Group Reserves) and 'in the case of need', General Halder, Chief of the Army General Staff believed, 'these forces can be strengthened from the depths of 18. Armee.' He noted in his diary furthermore that 'if the enemy should attack, we are strong enough and the bringing up of reserves will not be required', concluding, however, that 'success in attacking apart from winning territory (by Panzer Korps) Hoepner is hardly to be expected'.[30] Army Group Command B also concluded from these observations that 'the enemy is bringing up new forces from the depths'. Col-General von Bock remarked in his notes: '… At 1100 hrs the first railway transports were reported, also soon after numerous motorized columns, crossing the French-Belgian border. Now they are coming! French have landed at Flushing … the picture is slowly become clear … that perhaps the enemy will embark upon his attack across this line (Namur–Leuven–Antwerp)'.[31]

At 1630 hrs Army Group B HQ received a report issued by Army Group reconnaissance (at 1615 hrs) with the information: 'Unloadings at about 1530 hrs at Ghent (here motorized units), at Courtrai, in Gramont (here tanks), at Ath, at all railway stations on the Brussels–Leuven stretch.'[32]

Thus the Battle for Belgium was approaching its climax. Despite the surprising initial successes of the German forces, the outcome was not certain. All the same, the enemy had completed the hoped-for change of direction by his north–west wing and in doing so had fulfilled one of the most important preconditions for the success of the 'Sichelschnitt Plan'!

On the night of 13 May, Army Group Command B urged 18. Armee once more to take 'Fortress Holland' quickly because the possibility existed that 'British forces' were reinforcing the enemy at Amsterdam: they ordered that once Rotterdam was occupied, 9. Panzer Division was to proceed to Amsterdam. The escape of the beaten Dutch Army from the northern part of the 'Fortress' had to be prevented.[33]

Not until the early hours of 14 May did it become certain that 'in the night the enemy, by leaving behind a skillful fighting rearguard and under cover of the thick morning fog, had abandoned the Grebbe Line.' Both the Army Group order and also the new situation had been taken into the reckoning in the new instruction of AOK 18 at 0811 hrs in which instructions were given that: 'XXXIX Armee Korps is to advance *en masse* to Amsterdam-Leiden. It is important to capture "Fortress Holland" before the main body of the Dutch Army escapes the new waterline … or can even be deployed against Rotterdam.'[34] In order to take 'Fortress Holland' faster, the Commanding General of 18. Armee, General von Küchler, ordered XXXIX Armee Korps to issue an ultimatum demanding the surrender of Rotterdam, the decisive gate for entry into the Fortress. The destruction of the city was to be threatened and 'if necessary' carried out.

Despite the negotiations begun on the morning of 14 May between the Germans and the Dutch, the bombing ordered for 1500 hrs could not be stopped in time. Sixty per cent of the bombers which took off dropped their payload (60–90 tonnes of 50-kg and 250-kg bombs) on the Old City which was almost totally destroyed, not least because the spreading fires could not be extinguished sufficiently quickly.[35]

At 1530 hrs, XXXIX Armee Korps reported to AOK 18: 'Bombing attack 1500 hrs could not be halted. Occurred during negotiations. Continuation in question. Attack postponed provisionally.'[36]

Under the influence of the heavy air raid, all connections cut off, the Dutch military commander of the city decided to offer unconditional surrender. *At 1710 hrs* he appeared personally at the XXXIX Armee Korps command post so that at 1830 hrs General Schmidt was able to inform AOK 18 that the city had changed hands.

That same evening, SS-Leibstandarte Adolf Hitler went through the burning city and relieved the southern group of the encircled 22. Airborne Division while elements of 9. Panzer Division reached the northern exit and the road to Amsterdam. At 1800 hrs, AOK 18 issued the order for the continuation of the attack against 'Fortress Holland'.

It never came to it, however. In view of the almost hopeless operational situation, the destruction and capitulation of Rotterdam (Utrecht had also capitulated), and the Allies having given it up, at 2030 hrs General Winkelmann, Commander-in-Chief of the Dutch armed forces, made a radio broadcast offering the cessation of hostilities with the exception of the island of Zeeland.

At 1020 hrs on 15 May accompanied by staff officers, he went to Rijsoord to complete the capitulation in 'a dignified manner previously laid down by the Commander-in-Chief, 18. Armee.' After General von Küchler had expressed the high esteem of the German Wehrmacht for the defeated enemy, he made known the conditions. At 1145 hrs both men signed the instrument of capitulation to end the campaign in the Netherlands after five days of fighting.[37]

As at 1400 hrs on 14 May, 6. Armee had reached the general line Oostmalle–Aarschot–Longueville–Longchamps area (north of Namur). By evening XVI Armee Korps straddled Ernage. 'It had stood the whole day advancing slowly while exchanging fire with enemy tanks and suffered the difficulties of a forefield destroyed according to a plan,' the Army War Diary recorded. In the subsequent push against the Dyle defences (well built with anti-panzer obstacles) the foremost elements of IX Armee Korps arrived in the evening at the area 20 kilometres west of Herenthals, XI and IV Armee Korps as far as Aarschot–east side of Leuven–district north-east and south-east of Wavre. XXVII Armee Korps surrounded the northern front of Namur and saw to the remaining Liège forts.

On the afternoon of 15 May it was apparent that all efforts by the armee to penetrate the Dyle Line had come to nought. Therefore Col-General von Reichenau decided at 1630 hrs to halt the advance along the whole front and re-start it on 17 May after a plan had been drawn up. (The front here ran from Nylen–Bael–Rotsclaer–Hamm–Ottignies–Gembloux–Meuz–Leuxe–Tillier).[38]

2. The Breakthrough on the Meuse Front (Southern Wing) 10–15 May 1940 (Maps 1–4)

At this stage we now turn to the front sector of Army Group A. While the northern wing of the German advance (Army Group B) – as depicted – drew the enemy towards itself in central Belgium, the southern wing (Army Group A) had moved up smartly to the Meuse. The success of the bold German operational plan depended decisively on the breakthrough here being made in time so that the fast units heading west for the Somme estuary, covered by advanced infantry divisions on the flank, could push forward before the enemy had recognized the build-up of this concentration and brought up his operational reserves to this threatened sector. In the Wehrmacht bulletin of the opening days therefore, the successes in Belgium and Holland were emphasized deliberately in order to mask the measures in the southern sector![1]

Great demands were made of Panzer Group Kleist within Army Group A. The difficulties of organization were large (arranging 300 kilometres of long individual columns on the march, supplying them with fuel, ammunition and provisions, traffic control). Moreover panzer and motorized units – a total of 41,100 vehicles (including 1,250 panzers and 302 armoured reconnaissance cars) – had to move through trackless terrain (thick woodland, deeply indented river valleys, few and narrow roads) and then cross the Meuse. For this purpose Group Kleist split down into three sub-groups:

1. Sub-group: XIX Armee Korps (Guderian) with 1., 2., 10. Panzer Divisions and Infantry Regiment Grossdeutschland.
2. Sub-group: XXXXI Armee Korps (Reinhardt) with 6. and 8. Panzer Divisions.
3. Sub-group: XIV Armee Korps (Wietersheim) with 13., 2. and 29. Infantry Division (mot.).[2]

On the afternoon of 10 May the panzer group fell on advanced French and Belgian units which offered little resistance. The enemy stalled so as to avoid having to fight on the Meuse Front.

In the evening XIX Armee Korps, whose advance had been delayed by much congestion on the roads, reached Burnon–Strainchamps–Fauvillers–Rulles–Etalle (7 to 15 kilometres from the Belgian frontier; the second sub-group being diverted to the Kyll sector.[3]

The same day 4. Armee, operating on the right wing of Army Group A and having met no resistance worthy of note, had pushed forward to the line Malchamps–Vielsalm–Houffalize (excluding town). Its commander, Col-General von Kluge bemoaned the 'poor street discipline' of some units but the enemy air force did not delay his advance.[4]

Meanwhile 12. and 16. Armees had reached Mabompre–Bastogne–Arlon–Aubange–Esch (not the town)–Frisingen.[5]

On 11 May the German advance was halted in many places by barricades and destruction to roads.

At 1105 hrs Col-General von Rundstedt 'on the basis of another personal instruction by the Army Commander-in-Chief' had ordered Group Kleist 'with *all elements*, and also 10. Panzer Division, 'to force the crossing of the Meuse as quickly and in as much strength as possible without regard to the possible threat to the flank from the south-west.'[6]

On the whole the operations on this day went off as planned. While Group Kleist with forward companies of 2. Panzer Division had got to the Semois at Vresse, those of 1. Panzer Division to Bouillon and those of 10. Panzer Division to Cugnon that evening, 4., 12., and 16. Armee were spread along the general line Sprimont–Ferriéres–Champlon–Libramonth–Bercheau–Longwy–Hellingen–Mondorf.

At 4. Armee in the morning, 5. and 7. Panzer Divisions were merged under XV Armee Korps (Hoth) and the Korps, elements of which had crossed the Ourthe at 1100 hrs, received the order at 2045 hrs '*Forward to Dinant*'.[7]

The weaker and inferior enemy spearheads thrown into southern Belgium were evidently intended to gain time to organize the defences on the Meuse by crossing Semois and the Meuse to the Maginot Line. The intention of Army Group A for 12 May was 'to defeat this enemy and force the crossing of the Meuse between Dinant and Sedan – XV Armee Korps and Group Kleist leading.'[8]

On 12 May enemy resistance stiffened for the first time and around Emptinne (20 km north-east of Dinant) XV Armee Korps encountered forty enemy tanks; these were overwhelmed and at 1935 hrs elements of 7. Panzer Division forced their way into Dinant.

Col-General von Kluge remained personally at XV Armee Korps on 12 May 'in order to keep urging them on'.[9] XIX Armee Korps also made good progress, taking the northern bank of the Meuse at Sedan and the city. At the same time XXXXI Armee Korps was reported with advanced companies of 6. Panzer Division 25 km west of the Belgian border; XVI Armee Korps (former third sub-group)[10] headed west with the greater part of its units (29. Motorized Division leading to Rottes).

Otherwise, the front on the evening of 12 May was:

4. Armee:	V Armee Korps,	Beaufays, Rotheux.
	VIII Armee Korps,	Warzée–Bend–Bonsin
	XV Armee Korps,	Dinant
	II Armee Korps,	Edges of woodland south of Wanlin.
12. Armee:	III Armee Korps,	Maissin–Jehonville with XVIII Armee Korps following up behind III Armee Korps as ordered.
	VI Armee Korps	Vouillin–Orgée with leaders of foot columns. St. Pierre–Grandvoin
16. Armee:	(VII, XIII, XXIII Armee Korps) as on 11 May. Here the movements were continued as planned in order to begin the assault on the Maginot Line.[11]	

Probably the most important decision of the day was *when* and *where* the Meuse was to be crossed. From Ic-reports and air reconnaissance, Army Group A was not able to obtain a clear picture 'of the situation at the Meuse'. Therefore Army Group Command wanted to have a report from commanders on the spot, 'the successful crossing and tempo' naturally being decisive for the future prospects of the operation. At this point in time the heads of Army Group A were still wanting to know what 'measures for a planned river crossing' were required in case the panzer and motorized units ran up against a powerful defence of the Meuse 'as they basically expected from the French leadership.'[12]

Lt-General von Sodenstern, Chief of Army Group A General Staff, therefore accompanied Luftwaffe General Sperrle (Chief, Air Fleet 3) to the Group Kleist command post. In the discussion which followed, Sodenstern and Kleist came to the following accord:

1. The Panzer Group had to expect 'a firmer response by the enemy' behind the Meuse than in the fighting up to this point: however, based on reports received, it was convinced that even now, to 'quickly seize the opportunity' would bring success. The panzer and motorized divisions could go through the Meuse Front if they only 'first of all set foot on this or that place along the western bank.'
2. In order to benefit from the element of surprise, Group Kleist would attempt *this very night* to gain the western bank in order 'to bring up strong forces in the morning.' Meanwhile the Group's artillery was arriving.
3. Should the enterprise fail, the attack would go ahead as planned at 1600 hrs on 13 May.

It was agreed with Air Fleet 3 to have the Flying Korps start the softening-up process at 0800 hrs (this could not be done, however, because it was not possible to pass the necessary instructions during the night.) Between 1400 and 1600 hrs the bomber attacks 'would be increased in continually repeated waves' of the 'greatest violence'.[13,14]

Against Kleist's conviction, General Guderian finally got his way in the matter of where XIX Korps would attempt the crossing. The orders were to cross west of the Ardennes Canal which he thought 'would cause postponements and lose us time,' and therefore he decided to cross east of the Canal.[15] The result, certainly undesired, was that the korps was forced in a direction more southerly than westerly. The objective for 13 May 1940 remained: with all means available, using every opportunity, force the crossing of the Meuse.

The fourth day of battle had to bring the first decision on the south wing: it was most important that the German attack spearhead lost no time at the Meuse. At 4. Armee, XV Armee Korps reported at 0610 hrs on 13 May that it had crossed the river south of Houx (about 8 km north of Dinant): at 0645 hrs the crossing also succeeded at Yvoir. By evening the Korps reached the Flavion sector. Towards midnight German forces were attacked by enemy fighter-bombers and tanks (4.1e.Cavalry Division) at the bridgeheads, but the most advanced elements were only forced back to the river embankments.[16]

In the meantime at Monthermé-Sedan, Group Kleist had also been successful. Col-General von Rundstedt, who had 'gone forward' in order to exercise 'his personal influence on the development of the Meuse crossing' was able to report to Army Group Command at 1930 hrs through his adjutant Lt-Colonel Tresckow:

'The crossing of the Meuse prepared and supported by Air Fleet 3 has been successful at two locations.' 2. Panzer Division had occupied Nouvion and Donchéry on the north bank of the river while 1. Panzer Division had taken the south bank of the Meuse with infantry and crossed the Frenois-Sedan road. 10. Panzer Division had pushed forward south of Sedan and elements had crossed the Meuse at Wadelincourt. Towards evening 6. Panzer Division had reached the area south of Monthermé.

These surprising and unexpected successes motivated Col-General von Bock, Commander-in-Chief of Army Group B, to conclude: '*The French really seem to have been abandoned by all good spirits, or otherwise they could, and should have prevented that.*'[17] In fact, the German commanders found it incomprehensible that the enemy had not occupied the sector Namur-Sedan (extension of the Maginot Line) quicker and with more powerful forces: particularly since the field positions had been poorly developed. While on 13 May 12. Armee had come to a standstill at Bouillon with the spearhead (an enforced stop to make space for Group Kleist, XXXXI Armee Korps!), 16. Armee had reached the line Francheval–heights and also Carignan-Marville: it was intended to advance to Marville on 15 May in order protect the south flank here.

For 14 May, Rundstedt ordered that, after establishing a large bridge-head and with the protection of the southern wing between the Canal des Ardennes and Meuse, the attack spearheads were to push forward vigorously towards *Hirson-Montcornet* and *Rethel*.[18]

On 14 May, 4. Armee had become involved in heavy fighting. To begin with, the bridgehead had had to be expanded. During the morning this gave rise to a crisis. At 0630 hrs, General Rommel, commanding officer of 7. Panzer Division, reported that after the first bitterly fought encounters with elements of the French 9.Army (4.le.Cavalry Division), his Division was 'at the end of its strength'. As the 4. Armee War Diary remarked, the XV Armee Korps bridgehead was 'therefore much smaller than previously thought' and the situation there 'insecure'. Not until after 1100 hrs did the tension subside. At 1230 hrs the Korps reported to the Army: 'Crisis overcome. Sommières in German hands. Infantry regiment no longer encircled, now west of Onhaye. Our own losses are unfortunately not light.' Finally the enemy resistance abated somewhat so that by 2100 hrs XV Armee Korps had captured Anthée.[19]

Meanwhile, during the night of 13 May, XIX Armee Korps succeeded in setting up a narrow bridgehead at Villers-sur-Bar–S.Aignon–Noyers from where an advance could made towards Chéhery – defended by forces of X French Army Corps. On the morning of 14 May, Col-General von Rundstedt drove to the XIX Armee Korps command post. According to the Army Group A War Diary there was 'full agreement' regarding the assessment of the tactical situation and XIX Armee Korps received the task of protecting the southern flank and expanding the bridgehead, thus 'creating the pre-conditions' for an immediate advance *westwards* across the Canal des Ardennes (south of Sedan). Rundstedt took the opportunity to emphasize the overriding importance of winning territory towards the Channel coast.

In the late afternoon, this was the picture of the Meuse Front which had formed. XXXXI Armee Korps had been in action crossing the river at Monthermé and Nouzonville. In the loop of the Meuse south of Monthermé it had battled for itself a small bridgehead. XIX Armee Korps had been able to extend its defensive flank farther southwards, and after warding off counter-attacks by X French Army Corps, the Canal bridges at Bencourt and Malmy had fallen 'undamaged' into their hands.

The intention of Group Kleist for 15 May was to push on westwards. The gradually approaching XIV Armee Korps was to turn off to the south, relieve the panzer forces there and take over protecting the flank in the area of Ronucourt.[20]

In order to bring the fighting involving 12. Armee, whose most advanced elements had reached the Meuse (III Armee Korps), 'into a certain harmony' with Group Kleist, the latter was subordinated temporarily to 12. Armee, initially at least, until the bridgehead had been adequately secured and supported.

Army Group Command had by this time the impression that the enemy, though brave, was fighting without coherence: 'apparently' the tempo of the German advance had come as too 'surprising' for him. Forces were being sent down from Paris either for a counter-attack against the bridgeheads or to erect a new defensive Front.[21]

These successes of the first days of the attack prompted OKW (Commander-in-Chief of the Wehrmacht) to issue a new Instruction (No.11) on 14 May for the future conduct of operations. The enemy had not so far succeeded, it stated, in recognizing the centre of effort of the German offensive. The enemy was continuing to assemble strong forces against the Antwerp–Namur Line while neglecting the sector in front of Army Group A.

This situation and the swift breakthrough at the Meuse met all preconditions for an advance north of the Aisne to the coast with strong, fast forces. Army Group B fighting north of Liège–Namur would now tie down the enemy with the forces presently at its disposal and draw the enemy to itself while *all fast units must be channeled with all speed to the spearhead of Army Group A*.[22]

In carrying out this Instruction, OKH ruled that at this stage all the requirements had been met to 'continue the advance in the sense of Deployment Order *Gelb*' in the direction of the lower course of the Somme.[23]

Army Group B was given the task of breaking the last resistance of the Dutch Army and offering OKH as soon as possible the fast units deployed there 'stating the place and time of availability for operations.'

The northern and eastern fronts of Fortress Antwerp had to be closed down simultaneously with tying down the enemy in the Dyle Line. With the main body 'of its forces the Army Group will if possible continue the advance across the Wavre–Namur Line in the direction of Ath.' XVI Armee Korps, including 20. Infantry Division (mot), was to pull out at the latest upon reaching the Genappe–Charleroi Line and place itself at the disposal of OKH.

Army Group A was ordered to 'proceed to the West after crossing the Meuse between Sambre and the Canal des Ardennes. The right wing of 16. Armee is to head as far as the Canal des Ardennes in the area of Chesne. AOK 2 is to insert itself between AOK 4 and AOK 12. The armies are then first to proceed against the line Beaumont–Rethel in such a manner that 4. Armee can advance with the concentration of its effort south of the French border fortifications and centred on *Douai*, 2. Armee centred on Bapaume: 12. Armee will take the line La Fère–Laon–Rethel to defend the left flank of the attacking group.' In this way one group each of fast troops of 4. Armee and 12. Armee would push ahead. The decisive factor was that the panzers should have the greatest possible fire power in the combined attack.

The morning report of *Foreign Armies West* (OKH) of 15 May 1940, 1145 hrs, had summarized the enemy situation as it lay in the path of Army Group A as follows:

'...*French 9. and 2.Armies*:

a) The bridgeheads between Namur and Givet have been expanded against little enemy resistance ... no new troops have been noted. It is not yet recognized in which Line we have to expect strong resistance once more...

b) ......?

c) The enemy south of Sedan has been deeply shocked by the fighting of the last few days; more than 4000 to 5000 prisoners are being brought in here...

d) Before our attack on Carignan the enemy withdrew without resisting, probably to the strongly defended position east of Mouzon.

e) Up to the evening of 14 May, the enemy had not brought up reserves over the Hirson-Rethel Line, nor from the south against the breakthrough area.'[24]

On the *right wing of Army Group A*, at the seam with Army Group B, the spearhead of 5. Panzer Division was meanwhile threatened on the flank by an enemy group advancing from the area Charleroi-Namur to the south-west (principally 1. French Tank Division). Despite a fast reaction, the left wing of Army Group B had not been able to prevent this especially since 269. Infantry Division had not reached the area north of Namur and 6. Armee had halted its advance along the entire Front. 4. Armee therefore had to decide either to wheel its left wing more northerly or maintain its set direction of advance. Furthermore it also had to assess how to pass through the French border fortifications between Maubeuge-Fournies in the case that 6. Armee resumed its advance' westwards.

At 1330 hrs the Ia of Army Group A, Colonel Blumentritt, informed General Brennecke, 4. Armee Chief of the General Staff, by telephone that on the orders of the Army Commander-in-Chief the Armee had to 'proceed towards Beaumont and Chimay'. This was the next objective after breaking through the French border fortifications on the Maubeuge–Fournies Line with the centre at *Douai* (therefore more north-westerly). The left neighbouring army (12. or perhaps 2. Armee after insertion) was heading for Bapaume.

When the Chief of Army Group A General Staff, Sodenstern, spoke with Brennecke that evening, the latter pointed out that 4. Armee 'must look to the *West and North*'. Sodenstern replied, that as far *as the tempo and execution* of ongoing operations were concerned, the Army Group *did not regulate 4. Armee.* For the remainder, at midnight Col-General von Kluge ordered for 16 May: 'the Armee with its left wing (II Armee Korps) protected on its northern flank will reach the French border and *assimilate it.* Surprise attacks will only be made against the French border fortifications if the weakness of their occupation promises certain success...'[25,26]

XV Armee Korps would cover the Armee's *northern flank* from Florennes (excluding town) to Walcourt. To the West only the l'Eau sector was to be occupied initially. The Korps would then remain at readiness and in strength so that it could head either *to the* West *or else* to the North should the enemy make a renewed attack. The *attention of Army Group Command A* was to be drawn to this and also in the next few days to the '*possible danger of the always lengthening southern flank.*'[27]

All measures were 'continually' examined and improved in order to 'guarantee the uninterrupted bringing up of divisions both from behind the 16. Armee Front via Sedan in the general direction of Laon, and in the 12. Armee stretch via Charleville and north of Hirson and Vervins-Marle.' AOK 2 was to be responsible for the organization of reserves.

Regarding the fighting of 15 May the War Diary KTB–A observed: '... the day passed according to the expectations of the Army Group Command.' The most advanced elements of the motorized forces ahead of 4. Armee and 12. Armee had reached the general Line Cerfontaine (10 km west of Philippville)–Liart (25 km west of Charleville). Enemy tank attacks from the Charleroi area had been warded off. South of Sedan also XIX Armee Korps had beaten off an enemy tank attack in which 'the enemy incurred substantial losses of materials'. After heavy fighting and unparalleled coverage of distance, the most forward infantry had kept up very close behind the motorized units. 16. Armee, after wheeling south, had meanwhile taken terrain for the ordered defensive Front facing the Maginot Line (south-east of Sedan-Longuyon).[28]

Despite the situation in the 6. Armee Front sector, during the night Army Group Command A came to the 'definitive assessment' that 4. Armee should be able to protect its northern flank with 'its own forces'; for the continuation of the operations towards the Somme it was quite especially important that *the left flank of 12. Armee was protected at the right time*. For the first time the matter came up 'that it could become important to halt the motorized forces at the Oise *temporarily*.'[29] Rundstedt laid the greatest emphasis on preventing the enemy 'under any circumstances' achieving even local successes at the Aisne or – later – in the Laon area. This would have a more damaging effect for the entire operation than the case of 'a temporary interruption to the tempo of our motorized forces.'[30]

The German operations on the southern wing were now favoured greatly by the better road conditions for the fast units west of the Meuse: the area for spreading out was greater and the terrain more open. This gave the motorized units the opportunity to move faster and with more fluidity.

In this period (and until 20 May), Air Fleets 2 and 3 were able to carry out the following missions – in general terms – in untiring day and night operations: first, they had destroyed most of the enemy ground organizations and broken the resistance of the border fortifications. In this way they gave indirect support (e.g. by destroying the transport connections) and immediate support to operations of the German Army (above all VIII Flying Korps to Panzer Group Kleist). By 14 May 'air superiority' had been won, a little later even 'air supremacy'. While Air Fleet 2 protected the northern flank of the German advance to the

Channel coast after the successful crossing of the Meuse, and additionally bombed enemy shipping, Air Fleet 3 secured the southern flank by attacking enemy troop movements and reinforcements. Furthermore they defeated the French Air Force.

On 15 May there was a change in command at the Luftwaffe so that from now on I and IV Flying Korps (long-range units) were subordinated to Air Fleet 2, and II, V (both long-range units) and VIII Flying Korps (short-range unit) were merged into Air Fleet 3.[31]

3. The Pursuit to the Scheldt and Advance to the Channel Coast 16–20 May 1940 (Maps 1, 4 and 5)

On the morning of 16 May, General Halder entered in his notebook: 'The breakthrough wedge is developing in almost classic form. West of the Meuse everything is proceeding smartly. Enemy tank attacks are being beaten off. The marching achievements of the infantry are outstanding.'[1]

It was important now to create through Visé or Maastricht a feeder route to get forces to the spearhead in the south (XVI Armee Korps and 9. Panzer Division). It appeared that the French were moving up reserves from Dijon and Belfort to the left side of the wedge, those which he had sent from the Charleroi area against the German right wing had been 'smashed to the ground'. So far the enemy had probably not drawn on his 'Great Reserve', and it remained to be seen where he intended to deploy this. On the whole, so the Chief of the Army General Staff reckoned, the enemy would still be able to bring up 30 divisions against the breakthrough wedge when he decided it was time for the 'final decisive battle'. 'We can free more reserves from (the sector of) Army Group C and if necessary feed them to the left wing…. The overall assessment of the situation and the ratio of forces is therefore very favourable,' General Halder concluded.[2]

When the left wing of Army Group B ran into enemy delaying resistance on the approach to the Dyle Line, Army Group Command A feared that the enemy would make a renewed attack against the open flank of 4. Armee (left side neighbour of Army Group B) – south-west of Charleroi

– and radioed OKH 4 at 0752 hrs: 'The Army Group instruction that advanced elements are not to cross the French fortifications south-east of Maubeuge, and are to *secure* adequately to the north (facing the Sambre), is gaining increased significance'.[3]

When Col-General von Brauchitsch (Commander-in-Chief German Army) arrived at the 4. Armee command post at 1447 hrs, General Brennecke made the following report on the situation: The enemy hit hard, particularly where he was well entrenched, though his tank attacks were not always very skillful. So far he had lost two to three divisions. On 15 May the enemy had, for the first time, dropped bombs aimed at the bridges over the Meuse, but without success.

Brauchitsch took this opportunity to inform him that the enemy was still holding his positions ahead of 6. Armee: in view of the way the situation was developing it was on the whole very possible that the concentration of effort of the operations would be transferred to 4. Armee. Next he announced the attachment of XVI Armee Korps to 4. Armee: other divisions would follow. Brauchitsch went on to say that 4. Armee, after forcing its way through the French line of fortifications, would probably have to pause, particularly the panzer divisions, which had to be held 'on a tighter rein.' One did not know but possibly it might resume soon and in the direction of Douai if the enemy decided to evacuate the Dyle Line at the approach of 6. Armee. 'If he stays there, however, it may be necessary to divert 4. Armee more to the north or north-west.'[4] In any case, the Armee had to 'pay special attention to its north flank, and plug the gap between XV and XIII Armee Korps at Berzee.'

In the evening XV Armee Korps with 7. Panzer Division broke into the French line of bunkers west of Clairfayts while 5. Panzer Division, left wing Beaumont, secured to the north and north-west. The remaining Korps of 4. Armee closed up. Meanwhile, Army Group Command A had decided on the morning of 16 May to temporarily halt the attack heads of its armies' fast units. The instruction was passed by telephone to 4. Armee and 12. Armee 'only to cross the line Beaumont–Hirson–Montcornet–Guignicourt with advance detachments', the bridges over the Oise between Guise and La Fère were to be taken intact; in the south, the Aisne was to be protected. The motorized units were to close up to the West, the infantry corps sent to follow.[5] The same evening Rundstedt made the 'crossing of the Sambre-Oise Line' dependent on his approval and ordered − 'with the full approval of the Commander-in-Chief German Army' − 'all units to close-up for the further advance to the West.' Rundstedt, Commander-in-Chief of Army Group A, had certainly had justified reasons for this *first close-up order of 16 May 1940*: the threat to his northern flank had still not been removed, and without doubt the panzer and motorized units were well strung out to the rear.[6] Up to this point it was primarily the 'panzer heads' which had done the fighting while the greater part of the units were often 'many kilometres farther back on the road' and 'frequently never saw action'.

'Army Group Command was probably in no doubt that the motorized units, by seizing the opportunity ahead of 12 Armee' could cross the Oise between Guise and le Fère 'without effort' (this was also the conviction and wish of the senior commanders, especially the Guderians and the Kleists), yet 'the risk attaching to it − from the standpoint of the whole operation − was not acceptable.' The long drawn out *southern flank* between La Fère and Rethel was − especially in the Laon area − too vulnerable. It almost asked the enemy to attack it. 'Even a local success by the enemy would imperil the continuation of the operation for days at least, if not put the whole thing in question.'[7]

Meanwhile Army Group B had issued a new instruction in the early hours of 16 May to the armies subordinated to it:

'The Dutch armed forces capitulated on 15 May. Belgian-British-French forces are holding the line Antwerp–Dyle–Namur.

'The Army Group is to occupy Holland and break through the Dyle positions, primary thrust direction, *Ath*.

'*18. Armee*

'… Holland securing the coast including the island of Walcheren. It blocks the Scheldt Estuary. The fortress front of Fortress Antwerp along the 18. Armee strip is to be subjected to an onslaught. As soon as possible partial attacks are to be made to tie down the occupants.

'(It) (i.e. 18 Armee) is to prepare to take over command of IX. Korps from the north wing of 6. Armee leading the way towards Antwerp. The hour when command is to be transferred is awaited…

'6. *Armee*

'a) is preparing on 16 May to continue the advance and on 17 May in echelon formation right will break through the Dyle position thrusting to Ath. The Antwerp eastern front will be covered by the heavy attack, and secured facing Namur.

'If established by scouting parties and night reconnaissance that the enemy is wavering, he is to be pursued immediately...'[8]

When the enemy pulled back as a result of the dangerous panzer breakthrough west of the Meuse, General *Hoepner* (Panzer Korps, XVI Armee Korps) decided on 16 May – in agreement with Bock and Reichenau – to take up pursuit of the retreating enemy at Wavre. Hoepner advanced to the south-west with both panzer divisions, crossed the Dyle river and pursued to Tilly. The northern wing of 6. Armee followed at first hesitantly, the more so because British counter-attacks either side of Leuven in the early hours had forced XI and IV Armee Korps on the defensive for a short time.[9]

By that time Hitler had ordered all Army Group B fast units, which had fulfilled their most important assignment and attracted strong enemy forces towards themselves, to follow at all costs the spearhead of Army Group A; therefore OKH had already ordered Army Group B on 14 May to take XVI Armee Korps of 4. Armee (Army Group A) under its command. The attack south of Wavre had occurred unexpectedly. The OKW therefore declared itself in agreement that the motorized forces on the left wing of 6. Armee with the right wing of 4. Armee should proceed towards the enemy (west of Charleroi). Col-General von Bock and von Reichenau had both argued to Wehrmacht High Command (OKW) and Army High Command (OKH) that withdrawing panzer forces to the rear would only delay the advance of XVI Armee Korps, but they had not managed to force through their opinion.[10]

By evening the centre and south wing of 6. Armee had arrived at the Nivelles line south of Brussels: the British were fighting a delaying action over the Lasne-Ysche to Brussels opposite the Korps on the northern wing and at the same time maintaining the Dyle Line either side of Leuven. IX and XI Armee Korps reached the Antwerp line of forts from Broechem – Koningshoyckt providing cover by their advance.

For 17 May, Army Group B gave 6. Armee the task of pursuing the enemy towards Tournai 'without let-up' while 18. Armee was to take Walcheren and carry out attacks against the Antwerp fortified front. The intention of the enemy remained unclear for the time being. Col-General von Bock wrote in his notes: 'Everybody is trying to solve the mystery of what the enemy is really attempting to do. Perhaps he is trying to hold, against me, Antwerp, the "Reduit National" – around Ghent and Bruges (and also) the Dendre Line but the latest Luftwaffe reports make that seem questionable.'[11]

For the operational assessments of OKH on 17 May Halder's notes are especially informative: 'The morning picture,' as he wrote in his diary, provided his conclusions regarding the enemy situation: the enemy had still taken no decisive measures to close the breakthrough area! He had brought up at least six divisions to the south and was waiting there, his forces being insufficient to advance.

On the basis of the apparent overall situation on the morning of 17 May, the Chief of the Army General Staff inferred that *perhaps* it was *reasonable to continue the operation in a south-westerly direction*. It could be left to Army Group B brought *up in staggered formation* to dispose of 7. French, the British, and 1. French Armies. To do so it would have to wheel at Lille to the coast, and then 4. Armee could attach.

As the enemy was not attacking out of the Antwerp Front, the Army Group was in the situation of being able to concentrate its effort on its southern wing. In order to continue the operations to the south-west, Army Group A should not bind any forces 'to its south flank', but rather continue striving to the West in staggered formation. Because the enemy was too weak to attack in this sector, Halder saw no danger in such a forward thrust.[12]

The centre of effort of this new operation to the south-west would centre on Compiègne and keep open the possibility for the right wing to wheel via Paris to the south-east. Halder noted: 'A great *decision is to be made!*'[13]

At midday the same day, Halder was summoned to a situation conference at OKW. By all accounts there was once more (between Brauchitsch and Hitler) 'little meeting of minds'. The Führer emphasized that he 'saw the major danger from the south.' (Halder observed later in his diary, 'I see at this time no danger at all!'). As soon as possible the infantry divisions had to be brought up to secure the southern flank. The fast units alone were not sufficient to make a thrust to the north-west. Halder remarked on 17 May: 'A really unpleasant day. The Führer is enormously nervous. He is *made anxious by his own success*, does not want to risk anything and therefore best of all would like us to stop. The pretext is concern about the left flank. A conversation between Keitel (Chief, OKW), given the task by Hitler of talking with the Army Group, and his own visit to Army Group A, has caused only uncertainty and doubt.'[14]

Army Group A gave the endangered southern flank much more attention on this day and a certain release from tension resulted. The foremost infantry divisions, marching behind 16. Armee in unbroken order, reached the Sedan area in the evening while the Group Kleist panzer units between La Fère and Rethel gave them cover. Rundstedt then decided to free a strong vanguard from Group Kleist to the Cambrai–St. Quentin sector in order to keep open the most important bridges over the Somme-Scheldt Canal for 18 May. The major body of Group Kleist was to close up at the Oise, 12. Armee infantry following. Halder had also spoken to this effect by telephone at 1330 hrs.[15]

This same day *Hitler now visited the HQ of Army Group A*. At 1500 he arrived at Bastogne and had the Army Group commander give him a general summary of the situation. Rundstedt took the opportunity to make special mention of the vulnerability of the southern flank and described 'the measures already taken and those intended to secure it.'[16]

According to the Army Group A War Diary, the Führer was 'in full accord with the assessment of the situation' and approved Rundstedt's arrangements. He underlined in particular the significance 'which the southern flank has not only for the operation of the whole Army, but especially politically and psychologically. Under no circumstances must it at this time receive a reverse anywhere, which would give not only the military, but also the political leadership of our enemy a disastrous boost... *At this moment it is not so very decisive to push forward to the Channel coast*, but much more *in the very short term to create an absolutely reliable* defensive preparedness on the Aisne, in the Laon area and later on the Somme. All measures are to be geared to this end *even if it should mean a temporary loss of time with regard to the push to the West*.'[17]

Shortly afterwards this decision of Hitler's found embodiment in Army Group Order No.2, of which extracts read:

1. The overall picture of our observations of the enemy hitherto lead us to conclude that the enemy is assembling a strong battle group in the area east of Paris in order to unleash the decisive thrust against our open southern flank between Compiègne and the Argonne Forest.
2. The Führer and Supreme Commander has therefore ordered the immediate closure by infantry forces of the open flank between La Fère and Le Chesne, and the restoration of the defensive preparedness within this Line (XVIII and III Armee Korps).
3. A strong vanguard of fast troops ahead of 4. Armee and 12. Armee will capture immediately the sector Valenciennes–Cambrai–St. Quentin and hold the most important bridges open for a later advance to the West. The *mass* of fast troops will close up in the Maubeuge–Guise–Crécy–Marle–Vervins–Hirson area, hold the bridges open and be ready to move out upon receipt of a special order.'[18]

By evening the leading units of Army Group A had reached (from left to right): area south-west of Carignan (16. Armee)–La Capelle line–St-Gobert-Dercy (vanguard Oise/12. Armee)–east of le Cateau (4. Armee).[19]

On the same day Army Group B had continued with the pursuit of the enemy using 6. Armee on the whole Front; the most advanced elements by 2000 hrs were on the line of the Senne sector and at Obaix. Panzer Korps Hoepner, which had received the order from Bock that evening to advance to Valenciennes via Mons, had this order countermanded by the Army Commander-in-Chief and was sent instead to join 4. Armee by the fastest route via Beaumont. Army Group B was therefore deprived of the last of its fast units, much to the disapproval of its commanders. This meant that in the fighting to come, the Army Group would have no option but to confront the enemy in tiring frontal encounters gaining ground step by step: a rapid push to one of the desired sectors was no longer possible.[20]

The morning picture on 18 May showed the enemy making an 'orderly' withdrawal north of the Sambre, apparently being in the process of thrusting strong forces from Belgium 'in front of the Western Front' of the German breakthrough wedge. Troops were being unloaded between Aisne and Meuse. OKH assumed that the enemy was intending to set up a new defensive Front here, for no 'attack groupings' had been identified. In the German estimation the French OHL reserves 'were present at least in small elements.'[21]

On the basis of this situation Halder came to the conclusion: 'The fact that the Allies are evacuating Belgium step by step' (the German flag had been raised on the Antwerp town hall!) and that 'with the greatest haste they are making the effort to implement emergency measures to set up a collection centre' proves that 'my understanding of yesterday' was correct. 'The *whole operation* must be continued *in a south-westerly direction* and without the slightest halt with *concentration of effort south of the Somme*: every hour is precious.'[22]

The OKW, on the other hand, thought differently. When Brauchitsch and Halder were summoned to a situation conference at 1000 hrs, Hitler expressed 'an incomprehensible anxiety about the southern flank'. As the Chief of the Army General Staff noted, the Führer raged and roared 'that we were on the way to ruining the entire operation and exposing ourselves to the danger of a defeat.' From the outset, *he refused to allow the operation to continue in any westerly direction*, let alone south-westerly. Moreover he supported the *north-west train of thought*, therefore diverting Army Group A in the direction of Arras-Calais.[23] As Jodl recorded in his diary, 18 May was a day of 'great tension'. OKH wanted to 'reinforce the southern flank with the greatest urgency and this had not been done. The infantry divisions were still marching westwards instead of turning south-west.' This left 10. Panzer Division and the 2. and also the 29. Motorized Divisions protecting the flank. Hitler ordered OKH 'in no uncertain terms' to 'take the necessary measures forthwith' and turn away the 1. Gebirgsjäger Division and also the 4. Armee rearward echelons advancing to the south and south-west.[24]

Clearly on the night of 17 May OKH had not gone ahead with Hitler's orders apparently based on his reading of the situation map of the evening of 17 May, for at 0200 hrs Army Group A received the following telex from OKH in which it was stated:

'As no serious resistance is to be expected at the current time ahead of 4. Armee and 12. Armee, the *securing* of the *left flank* seems highly important, the swift bringing forward of infantry divisions to the Aisne both sides of Rethel and especially in the direction of Laon is to be attended to. The fast units are to be freed for operations to the *north-west.*'[25]

Col-General Keitel, Commander-in-Chief of the OKW, who had flown to Army Group A on the morning of 18 May on behalf of Hitler to inform them that the Führer 'on the basis of the situation map placed before him by OKH was very concerned about the open southern flank', was told that the Army Group had already received orders to erect a defensive Front as soon as possible between La Fère and Le Chesne. All measures had been directed towards doing this. Keitel returned to Führer-HQ with a much more favourable impression of the development of operations, especially since the morning situation of 18 May recognized the turning of the infantry divisions towards the south. Thus Keitel was able to telephone Army Group Command A during the course of the day with news that the *Führer* had expressed his total satisfaction *respecting the measures taken by the Army Group* and at this stage now *felt reassured about the southern flank.* Now as before the quickest possible release of the motorized units out of this Front was urged.[26]

At midday the Chief of the Army General Staff noted: '… Antwerp has fallen, Cambrai (11.30), St. Quentin (9.00) reached. The picture is now becoming much clearer that the enemy is taking back his Belgian Front, apparently with an intermediate position somewhat north of the French national frontier and is attempting to cover these movements with fierce resistance to our 4. Armee in the Maubeuge-Valenciennes region.' Furthermore the enemy was striving to set up a collection line for forces he was shifting from Belgium and the south towards the Valenciennes–Cambrai–St. Quentin–La Fère line. 'We must go through them before they stiffen … (and) preserve the opportunity' to advance across the Somme at Péronne and Ham!'[27]

At 1350 hrs, therefore, OKH ordered that the mass of the fast units *'further increasing the security of the southern flank'* were to take the Cambrai–St. Quentin Line, *OKH had a further movement in mind.* Forward elements were to capture Péronne and Ham, motorized units hanging back were to be 'accelerated' up. 'As few as possible' forces were to be expended against Maubeuge and Valernciennes.[28]

When Halder made a fresh report to the Wehrmacht Commander-in-Chief at 1800 hrs, he succeeded finally in obtaining 'freedom of movement'. As he noted at the time, he had now 'finally got the right thing, but after general annoyance and in a form which looked outwardly like a policy decision of the OKW.'[29]

Thus *at 2048 hrs OKH* was in a position to issue to Army Groups A and B the following instruction for the continuation of operations: 'The intention of OKH is to *resume the advance on 19 May at the earliest possible point in time* with the aim of destroying *the enemy forces north of the Somme* and in the area of Belgium.'

Army Group A was to capture Arras deploying its fast forces in such a way 'that the advance in general can be continued in a general northerly or westerly direction.' The left flank on the Somme was to be given cover...

'Army Group B will attack with the concentration of its forces on the left wing.' The 'Luftwaffe has the task of supporting the advance of the fast forces in the region between the French national frontier and the Somme, and to protect the left flank at the Aisne and Somme.'[30]

Thus the temporarily reined-back German operations resumed motion. The same evening Rundstedt embraced the decision to place all fast units under the leadership of 4. Armee for the decisive thrust to the north-west. What he wanted to avoid at all costs was the danger of a 'spreading out'.

According to Army Group Order No 3, 4. Armee was to advance structured as follows:

Organization for the Advance of 19 May 1940
AOK (AOK–4)

Group Hoth	General Commanding XV Armee Korps
XVI Armee Korps	(3, 4. Panzer Divisions, 20. Infantry Division motorized.)
XXXIX Armee Korps	(5 and 7. Panzer Divisions, 11. Rifle Brigade., SS-*Totenkopf*.)

Group Kleist	General Commanding XXII Armee Korps XXXXI Armee Korps (6. and 8. Panzer Divisions)
XIX Armee Korps	(1., 2., 10. Panzer Divisions)
XIV Armee Korps	(29., 2, and 13. Infantry Divisions motorized) Initially still with OKH 12.
VIII Armee Korps	(28., 8. forward, 267. and 87. following at the rear.)
II Armee Korps	(12. and 32. forward, 62. and 263. following at the rear.)
V Armee Korps	(with 251. at the rear)
I Armee Korps	(with 1., 11., and 46. Infantry Divisions at the rear.)

Armee reserves: 211. Infantry Division, SS St *Der Führer*, 9. Panzer Division, SS-*V(erfügungs?)*-Division, SS-Leibstandarte *Adolf Hitler*, 81., 290., 292., 293., 294., 298. Infantry Divisions.

From Army Group Reserves   4. and 27. Infantry Divisions

Working in cooperation   I and VIII Flying Korps[31]

Meanwhile Army Group A had succeeded in diverting to the south all 12. Armee divisions it could contact, and command of the defensive Front had been transferred to OKH 12. While XV Armee Korps with 7. Panzer Division (leading elements!) reached the area south-west of Cambrai during the evening, and XXXXI Armee Korps was approaching Le Catelet, XIX Armee Korps had already passed through St. Quentin.[32]

On the northern wing of the German advance, 6. Armee – only now fourteen infantry divisions strong – was pursuing the enemy with its centre of effort on the southern wing in the direction of Tournai. Towards the Dendre Line, Ninove–Enghien–Soignies–Roeulx it closed up, and east of Ninove became entangled in a bitter rearguard action against British forces. The same day Antwerp and Brussels were surrendered.[33]

Col-General von Reichenau ordered for 19 May: 'Advanced elements of 4. Armee have reached Valenciennes and Cambrai. This rapid advance makes planned enemy resistance at the Dendre unlikely.' A quicker rate of advance was therefore justified 'provided always under the protection of

heavy artillery … Army Group has … specified the direction as westerly.
The centres of effort for the advance are:

IX Armee Korps Line Ghent-Audenarde.
XI Armee Korps Audenarde–Renaix road (inclusive towns).
IV Armee Korps high ground east of Tournai.
XXVII Armee Korps Péruwelz.'
IV Flying Korps (General Keller) was to support the advance of
6. Armee.[34]

On the evening of 19 May the vanguard reached the Scheldt both sides
of Tournai. XXVII Armee Korps followed in echelon formation left and
to the rear with its southern wing in the Mons district. AOK wanted to
allow the enemy no time to gain a fresh footing whereas Col-General
von Bock did not give serious credit to the possibility that the Allies
would make a massed counter-attack ahead of his path since they had
at most only 20 divisions. Army Group Command did not understand
why the enemy, in view of the dangerous situation, was not attempting
to take a large step backwards.[35]

On 20 May 6. Armee was everywhere at the Scheldt with the leading
sections of its force and the commander decided, therefore, to break
through on either side of Tournai to Seclin.[36]

After concluding the operations in Holland, 18. Armee had become
involved meanwhile in the fighting along the northern wing of Army
Group B. The blowing up of the large Scheldt tunnel delayed initially
a faster advance towards Antwerp but at 0950 hrs on 18 May, units of
208. Infantry Division raised the Reich war flag on the city town hall.
The armee received at this point the order to proceed south of Antwerp
to Ghent, pursuing the enemy across the Scheldt as quickly as possible
to seize the coast.

On 19 May the armee set off for the attack after regrouping: to the
right XXVI Armee Korps with 208., behind it 225. and 256. Infantry
Divisions coming forwards only slowly because the divisions had to
follow one another across the only undamaged bridge over the Scheldt
while under heavy enemy artillery fire: to the left the newly attached
IX Armee Korps built bridgeheads over the Dendre south of Termonde.

By 1740 hrs on 20 May the armee had pushed forward to the Canal de Gand (north-east of Ghent) at Wachtebeke, and at the same time 56. Infantry Division reached the area west of Mechelen where in the evening it fought off French counter-attacks from the line of bunkers around Ghent.[37]

The outstanding event of *19 and 20 May 1940 was that the German panzer spearheads reached the sea.* At 2100 hrs on 20 May the 2. Panzer Division (XIX Armee Korps) vanguards arrived at Abbeville while 8. Panzer Division (XXXXI Armee Korps) won through to the sea around Montreuil-sur-Mer at midnight.[38]

General Jodl, Chief of the Wehrmacht Command Office at OKW, noted in his diary: '… The breakthrough is looming ever larger… On 20th (May) we already have all panzer and motorized divisions with the exception of 9. Panzer Division in the breakthrough wedge. Whereas we were fearing on 19th that the main body of the Anglo-French Army had escaped to the south, it is becoming ever clearer on the 20th that they still have 20 divisions north of the Somme. The important thing now is to close the gap at Abbeville and that Korps Kleist reaches it on the evening of 20th…'

Meanwhile on the morning of 20 May, Hitler had announced the new guidelines for the continuation of the operations against the French Army (second phase). He was demanding:

1. the wiping out of the enemy north of the Somme and the occupation of the coast;
2. thus enabling the push between Oise and the sea to the Seine and
3. then joining the main principal advance both sides of Rheims (north-east of Paris) in a south-westerly direction, accompanied on the right flank east of Paris by fast forces.[39]

Jodl also recorded that on 20 May the Supreme Commander of the Wehrmacht was 'beside himself with joy', speaking *in words of the highest recognition of the German Army and its leadership.* Yes, he even occupied himself drafting the peace treaty which had to read: 'Return to the German People of the Territory and other Assets stolen from them 400 years ago'. He wanted to hold the first negotiations at Compiègne as in 1918. The British could have 'a special peace settlement at any time' provided they gave back their colonies. Jodl's entry of 20 May concluded with the sentence: 'As to the Führer's emotional words upon receiving the telephoned information from the Army Commander-in-Chief (capture of Abbeville) there is a special note by the Chief of OKW (i.e. Keitel) in the files.'[40]

On 19 May Halder was under the impression that the German panzer attack was to be towards Arras against the bulk of the retreating enemy. 'It will be a great battle lasting several days in which we have the advantage of the initiative, the enemy the advantage of the greater concentration of troops. Since we have besides the benefit of all the factors of morale and the extraordinary effect of our superior Luftwaffe, as far as I am concerned success is certain...'

During the afternoon enemy attacks were reported against the right wing of 4. Armee (from the Mons-Valenciennes direction); while it seemed to unsettle the OKW, Halder welcomed it. 'For north of it, the left wing of 6. Armee will go into the back of this attack.' In the evening the Chief of the Army General Staff received the report that Kleist's spearheads had crossed the last great obstacle before reaching the sea, the Canal du Nord, although they were expecting an enemy attack across the Ham–Cateau–Porcien line. Halder noted: '... Let them come! We have depth and strength enough!'[41]

The situation map on 20 May showed Halder that the left wing of Army Group B was making good progress. Between these forces and the right wing of 4. Armee, however, apparently strong French elements had 'squeezed themselves in' and were trying to break out to the south. Halder was of the opinion that, 'we shall see similar phenomena in the vicinity of the two wedges pressing ahead close together' more frequently as time went on. It remained to be seen if Group Kleist, which 'is getting ever closer to the Somme and perhaps might even have to *cross* the Somme for the south, is working with Bock in a major encircling movement, or if Bock is not to a certain extent driving the wild game to pass in front of Kleist.' Halder considered this perfectly possible considering the 'ambitious pressing forward by the Officer Commanding Army Group B.'

From the attempt to force the enemy to accept battle with a reversed front north of the Somme, a 'quite common encirclement' could ensue in which Bock, 'would surface on the most extreme wing. The more the way was paved for such a development, the more would Kleist be forced in a *south-westerly* direction.[42]

4. The Crisis at Arras, 21 May 1940 (Maps 1, 4 and 5)

On 21 May the enemy resistance stiffened against Army Group B. 18. Armee, operating on the northern wing, was unable to cross the Canal de Gand with its weak vanguard and it was therefore decided to close up and await the arrival of 225. and 256. Infantry Divisions still on the eastern banks of the Scheldt.[1]

Towards 1400 hrs, the Chief of Army Group B General Staff, Lt-General von Salmuth, located in Brussels, briefed the 1a of the Army Group on the situation at 6. Armee.

It seemed that the enemy had stopped along the entire Front, supported by much artillery. Until now the Armee had only created 'weak bridgeheads' on the western bank of the Scheldt which had driven off enemy attacks.

AOK intended to transfer the centre of effort to XI Armee Korps (right wing) and east of the border fortifications, if possible, to advance in a north-westerly direction. Col-General von Reichenau did not want to get bogged down 'frontally'. He believed that 4. Armee west of the border fortifications was strong enough to overrun them from the rear.[2]

Col-General von Bock made OKH aware a short time later that 'how very much it was important in the situation which had now arisen in front of the Army Group to gather all forces at Lille.' Furthermore he now *considered that the time had come to subordinate forces of the right wing of 4. Armee to Army Group B* in order to guarantee the uniform control of the attacks against the fortifications.[3]

At 1500 hrs, Army Group B reported to OKH that they wanted to transfer the centre of effort of the operations to the right wing of 6. and to 18. Armee with the objective of driving a strong wing 'along the coast'. The precondition for this was that Army Group A should advance northwards across the line Valenciennes–Arras–Abbeville. As it now appeared, Bock wanted to create the encirclement so as to wipe out the enemy in a *pincer* attack.

Towards evening OKH responded: regarding the objectives of 6. Armee, nothing had changed. It was not to destroy the enemy but *pin it down* without ramming its own head against the Lille fortifications. The Chief of the Army General Staff laid particular stress on having 6. Armee prevent enemy attacks from Lille against the wing of 4. Armee.[4]

Bock was not satisfied with this decision and declared himself in agreement with the intention of 6. Armee to attack with its strong right wing. The second order from OKH, which put renewed emphasis on the decisive forward movement of the *left* wing of 6. Armee, came too late. Bock telephoned Halder at once and told him that he 'could not change anything now. As for the rest, 6. Armee would also proceed on its southern wing.' When the Chief of the Army General Staff mentioned the heavy attacks against 4. Armee's northern wing, Bock replied, 'The attacks can't be all that heavy' since for its development with heavy forces the space between 6. Armee and 4. Armee was 'much too narrow.'[5]

On the morning of 21 May Halder confided to his diary: '… The day has begun in fairly nervous mood. According to reports received there is fairly heavy pressure on the 4. Armee northern flank….'

When Lt-Colonel Kinzel, OKH liaison officer to 6. Armee, informed OKH of Reichenau's new intentions at 1700 hrs, Halder made it 'unequivocally clear to him that the important thing was to advance with the left wing in order to help 4. Armee.' Because the decisive outcome lay on the heights of Arras, 4. Armee had to get there as quickly as possible with infantry divisions. If 6. Armee stayed back on its left wing, 4. Armee would be forced to halt at Valenciennes. Then the Chief of the Army General Staff expressed the point of view that *the battle would be won* once German troops reached the heights of Arras.[6]

If we turn briefly to the decisive events in the front sector of 4. Armee, without doubt 21 May here was marked by critical fighting: at Maubeuge (VIII Armee Korps), Mormalwald (XVI Armee Korps) and particularly at Arras (XXXIX Armee Korps).

On the morning of 21 May, Col-General von Kluge reported to the Chief of Army Group General Staff A at 1040 hrs 'that 4. Armee is involved in fairly heavy fighting on its right wing in the Valenciennes-Mormalwalk area' ... incidentally the fast formations had turned north towards the Arras–St. Pol–Hesdin–course of the Authie line.

It had always been his intention ... to reinforce the left wing of the Armee with panzers. Meanwhile the OKH Order had arrived to the effect that the panzer forces coming up were not to attach to Group Hoth but to Group Kleist. This was 'obviously' carried out.[7]

Indicative of Kluge's appreciation of the situation that day were some comments directed to his Staff: It had to be carefully considered 'if one should just maintain the encircled units in Flanders' in order to *use them with the main body of the Army against the French Army*. The latter would otherwise have the opportunity to erect a proper defensive front against which our own attack later would not be easy![8]

At 1142 hrs however, Colonel Blumentritt telephoned through the new instructions of the Army Commander-in-Chief: 'Advance the panzer spearhead to Calais and Boulogne. Build bridgeheads at Abbeville–Amiens–Péronne and in the direction of Noyenne.'[9]

The only temporary crisis during the first phase of the Western Campaign occurred around Arras on 21 May.[10] That morning, XXXIX Armee Korps (Group Hoth) was south of the town still held by strong British and French forces. Following information from the Commander of Group Hoth, the korps was to press forward either to Pernes (north-west) or Béthune (north). Additionally it had the task of capturing the Scarpe bridges. 4. Armee had reserved for itself a move farther northwards. At 1445 hrs Command Headquarters ordered its attached divisions to take the Scarpe river at Acq and Aubigny-Savy in company with 7. Panzer and SS-Totenkopf. For this purpose, these two divisions had to pass south and west of Arras in order to then turn northwards. Meanwhile 5. Panzer Division could not attack east of the town simultaneously as envisaged. Thus the right flank of 7. Panzer Division was totally exposed to the heavy enemy presence in Arras.

The vanguard of 7. Panzer Division (Commander, Major-General Rommel) had passed east of Beaumont at 1500 hrs, heading north, when the main body of the Division was surprised at 1530 hrs by several strong tank attacks on the flank along the line Tilloy–Arras road–Beaumetz, and forced on the defensive. Other enemy tanks, advancing from Achicourt, rolled over the Division's Rifle Regiment 6 to the south-west and confronted SS-*Totenkopf* Division west of Wailly. The situation soon became more critical and the advance of XXXIX Armee Korps came to a standstill. Before the newly sent-up 11.Rifle Brigade could arrive in the area under threat, more enemy tanks broke through to Henin-Broiry (south-east of Arras) and found columns and the Divisional Staff of SS-*Totenkopf*. The Panzer Regiment of 7. Panzer Division, which had already pressed through to the Scarpe river south-west of Acq had to be recalled. Finally numerous Stuka attacks between 1830 and 2030 hrs brought a tangible relief. The enemy was forced to return to Arras, but not until late evening was the situation passably stabilized. At the same time, 5. Panzer Division had also been obliged to ward off heavy tank attacks coming from Arras.[11]

The account in Rommel's Battle Report reads: 'Between 1530 and 1900 hrs (south-west of Arras) very heavy fighting occurred against hundreds of enemy tanks and supporting infantry. Our own anti-tank guns are not effective against the British heavy armour, even at close range. Our defensive Front consisted of anti-tank guns. The enemy broke through the line and shot down or crushed the guns, killing most of the crews. I.Rifle Regiment 6 and Anti-tank Detachment 42 had especially severe losses....Finally the very hard battle ended in our favour by means of our successful defensive fire, above all from the combined batteries of Artillery Regiment 78, Anti-tank 42 and all the flak. The enemy was forced to retire to Arras with heavy losses (43 tanks destroyed).'[12]

Meanwhile Army Group Command A sent AOK 4 the following *new instruction* at 1640 hrs: '4. Armee is to prevent a breakthrough by enemy forces along the line Douai–Arras–Boulogne and is also to advance with panzers *to Calais*. Bridgeheads are to be erected and held on the bridges at Abbeville and Amiens. I Armee Korps is being reincorporated.'

Shortly afterwards the Army Commander-in-Chief telephoned the Commander of 4.Army for a report on the situation which he received as follows: On the right wing the situation at Maubeuge was being cleansed. The enemy was still fighting stubbornly but had orders to halt. At Mormalwald a major cleansing process was in process: the enemy forces there were being overcome. 3. And 4. Panzer Divisions were still in action: these had the task of standing west of Arras in the early morning because von Kluge *intended to assemble all panzer divisions in the area between Arras and the sea.* Montreuil was in German hands. The intention for VIII Armee Korps was to send it tomorrow into the area Valenciennes, Denain, Bouchain. II Armee Korps stood south-west of Cambrai.

Kluge then added, regarding *the enemy attack at Arras:* the Luftwaffe had the impression that *the enemy was attempting to break through from north to south.* Their columns had been attacked by the two Flying Korps *Grauert* and *Richthofen.* His own intention was to attack the enemy troops coming from the north.[13]

When the situation at Arras came to a head towards evening, von Kluge gave II Armee Korps the following order personally at 1830 hrs: 'Enemy has broken through at Arras with tanks direction Beaumetz. General Hoth has requested urgently that 12. Infantry Division be alerted and march. Correspondingly it is to march and a vanguard is to take spot height 122 at Monchy and secure to the right. It will then be subordinated to General Hoth.'

Group Kleist reported at 1940 hrs that the enemy had attacked St. Pol and Hesdin from the north but had been repulsed. Subsequently the Group received the telephoned order: 'On 22 May the Armee is to attack the enemy advancing from the north and force him back across the line Arras–St Pol–Hesdin–Etaples. This line may only be crossed with the approval of the Armee.'

At 2208 hrs the conduct of this attack was discussed between von Kluge and General von Kleist in a telephone conversation:

… He (Kleist) will be *prepared early tomorrow morning to advance to the north*, with XXXXI Armee Korps to Calais, with XIX Armee Korps to Boulogne. He asks that Group Hoth be allowed to accompany him in order to protect his right flank. Kluge requested the building up of a pronounced centre of effort for the operations on the line Avesnes–le Comte (about 20 km west of Arras)–St. Omer. General von Kleist replied that he had *already done so to its right.* Kluge stated that he agreed, but on the condition: 'All proceedings first on my order. It will happen once the situation at Arras has been mopped up.'

Shortly before midnight a long telephonic exchange of views occurred between the Chief of AOK 4 and Army Group A (1a) for the War Diary (in extracts): '..The enemy breakthrough at Arras has been sealed off. The northern part of Mormalwald has been cleansed – all quiet on the southern Front. The bridgeheads are holding, apparently there has been no enemy activity against them. Von Kluge reserves to himself the right to order the crossing of the line Arras–St. Pol–Hesdin–Etaples in order to guarantee the orderly setting up of the panzer wedge and the cleansing of the situation at Arras.... Today *was the first day* in which *the enemy had scored successes.'*

Colonel Blumentritt replied that the Army Commander-in-Chief had expressed clearly that creating order in the area north of the Somme would take several days. The bridgeheads were important for the later, second phase.[14]

CHAPTER III

The Allied resistance to the German attack, 10–21 May 1940 (Map 2a)

An overview
Dr K. J. Müller

On 10 May 1940 the Allied armies moved up to the French northern and eastern borders in two Army Groups. At the French-Belgian border from the sea to Longuyon stood Army Group 1 commanded by General Billotte on a front of over 300 kilometres in length.[1] Seventh Armee Giraud[2] formed its left flank; the British Expeditionary Force (BEF) joined it; followed by First French Army[3] to which the French Cavalry Corps (CC) of General Prioux was subordinated. Adjacent was 9. Armee Corps[4] and Second Armee[5] Huntziger holding the Maubeuge–Longuyon sector; to its right in the east Army Group 2 under General Prételat occupied the Maginot Line.

Initially the BEF was not attached to Army Group 1 but under the direct control of the Allied Commander-in-Chief General Gamelin and the Commander-in-Chief of the Allied North-east Front, General Georges. Not until after the German offensive was under way was it decided on 12 May, at a conference at the Chateau de Casteau[6] at Mons, that the Commander-in-Chief of Army Group 1 would coordinate all Allied armies in Belgium and Holland.

After the Wehrmacht began the campaign in the West in the early hours of 10 May by invading Belgium[7] and the Netherlands,[8] these two nations appealed to the Western Powers for help. A few hours later Army Group 1 entered Belgium to trigger the Dyle Plan envisaged for this eventuality.[9] According to the Plan, Army Group 1 would wheel on its right flank (pivoting in the area of Sedan) to form a line Antwerp–Louvain–Wavre–Gembloux–Namur–Givet–Sedan. On its left flank 7. Armee Giraud had to advance through Walcheren, South Beveland, and the estuary of the Scheldt into Holland and then as far as Breda in order to link up with the Dutch Army and also cover Antwerp from the north and north-east.

The Dyle Line was based not only on the fortifications at Antwerp and Namur and additionally from Givet on the existing French border fortifications, but also on the courses of the Demer and Dyle rivers and by the Meuse from Namur. Only between Wavre and Namur, in the Gembloux sector, were there no natural obstacles: therefore, it was here that the Cavalry Corps (CC) of First French Army would intercept the enemy attack.

In the winter of 1939, the Allied High Command had initially adopted the so-called 'Escaut Plan' which would bring any German offensive to a standstill by wheeling the mass of its forces into a line Antwerp–Ghent–French border along the Scheldt (*Escaut*).[10] The Allied leadership then thought again, and now they believed it possible to find time to build their defensive front on the river Dyle. Advanced troops of the Belgian Army would give cover at the Albert Canal ('*position de couverture*') while the cavalry corps would be thrown forward quickly to the Dyle to intercept the first enemy hordes. In addition there would be delaying tactics such as the destruction or blockading of roads, bridges, and other means of communication which would be bound to halt the German advance.

This assumption very soon proved faulty after the campaign began. One of the basic pre-conditions of the Dyle Plan was not met, a loss which was to have a fateful influence on the course of the battle for Belgium and Northern France, and indeed on the whole campaign.

The massive German blow forced the Belgians on the Albert Canal and south of Liège back to the Dyle position quicker than expected. Essential for the rolling up of the *position de couverture* was the surprise capture of Fort Eben Emael and the capture intact of the bridges Veldvezelt and Vroenhoven over the Albert Canal near Maastricht.

As a result of this unexpectedly fast German advance, the Allied commanders were forced to reconsider the Dyle Plan. General Georges decided to run with it, however, but accelerate the advance of the Allied armies[11] and delay the enemy by any means possible.

While the main body of Army Group 1 continued with the occupation of the Dyle Line, the forward Allied light mechanized Divisions made contact with the enemy on 11 May. Between 12 and 14 May, principally in the Méhaigne–Hannut region from Tirlemont–Huy and from Perwez–Waret–Marchovelette fierce fighting ensued between the French cavalry corps and German panzers. On 14 May the mechanized divisions pulled back to the Dyle Line, and on 15 and 16 May fighting broke out in the sector of First French Army and the BEF around the Dyle position.

Meanwhile a crisis had occurred farther south in the domains of 2. Armee and 9. Armee which would be decisive for the campaign. It arose from a combination of *two factors*: (i) from the fact that the time factor for the carrying out of the Dyle Plan had been *incorrectly estimated* and (ii) as a result of the erroreous assumption by the Allied commanders[12] that the German *main thrust would come through the Belgian plain* against the centre of the Dyle position, and certainly not in the area south of Namur because – as was believed – the mountainous Ardennes region was impassable for a force of massed panzers.

The result of factor (i) was that only parts of the two French armies had arrived in time, and those that were there had not yet adequately structured their front for an effective defence[13] by the time when the German forces appeared at the Dyle position. Factor (ii) resulted in the main body of Army Group 1 with the best and most powerful forces proceeding farther north: 2. Armee and 9. Armee, on the other hand, were made up principally from divisions of series A and B whose equipment was less modern and whose officer corps possessed a high percentage of reserve officers.

On 13 May at 2. Armee in the Sedan area and in the 9. Armee sector at Givet and Dinant (Houx, Anhée, Yvoir) after the German advance across the Meuse had begun with strong Luftwaffe support, the front here collapsed after vain attempts, disconnected and hesitant, to destroy or at least isolate the bridgeheads.

The Allied commanders deployed bombers, mostly RAF machines, against the Meuse bridges at Sedan, Dinant and Givet and the two bridges over the Albert Canal near Maastricht.[14] Especially after the critical situation at 9. Armee had become evident,[15] great efforts were made to prevent the Germans crossing, or to destroy the bridges. Meanwhile, due to the inferiority of their fighter protection and the heavy German flak, the Allied air forces suffered very heavy losses[16] and very soon it was necessary to limit activity to night attacks. Some of these attacks were carried out with great courage but even so they neither halted the German operations nor interfered with them decisively.

Equally, up until 15 May – apart from local, independent attempts – effective counter-measures were not organized in the 2. Armee and 9. Armee spheres. All army group orders got no further than the paper they were written on,[17] the army commanders did not react with sufficient speed and determination while the troops themselves were sorely demoralized by the combination of Luftwaffe and panzer attacks. One tank division 1st DCR (*Division Cuirassée de Reserve* – Armoured Division) brought up to 9. Armee for a counter-attack on 14 May was too long in the preparation, dissipated its energies and was lost in vain.

By 16 May most of 9. Armee had already been wiped out, and 2. Armee battered. Their remnants built a defensive front south of Sedan to the north. 1. Armee organized a flank protection to the south at the river Sambre. German panzers flooded westwards through the breach between Namur and Montmédy–Stonne; Army Group 1, the Belgian Army and the BEF all came under threat of being cut off.[18]

In this situation, the Commander-in-Chief of Army Group 1 decided on a general retreat to the Scheldt Line (Escaut) in three stages over the Senne and Dendre Lines. On the whole this operation was carried through to plan successfully by 19 May in the areas held by the Belgian, British, and First French Army.[19]

If one conducts a survey of the rapid succession of events between 16 and 19 May on the Allied side, apart from the retreat to the Scheldt the following phases of the operations can be ascertained:

Initially the Allied commanders made the effort to intercept the panzer breakthrough by setting up blocking fronts, but the orders to build interception positions both on the Aisne–Canal de l'Ailette–Oise–Sambre Line and also the Valenciennes–Bouchain–Cambrai–Le Catelet–St.

Quentin–Canal de Crozat–Oise Line proved unfeasible because of the fast tempo of the German breakthrough. Furthermore the French High Command also failed to assemble any strategic reserves for deployment in a decisive counter-offensive.

The second phase of the development had been sounded in Order No.102 of the Commander-in-Chief, North-east Front. On the evening of 18 May at 2300 hrs, General Georges gave in, accepting the obvious impossibility of halting and sealing off the German breakthrough when he wrote:[20] 'In the case that the advance of the German panzer divisions westwards towards the Maubeuge–Péronne Front ... cannot be halted ... or they have already crossed this line – we will have to consider lengthening our barrage along the Somme from Péronne to the sea...' The hypothesis underlying this sentence – *the isolation of Army Group 1* – became reality on 20 May when the German panzer spearheads reached the Canal coast at Abbeville.

Meanwhile in the *political arena* problems no less serious had surfaced. The military crisis threatened to place a heavy burden on the Anglo-French relationship.[21]

On 16 May, Churchill had come to Paris at the urgent request of Reynaud. Once there, it became not only abruptly obvious to the British Prime Minister just what a threatening situation had developed in Belgium and northern France, but he also received the galling impression that the French leadership was looking on helpless and almost paralyzed at the vision of modern warfare unfolding on the battlefields of Artois and Flanders. He was – so he wrote later[22] – speechless when he discovered that the French had not set up any kind of strategic reserves. Consequently, the confidence which the British had invested in the virtuosity of the French High Command was sadly misplaced. Now an ear had to be lent to the loud complaints and accusations made a few days previously by Lord Gort, Commander-in-Chief of the British troops, that the orientation and coordination of the French High Command was deficient.

This sudden crisis of confidence affected Churchill to the extent that he already considered it possible that France would be forced to sue for peace.[23] British policy was now confronted by the difficult task of choosing between assisting an endangered ally with material help and moral encouragement, and not over-weakening its own defensive ability, for the margins were narrow.

A classic example of this dilemma for British policy revealed itself in the question of how far Great Britain would go in reinforcing its air support. From the opening days of the campaign the French were petitioning to a growing extent for increased involvement, particular by RAF fighter aircraft.[24] German superiority in the air and the rapid elimination of a large part of the French Air Force had made this necessary. Despite the urgency of these requests, which Reynaud had sent to London with the support of Lord Gort and Air Marshal Barratt, to make another ten British fighter squadrons available, the War Cabinet decided to send no additional fighters to France for otherwise the British home air defences would be endangered. When fresh energetic demands for RAF reinforcements were submitted on 15 May, the War Cabinet finally decided to send four squadrons to France and station six others at air bases in southern England from where they could fly over to France within the hour if the situation demanded it. As they saw it, this was the limit to which Britain could go to help their French ally otherwise there could be 'fatal consequences' for the home anti-aircraft defences!

During the further course of the campaign, all additional French pleas fell on deaf ears. Here was the tragic dilemma for the British policy towards France: the limited British material possibilities set narrow limits on what was possible to help its ally. British policy was therefore confronted by *two diametrically opposed options*: either to render France the military aviation it wanted, encouraging and reassuring its ally and holding the coalition together, or decline for fear of unduly weakening the English home air defences. It was here that this problem first came to light and would become ever more obvious until the French collapse.

As had already appeared likely on 15 May in the question of RAF reinforcements, this situation was to turn into a political issue of the first order which developed even further after the French surrender. Over the coming weeks, reproaches and suspicions were voiced loudly in various ways and later on, certain circles, particularly those supporting the Vichy regime, saw in the lack of Royal Air Force assistance proof for their assertion that Britain had left France in the lurch.[25] Anti-British propaganda in France *latched on to this only too willingly after the armistice.*

While the fighting in Northern France and Belgium raged, on the political stage two significant elements emerged for the Anglo-French relationship:

* the outbreak of a grave and highly questionable *crisis of confidence* during the prevailing military situation on the British side;
* *a dilemma of British policy towards France* which had first found its expression in the question of RAF aid, and which contained the seeds of the most serious political consequences.

Returning to the *military development*: when General Georges took into account in his Order No.102 on the evening of 18 May the possibility of Army Group 1 being isolated, he set out at the same time a couple of rather limited counter-attacks: 4th DCR (tank division) should attack the German advance in the flank in the direction of Laon–Crécy-sur-Serre,[26] and he recommended that Army Group 1 should operate its fast units towards Cambrai–St. Quentin to the south.

Next day the Allied Generalissimo, General Gamelin, intervened for the first time in the leadership of the operations with his '*Personal and Secret Instruction No.12*'[27] in which he suggested quite generally an operation against the rearward lines of communication of the German panzer division; Army Group 1 should open a route to the Somme. He outlined the decisive factor with the words, 'All is a question of hours.' Meanwhile there remained in practice either independent and therefore ineffective single actions or poorly organized and hesitant attempts to prepare.[28]

An operation which had psychological and also certain operational influence on the German side must be given closer attention: the British attack at Arras of 21 May 1940.[29] The BEF attacked with two assault groups,[30] crossed the Scarpe river to attack the flank of 7. Panzer Division and advanced about 5 kilometres south of Arras. After some tangled and unmethodical exchanges between tanks and panzers south of Agny the British withdrew, their attacking force too weak to hold the ground gained.

More interesting, because it is significant for the situation within the Allied Staffs, is the context in which this attack came to be ordered.

Originally the orders received by General Franklyn, Commander of 5th British Division who led the attack, had been to support the garrison at Arras and cut the German lines of communication by blockading the roads south of Arras. On 20 May the Chief of the Imperial General Staff[31] had flown to France to meet General Billotte and urge him to make an immediate and urgent effort to close the gap between the Somme and Army Group 1. Billotte agreed to an attack by two French divisions occurring at the same time as the British offensive. What was being planned now at the corresponding French Army commands was a greater offensive in order to restore contact between the separated army groups. General Franklyn had received no corresponding orders of the kind; as far as he was concerned his duty in its entirety was to support the garrison at Arras and carry out a limited operation to block off the enemy's rearward connections. Neither did he know about the wider scope of the attack, nor had he been informed that French troops would be involved in an offensive in the direction of Cambrai. The latter was not disastrous since this French attack planned for 21 May did not take place, but the former led to the British operation being undertaken with force too weak for the purpose and therefore, being under the aspect of the larger operation which the overall leadership had in mind for him, was unsuccessful.

On 19/20 May Gamelin was replaced by General Maxime Weygand. The next few days were dominated by the efforts of the new Generalissimo to effect the concept known as 'Manoeuvre de junction' – the so-called Weygand Plan.

Weygand's intention was to break down the isolation of Army Group 1 by energetic offensives. On 20 May in a telephone conversation he informed General Billotte[32] that Army Group 1 should advance towards Cambrai without regard to losses. Next day he went to Ypres[33] in order to negotiate personally with the commanders of the isolated armies on the spot. Here he developed his thinking on how he proposed to close the gap between Army Group 1 and the bulk of the Allied forces south of the Somme.

At the centre of the plan was a double attack: Army Group 3 (General Besson) would advance north while British and French divisions of Army

Group 1 would attack south at the same time in order to bring about the unification of the two Army Groups. Basically, therefore, the same line was being followed in this plan as had been indicated in the orders and instructions of Georges and Gamelin, it was simply clearer. The decisive factor, however, was that three days had been lost meanwhile!

Without wishing to go into greater detail about this conference, one must agree with the opinion of the British military historian Ellis[34] who writes that that meeting was less significant for the decisions taken, and much more for the lack here of real determination to carry out the planned offensive. Moreover, it revealed the lack of confidence and trust. In addition, questions which were important for the execution of the new plan were never clarified. The Belgians had pointed out at Ypres that their army was not in a position to retreat to the Yser as Weygand proposed it should. Billotte stated that First French Army could do no more than hold their lines: they were barely capable of defending themselves. Accordingly, Lord Gort, who to the annoyance of Weygand did not appear until after the latter had left, was naturally very dubious regarding what the participation of the French units in the planned attack to the south actually involved.

Between 19 and 21 May, therefore, *not only had valuable time been wasted*, but *the new plan was already from its inauguration under an evil star.* The next few days would impressively confirm that.

The efforts to carry out the Weygand Plan were overshadowed by the lack of determined leadership at Army Group 1; this began to have an increasingly unhealthy effect. On the journey from the Ypres conference to his headquarters, General Billotte suffered a fatal accident. Over three days passed before an official successor (Blanchard) was appointed, and even then an effective coordination of the three armies attached to Army Group 1 was not achieved. For example the Belgian Army remained five days without army group orders, and at the next discussions between Blanchard and Gort, Belgian representatives were rarely present.[35]

Just as on the one hand the effective coordination at Army Group 1 left much to be desired, the *instructions of the supreme Allied leadership* bore no relationship to reality.

On 22 May, Lord Gort received a note[36] from the Prime Minister in which there was mention of an attack by eight British and French divisions: this was apparently a remark[37] made by Weygand at the Supreme Allied War Council on 22 May and which was completely unrealistic.

The same day Weygand issued '*Ordre Operationel Nr. 1*' as the official order initiating his plan.[38] Characteristic of this order are not only the uncertainties regarding many details which it contained, but also the total glossing over of those critical remarks and reservations made by the Belgian King and General Billotte, and never discussed at the conference.

Likewise, on 22 May an order from General Georges arrived at Army Group 1 (*Ordre Operationel Nr. 17*) which contained no explanatory instructions regarding the Weygand Plan and ordered the setting up *of a defensive front* along the Somme. Apart from a brief remark concerning 7. Armee, no mention was made in it of any offensive action.

Under these circumstances the initiative for the execution of the '*Manouevre de junction*' passed almost completely to the individual Commanders-in-Chief of the Armees of Army Group 1. These decided first to pull back the front from the Scheldt to the Lys and the French border fortifications respectively in order to clear the way for the advance to the south by the required British divisions. This retreat was not possible until the night of 23 May, the relief of the divisions, therefore, at the earliest by the night of 25 May. Under these circumstances *a beginning of the offensive did not come into question* before 25/26 May.[39]

What Gamelin had said was needed on 19 May, was finally conceived on 22 May and enshrined in Operational Order No.1 as the '*Manouevre de junction*' originally scheduled to begin on 23 May, was thus postponed to 26 May. Because of the British operation at Arras on 23 May and the difficulties the French had in moving out, another postponement was necessary, and now the advance was set for 27 May.

CHAPTER IV

The decision to halt the German panzers, 22–26 May 1940 (Maps 5–8)

1. On 22 May

At midday on 22 May, OKH had the following picture of the situation on the Western Front:[1] In the Army Group B sector, opposite 18. Armee and 6. Armee, the enemy resistance continued to be strong, especially south of Ghent, in the uplands west of Audenarde and both sides of Tournai; also at Condé it had stiffened considerably. Nevertheless, 6. Armee had succeeded in building some local bridgeheads.

Before the Army Group A Front, the enemy had attacked 4. Armee (Group Hoth) at Arras on the afternoon of 21 May and had advanced to a line south of the town. From 0900 hrs a comprehensive counter-attack by XXXIX Armee Korps was carried out by 5. Panzer Division and elements of 20. Infantry Division (mot.). VIII and probably also XVI Armee Korps were still in action against the enemy in the area north of Maubeuge, Bavai and south-east of Valenciennes.

Group Kleist had advanced with XXXXI Armee Korps into the St. Pol, Hesdin, and Montreuil-sur-Mer region; the continuation northwards depended on how the situation around Arras developed. XIX Armee Korps had had the major part of its force close up near XXXXI Armee Korps and in addition had set up bridgeheads on the southern bank of the Somme between Abbeville and Amiens.

On the evening of 21 May, ground reconnaissance reported the area south of Abbeville to Hornoy free of the enemy. Almost at the same time in its situation report No.319, Foreign Armies West had warned that *the ports of Dunkirk and Boulogne* were *heavily occupied*, and a large number of transport ships had sailed. This gave rise to the assumption that 'apart from stores and rearward services, elements of British fighting troops were being shipped out from there.'[2] While 9. Panzer Division was proceeding to join Group Kleist via Philippeville, the whereabouts of the divisions of XIV Armee Korps (2., 13., 29., Motorized) were not known for the time being (lower Somme).

South of Le Cateau, II Armee Korps had entirely cleared the sector of the enemy. 12. Armee was along the entire front, right wing at Chany, on the Oise-Aisne-Canal and the Aisne. 263. Infantry Division was to relieve elements of 29. Infantry Division (mot.) on security duties between Ham and La Fère. XXXX Armee Korps was advancing westwards from the Vervins–Montcornet area.

16. Armee reported lively reconnaissance troop activity by both sides and a small amount of artillery harassing fire.[3]

Now we look at the events of 22 May individually. Without doubt the Wehrmacht leadership was troubled psychologically by the temporarily uncertain situation at Arras. In the early hours of 22 May, Hitler had his senior adjutant, Colonel Schmundt, call Army Group A headquarters for information regarding the development of operations. Colonel Blumentritt reported that the enemy forces which had broken through to the south on 21 May had forced 7. Panzer Division to pull back at some places. Hitler ordered accordingly that 'all fast units in any manner available in the area both sides of Arras and west of it to the sea, but the infantry divisions eastwards' of the town were to be deployed to cleanse the territory between Maubeuge and Valenciennes. Furthermore all other infantry divisions of 12., 2. and 16. Armees were to be brought up rapidly to the west.[4]

In order to speed up the execution of this order and make its importance clearer, and particularly in order to obtain a picture of the situation personally, Col-General Keitel, Chief of Wehrmacht High Command, flew out to Army Group A where he arrived at 0900 hrs. In his discussion with the Chief of the Army Group General Staff, he emphasized Hitler's instructions respecting the immediate importance of having infantry divisions release the motorized divisions from the Somme as quickly as possible, and of also having the Group Kleist panzer divisions 'ahead out of the flank protection' and extracted from the defensive fighting between Amiens and Abbeville. Only the motorized forces reach the attack wedge to the north in time, for that reason they had to be released from their burden of protecting the flank to the rear. Their purpose was to support and relieve the foremost panzer units. In order to achieve this, the infantry divisions had to move up on forced march to the west, at least with a vanguard.[5]

This order coincided no doubt with how Army Command A saw things and they issued the corresponding orders. Upon his return to Führer-HQ, Keitel informed the Staff at Charleville by telephone the same day that Hitler was in total accord with the measures taken by Rundstedt and was placing 'special confidence' in the person of the officer commanding the army group. The Führer had 'again and again' expressed his satisfaction regarding the 'leadership of the Army Group'.[6] Jodl wrote in his diary: '(Keitel) … has brought a very much more favourable picture with him than is shown on the situation map.' Kluge had deployed I Armee Korps south of the Sambre in order to lead it into the rear of the French border fortifications.[7]

At 1115 hrs and again with special urgency at 1700 hrs, Army Group Command issued instruction to AOK to that effect.[8]

Meanwhile, elements of Panzer Group Hoth, operating on the right wing of 4. Armee, passed west of Arras on course for the Scarpe. The only question now was whether Group Kleist would advance as ordered to Calais and Boulogne before the situation in the new 'focal point' had been clarified. Probably this type of enemy 'bridgehead' was not assessed as giving rise to concern, nevertheless there was no getting away from the fact that the German gap between Arras and Péronne was only 40 kilometres wide and through it the motorized and infantry forces of Army Group A had to be fed to the fast left wing. Fresh energetic enemy attacks from north and south against the German assault wedge could conjure up a critical situation. This was *inter alia* the perception of the commanding general of XXXXI Armee Korps who conveyed to General von Kleist by telephone his misgivings about the 'not to be taken lightly threat to the flanks'. He also took the opportunity to draw attention to the possibility of a 'serious danger' arising for the whole group if at the same time as the advance to the north, the high ground south-west of Béthune, with its panoramic view in all directions, were not occupied.[9]

These or similar considerations led to an agreement towards 0900 hrs between Rundstedt and Kluge 'first to clean up the situation at Arras and then advance with Group von Kleist to Calais and Boulogne.'[10]

By 1040 hrs, however, Kluge left it clear for Group Kleist to proceed in order to cut off the enemy south of Dunkirk having apparently arrived at a more favourable assessment of the situation. On the one side the fast units were to turn inwards to the line Gravelines–Aire, and on the other take the high ground south and south-west of Béthune. At 1300 hrs the leaders of XXXXI Armee Korps crossed the starting line to the north and the advance towards the Channel ports continued.[11]

Kluge, commanding general of 4. Armee, was soon confirmed in his decision by aerial reconnaissance which had reported the area south of the Somme – 'apparently to the Bresle' – free of enemy. The Ic-Report of the Luftwaffe stated: '… The morning reconnaissance … made no sightings on account of the weather situation. Later reconnaissance saw no railway traffic in the areas Dieppe–Forges–les Eaux–Amioens–Abbeville. No assembly positions were observed in the areas Aumal–Bauvais–C ompiégne–Péronne–Amiens.'[12]

Col-General von Brauchitsch, who had arrived at 4. Armee head-quarters at 1315 hrs for a conference, spoke forcibly in ordering the encircling belt to be tightened as soon as possible and with an advance also by II Armee Korps and VIII Armee Korps.[13] Enemy operations along the Somme Front were hardly to be expected, but in the morning Kluge had already ordered II Armee Korps to make all preparations for an advance east of Arras (centre line Henin–Liétard) as soon as 32. Infantry Division was available. VIII Armee Korps was to advance between Denain and Bouchain to the Scheldt Canal and set up a barrier there, erect protection for the flank facing Valenciennes and cleanse the Maubeuge area of enemy. The Commander-in-Chief of the Army laid particular stress on this korps establishing contact with the left wing of 6. Armee at Condé especially since 'the Führer had made mention of the gap in the German line near Valenciennes.'

Meanwhile the advance by Group Kleist on the left wing of 4. Armee to the north-north-east had gone to plan. The drive to the north-west by Group Hoth's XXXIX Armee Korps had been secured hitherto on its right flank by 5. Panzer Division along the Scarpe east of Arras to the north. Its task during the course of 22 May was to take over the march of 12. Infantry Division leaving 5. Panzer Division free for its attack west of Arras. While this was in process, at 0900 hrs, the enemy made a surprise attack with light tanks to the south across the Canal de la Sensée using the intact bridges at Wasnes–Féchain and struck deep into the flank of XXXIX Armee Korps, which at the time had no fighting troops and only the Group Hoth Staff at Boulon. At midday the spearhead reached Cambrai where a battalion of pioneers was at work on the bridge.[14]

Fighter and bomber aircraft of I Flying Korps and ground-attack aircraft of II./LG 2, drawn up on the airfield at Cambrai, and also fighters of IV Flying Korps supported by II. Flak Korps, cooperated in exemplary fashion and held back the enemy advance by air attacks until elements of 20. Infantry Division (mot.), 12. and 32. Infantry Divisions, assembled in haste, brought the enemy force to a halt.[15]

This had been the realization of a thrust ordered by Gamelin on 19 May to penetrate the area left empty behind the fast advance of the German panzer divisions. The enemy attack, carried out by the belated and insufficient force,[16] was broken off: the units involved (121st Infantry Regiment of 25th DLM (*Division Légère Mécanique* – Light Mechanized Division) with two motorized reconnaissance sections) returned to the north bank of the Canal the same evening.

On 22 May the Army Group A War Diary stated that 'the outstanding leadership of 4. Armee' had mastered all difficulties: 'at no hour had there been any doubt of their success.'[17]

In the evening report AOK 4 was able to inform Army Group Command of the following. The Armee continued with the encirclement of strong enemy forces. At Cambrai and Arras, attempts by enemy tanks to break through had been prevented in cooperation with Stukas. The Panzer Groups Hoth and von Kleist were advancing towards Calais, the Group Kleist vanguard had reached the region between Boulogne and St. Omer. 12. Infantry Division had been detached from II Armee Korps to block the Lecluse–Feuchy sector, advanced troops of 32. Infantry Division to the right of it. The enemy attacks of this date could hardly be assessed as an 'indication of a planned attempt by strong forces to break through to the south.' No enemy activity had been detected on the Somme Front.

Meanwhile, General von Kleist gave the units under his command the order at 1810 hrs: 'Main body not to advance over the Lys sector, vanguards only to the Aa sector.' This renewed order restraining the further advance of the panzers – 6. Panzer Division had already reached Lumbres – was certainly the effect on the one hand of the temporary crisis at Arras, and on the other traceable to the group wanting first of all 'to fight its way along the coast to Calais and Boulogne' and also then 'with its back free to strike decisively against the encircled enemy main forces to the east.'[18]

At the same time Army Group B – on the northern wing of the German attack – succeeded after a difficult struggle against the British in taking a stretch of the Scheldt 6 kilometres wide. 6. Armee (XI Armee Korps) erected a bridgehead on the line Petegem–Gyselbrechtteghem–Kerkhove Road– Avelghem. Meanwhile 18. Armee had prepared itself for an attack at the Canal de Gand, but here the day passed without any major fighting.[19]

On 22 May Air Fleets 2 and 3 bombed enemy troop aggregations in the areas of Roubaix, St. Pol, Béthune, Cambrai, and Arras and also attacked traffic in the ports between Zeebrugge and Boulogne. 'To the east of Paris' furthermore the railway stations at Vitry le Françoise–Fère–Champenoise–Nogent s.S. and Troyes, and targets on the latter's adjacent stretches of track were bombed. VIII Flying Korps noted the result for the first time: '… In the evening our Stukas suffered substantial losses from surprise attacks by numerous British fighter aircraft.' Elements of the previously reserved British homeland air defences had 'become involved in the aerial war on the Continent' from their bases in southern England. The situation in the air started becoming critical.[20] (See Map 4)

2. The objectives for 23 May

Army Group A intended to 'shore up' the front between Valenciennes and Arras 'by cleansing the situation' there, and with the help of Group Hoth on the uplands south of Béthune, with Group von Kleist at the Aa – between Aire and Gravelines – advance and occupy Boulogne and Calais.

Shortly after 2100 hrs, AOK 4 telephoned the two groups their respective individual orders:

a) 'Group Hoth is to advance to the right of the line Hesddin (about 25 km west of St. Pol)–Lillers (to Hoth)–Merville (to Hoth). It will be sufficient if the line Arras–Vimy Heights–Aire–St. Omer–Gravelines is reached.' Adequate infantry and anti-tank forces are to be deployed to the right of Arras. 'II Armee Korps is to prepare a 10-kilometre wide corridor east of Arras as the exit to the north... Departure is to be early. In no circumstances must the enemy break out from Arras.' The task in broad terms consists 'of taking the Vimy Heights, those west of Souchez and adjoining the line Chocque (west of Béthune)–bend in the canal south-west of St. Venant.' It was intended to give Group Hoth and Kleist a wide approach path each. OKH passed on the information that it was of decisive importance to 'take the *Vimy- and Loretto Heights*'. This was the expressed '*Order of the Führer.*'

b) 'Group Kleist has to occupy early the line both sides of Aire–St. Omer–Gravelines and create strong bridgeheads at the most important crossings. At the same time Calais and Boulogne are to be occupied. However, the latter is not the most important, *the centre of effort of the operation lies on the front wheeling east!* The old order remains in force for the Somme Front, the bridgeheads are to be strengthened. For the most part supplies from the land...'[21]

The task for 18. Armee was to cross the Canal de Gand and break through in the general direction of Thourout. Meanwhile 6. Armee was to advance towards Courtrai – tying down the enemy at St. Amand (21a).[22]

On the night of 22 May OKH issued another instruction:

> The immediate intention is to tighten the ring around the encircled enemy and keep the crossings over the Lower Somme open.
>
> *Army Group B* is to advance with its left wing to the Seclin area and then wheeling north, roll up the French border fortifications from the south, and throw back the enemy south and east of Lille.
>
> On the other front the enemy is to *be pinned down by attacks*. Attention is to be paid to economical use of manpower to achieve this. Army Group forces becoming released are to be offered to OKH as soon as possible.

The great *cities of Flanders*, upon the *preservation of which* the *political* leadership *lays value*, are to be spared if at all possible.

After reaching the line Béthune–St. Omer–Calais, *Army Group A* will wheel with fast forces towards the line Armentières–Ypres–Ostend – and *will capture* with infantry division as soon as possible the summits at Lens-St. Omer in order for the fast forces to set out from there north-eastwards. In the south the crossings over the Lower Somme are to be kept open, and after arrival of sufficient forces the bridgeheads expanded. East of Amiens the guard on the Somme crossing places is be transferred to the line Amiens–Roye–Noyon as soon as forces are available. The creation of bridgeheads over Aislette and Aisne is to be striven for.[23]

These new objectives show that OKH was adhering to the *Sichelschnitt* concept and intended to complete the 'great Plan'.

3. The order of 23 May to 'close up'

On the night of 22 May the British (I Army Corps) unleashed strong, surprise counter-attacks between Tournai and Condé in the front sector of Army Group B. At Bléharies (6 kilometres north of St. Amand) they succeeded in forcing their way through to the east bank of the Scheldt. They were making a fresh attempt, partly supported by tanks and artillery, to halt the German advance[24] and the fighting went on all day. At midday, British armour attacked on both sides of the Courtrai canal. The German defenders did not allow themselves to become disconcerted, and step by step the enemy was forced back by XXVII, IV, and XI Armee Korps. By evening XI Armee Korps stood at the Lys and had built bridgeheads at Vive St. Eloi and Harlebeke (north-east of Courtrai); at the same time IV Armee Korps reached Coyghem–Dottignies on the Menin road and was pushing closer to the line of French bunkers east of Roubaix–Lille. Nevertheless XXVII Armee Korps ran into fierce resistance at Maulde–Escautpont (north and south-east of St. Amand).

18. Armee was also making only slow progress forwards. The enemy north of Ghent remained unrelenting. XXVI Armee Korps had to fight hard at insignificant bridgeheads, but on the other hand elements of IX

Armee Korps broke through the Belgian bunker positions south-east of Ghent while 56. Infantry Division entered the town. On the southern wing of the army, 216. Infantry Division came up from the rear to the line Nazareth–Cryhauterm to the Lys (south-south-east of Deynze).[25]

The fighting on this sector of the front had shown that Army Group B was not making real progress on the north or south wings, but was moving forward better at the centre. Col-General von Bock therefore decided to transfer the centre of effort of the operations to the inner wings. What also may have played a part here was the idea of closing the encirclement south of Ostend–Dunkirk in a pincer movement, thus forcing the British to retreat. Following the OKH objectives, he also had the left wing support the 4. Armee attack south-east of Lille for which 217. Infantry Division was brought up. What was noticeable above all in the Cambrai–Valenciennes area of operations was the lack of a unified leadership.[26]

On 24 May, 18. Armee was to arrive either side of Ghent at Thourout, 6. Armee was to move up with its centre of effort at Seclin.

The Chief of the Army General Staff was not in complete agreement with these operational measures. What he thought they lacked was energetic attacks by XXVII Armee Korps against the seam between 6. Armee and 4. Armee so as to finally close the encirclement between Arras–Valenciennes–Lille. In his diary he expressed it thus:

> ...Korps Waeger (XXVII!) is advancing forwards too slowly on [the] left wing [of] 6. Armee near Condé. Instead of the promised 217. Infantry Division there is only the artillery of this division in the stretch of 269. Infantry Division. [In lieu] ... Reichenau is fighting his own private battle [in the area of] ... Audenarde, which is probably costing casualties and will bring no operational benefit. The attacks of XXVI Armee Korps north of Ghent are also without worth operationally.[27]

The Chief of the Army General Staff judged the advance of Army Group A more favourably. The measures it had taken coincided essentially with his views on how the operation should be run. The fast forces were approaching Calais (XIX, XXXXI Armee Korps) while the centre was pressing forward west of Arras for Béthune (XXXIX Armee Korps). 'The situation at the Army Group border is still rather unsettling,' he observed, 'the 4. Armee right wing is still rather thin near Valenciennes. 8. Infantry Division is "securing" between Valenciennes and Cambrai, but is still not completely there. 28. Infantry Division is continuing to mop up unskilfully behind Maubeuge. Instead of going for Valenciennes, 1. Division preferred Bavai and this has again lost us time' in the push to the west.[28]

Halder was thinking in terms 'of days' until strong infantry forces currently about 80 kilometres to the rear would arrive on both sides of Arras.

As it seems, *OKH* was gaining the impression at this time *that Army Group A was having serious difficulties in leading the large mass of 71 divisions.* Halder was right to pose the question if Army Group Command A would remain 'mobile and calm' enough for further operations![29]

As regards the enemy picture, the division Foreign Armies West came to the following conclusion on 23 May:

> … At Arras the British are still holding the town outskirts, besides which in this district there is … (a) mixed British-French armoured unit which has undertaken several unsuccessful thrusts to the west and south-west…from intercepted radio traffic it seems possible that (the) encircled enemy force intends a thrust against the rearward communications of Group Kleist advancing north. By the evening of 23 May however no reports had been received that such an attempt to break out had begun… The panzer attack on Lillers–St. Omer–Boulogne ran into stubborn but apparently (disorganized) … resistance. At Boulogne … elements of 1. mot. Infantry Division are in action; units of unknown type and strength were unloading there.[30]

On 23 May Group Hoth narrowed the Arras Pocket to further restrict the enclosed enemy and with its left wing advanced over the uplands south-east of Béthune (Loretto) to south of the town. At around this time General von Kleist had an exchange of thoughts by telephone in which he made the Commander-in-Chief of 4. Armee aware of the material losses of his group. First he pointed to his threefold task: he had to cover the Somme Front (South) and set up strong bridgeheads

(XIV Armee Korps, 100 kilometres of front line!), then he also had to take Calais and Boulogne (North, XIX Armee Korps) all while securing the territory in between. Finally, he had to wheel east (XXXXI Armee Korps) with a front 50 kilometres broad for the decisive attack in the ordered direction Ypres–Dunkirk. Kleist related that in the 14-day campaign to date, his divisions had suffered heavy losses in materials,[31] these were higher than 50 per cent amongst the panzers.[32] His group was therefore not powerful enough to take on 'a strong enemy' without replacements. (With regard to the crisis at Arras, AOK 4 had re-supplied first of all 9. Panzer Division and the SS-V. Division of General Hoth, not General von Kleist!)

Col-General von Kluge replied: '… all the more important then to safeguard the main highways … the main aim today is to take the high ground north of Arras (Vimy and Loretto).' Nevertheless Kleist informed OKH of his doubts. At 1730 hrs Lt-Colonel von Gyldenfeldt (liaison officer at OKH to Panzer Group Kleist) reported to the Chief of the Army General Staff that General von Kleist scarcely felt fully able to fulfil his assignment as long as the situation at Arras had not been totally cleansed; over 50 per cent of his panzers were out of action! Halder let it be known that in his opinion this crisis would be overcome 'in 48 hours'. *The troops had to be asked now more than ever to 'hold out' unquestioningly: he knew the size of the task they had been given.* There was no danger on the Somme Front.[33]

All the same, Kleist's reports to the Commander-in-Chief 4. Armee had apparently given him food for thought, particularly since aerial reconnaissance had made known two facts:

1. Strong enemy columns were leaving the area Courtrai–Dunkirk for the Béthune–Calais line.
2. South of the Somme, motorized columns were moving up from Beauvais to Abbeville and Amiens, from Montdidier to Péronne and from Château Thierry to Soissons.

Furthermore the Ic-Report of Luftwaffe High Command stated that at midday motorized enemy movements had been confirmed from the Gisors–Marseille-en-Beauvaisis region heading north.[34] Army Group

Command A was not at all surprised by these reports: they expected that AOK 4 would be able to handle this situation with their available forces.

In addition, the motorized troops of 4. Armee (XIV Armee Korps) had still not been relieved by infantry divisions on the Somme Front enabling them to proceed to join the fast wing. At 1640 hrs therefore, Kluge summarized his view of the situation to von Rundstedt as follows:

Fighting was continuing south of Calais. South of St. Omer there had been an advance and the heights of Loretto (west of Lens) were now firmly in German hands (at this time not yet! Author.), while II Armee Korps had set up a bridgehead east of Arras. It had to be decided for 24 May whether to proceed north or east of Arras. Kluge was of the opinion that the men in the field would certainly be happy if they could close up more tomorrow; therefore he suggested finally cleansing the situation in the Arras sector, have the motorized units on the left wing close up and if possible free 2. Infantry Division (mot.) at the Somme. Perhaps the Airborne Infantry Division could be used for this purpose (in the Abbeville–Amiens area)?

Col-General von Rundstedt was in agreement with this suggestion and ordered the 4. Armee right wing and centre to drive ahead but also close up.[35] All available infantry divisions were to make haste to the west. As regards the Airborne Infantry Division this idea could not be brought to fruition for lack of transport. Finally Rundstedt asked the Commander-in-Chief of 4. Armee if he thought the situation was 'tense'. The reply came back as 'That is not at all the case': Rundstedt seemed satisfied and revealed that he 'had feared that the enemy would make a thrust to the south via Velenciennes'. At 1810 hrs Col-General von Kluge informed the Chief of the Group Hoth General Staff by telephone that 'tomorrow the Armee would be basically stationary, also by the instructions of the Herr Col-General von Rundstedt.' It had to be closed up and brought into order in order to raise the striking power of the fast units; the present lines were to be held at all costs. Shortly before 2300 hrs von Kluge also brought the Chief of the Group Kleist General Staff, Colonel Zeitzler, up to date personally: '…On the whole Group Hoth will halt tomorrow, Group von Kleist too … so as to clarify the situation and close up.'[36] Not until 15 May would the operations resume as according to plan.

All the same, this new instruction to the subordinate commands was not totally comprehensible and even found rejection in some areas. Most wanted to continue the advance at once, feeling themselves to be with justification 'sovereigns of the battlefield'.[37] General Guderian asked permission to advance immediately to Dunkirk in order to complete the encirclement of the enemy.[38] General Reinhardt also urged for his korps to be allowed to proceed without interruption. With his panzer divisions (6. and 8.), by midday on 23 May he had set up several bridgeheads on the L'Aire–à la Bassée Canal extending to the general line La Crosse–Lynde–St. Venant (south of Cassel, 13 kilometres!). 'The General Command takes the view,' the armee korps war diary stated, 'that on the whole the enemy ahead of the XXXXI Armee Korps is not strong. It is very much more a case of French and Belgian forces being brought up quickly to parry at the Canal d'Aire à la Bassé the German advance to the north. This surprised the Allies as much as the turn to the east to proceed over the canal. The General Command *has no doubt that the korps will be equally successful going forward* as before if it tackles the enemy with vigour and with the same dash as in previous days.'

The Commanding General and the Chief of the Korps General Staff made Group Kleist aware very emphatically that a stay of any length in the present positions 'can only benefit the enemy'. 6. Panzer Division considered that 'contrary to the previous fighting', the 'from the operational point of view the dictated tempo of the advance had become slower than the tactical circumstances permitted.' On 24 May the division had left its bridgeheads at full strength at daybreak to attack an inferior enemy to the east.[39]

Repeated representations by General Schmidt (XXXIX Armee Korps) 'to use the favourable moment' were unsuccessful even though only weak enemy forces and some reconnaissance parties were all that lay in the path of 5. and 7. Panzer Divisions.[40]

At 2000 hrs AOK 4 ordered by telephone for 24 May:

1. *Enemy* has today only defended before the Armee Front.
2. On 24 May the Armee will advance east of Arras and will only close up north of Arras in order to advance further at the latest by 25 May.

3. Assignments:
   a) *VIII Armee Korps will* advance across the Canal de l'Escaut (Scheldt) between Valenciennes (not incl. town) and Bouchain (incl. town) over the line Orchies-Douai and will take possession of the Canal St. Amand–Douai. Echelon formation behind right wing.
   b) *II Armee Korps* will advance east of Arras in northerly direction across the line Liètard-Lens. Using strong echelon formation the Korps will take possession of the sector Canal de la Ht. Deule–La Souchez.
   c) *Group Hoth* will make all preparations for an advance in north-easterly direction on 25 May. Corresponding to the advance of II Armee Korps, the right wing of Group Hoth is to push forward, gathering up forces becoming freed. Arras is to be sealed off by progressive attack and cleansed.
   d) *Group von Kleist* is to take possession of the Aa sector from north-east Lillers to the coast and set up bridgeheads here. The situation in the coastal area, especially at Boulogne and Calais, is to be cleared up. Moreover all preparations are to be made for the continuation of the advance on 25 May.
   e) *The Somme Front* is to be removed from the command area of Group von Kleist (XIV Armee Korps) and will now fall under the command of AOK. It is to be held including the bridgeheads.[41]

Two hours later Lt-General von Sodenstern passed the following direction of Army Group to the Commanding Officer, 4. Armee: 'Strong enemy heading back on Courtrai-Dunkirk line towards Douai-Calais line, centre of effort apparently between La Bassée and Calais, direction south and above all south-west. *Powerful attempts to break through are to be expected.* 4. Armee will intercept any future breakthrough in the gained ground.' At the time, Army Group did not see the situation around 4. Armee as threatening but was preparing for attacks equally on the Somme Front, tied to landings at Boulogne.[42]

The Allied Measures of 23 May 1940[1]
Dr K. J. Müller

On the night of 23 May, the British Expeditionary Force, which had been at the Scheldt between Audenarde and Maulde with 44., 4., 3., 1., 2., and 48. Divisions since 21 May, was pulled back to the fortified border position between Bourghelles and Halluin while the right wing of the Belgian Army made an evasive movement to the Lys between Menin and Ghent.

On 23 May the BEF occupied the new front line with the following divisions: (from Halluin to Bourghelles): 4. and 3. (=II Armee Korps); 1. and 42.(=I.Army Korps). This released 2. and 48.Divisions to assemble south-west of Lille in order to defend the Canal Line. 44th Division remained available as HQ-Reserve.

Advanced units of both divisions moved up on the night of 24 May as X Force and Y Force (battle group) to the La Bassée–Aire Sector because the enemy pressure on the Canal Line had increased.[2]

The first steps to erect a thin defensive front had been introduced at the Canal Line on 17 May. That day a battle group had been put together as MAC Force[3] under Major-General MacFarlane to protect the right rear flank (HQ at Orchies).

On 20 May the detachment POL Force[4] had been formed to defend the sector from Pont Maudit (later lengthened to St. Momelin) to Carvin which aligned itself to the right of MAC Force. At the same time Colonel J. M. D. Wood expanded the Hazebrouck garrison as Wood Force.

North of POL Force, from St. Momelin to the sea beyond Gravelines were French troops of the SFF (Secteur Fortifié de Flandre); between them lay the British detachment USHER Force whose principal task was to hold the bridges over the Canal Line.[5]

On 23 May MAC Force took over the sector north of the Forêt de Nieppe after First French Army relieved it from its original sector. Only 139th Brigade of 46th Division remained between Raches and Carvin.

On 23 May the German panzer spearhead was approaching Calais, and that morning the attack on Boulogne had begun.[6]

In the approaches to Dunkirk, on the line of the Aa from the sea via Gravelines to St. Omer, the last position between Calais and Dunkirk, the occupation was *thin* on the ground: USHER Force, two French reconnaissance units (18th GCRA and 59th GRDI), a weak infantry regiment, a few pieces of artillery and for ground warfare coastal artillery of limited readiness.[7]

In the course of the day St. Omer was lost and between Forêt de Nieppe and Forêt de Clairmarais the bridges along a 25-kilometre stretch had fallen to the Germans.

Therefore, in the evening Admiral North[8] reported that the situation was very serious. A panzer and paratrooper attack on Dunkirk was looming. He intended to demolish all bridges around Dunkirk in order to hold the fortress area there with naval and air force aid.

In the sector of the French Cavalry Corps (CC) between Arras and Béthune, in the evening the German advance had reached the banks of the Aire Canal at Vermelles. As a result of that, the CC Front (1st, 3rd, 2nd DLM) ran via Carency and Lens to the Canal Line of La Haute Deule, Aire Canal to La Bassée (2nd DLM). (To the north-west a French battle group, TARRIT, remnants of 1st DINA North Africa Divisions) with the Boissieu reconnaissance unit attached itself to the CC.)

About 20 kilometres south of the Canal Line, FRANC Force had fought hard to hold the town of Arras and the surrounding countryside[9] since 19 May.[10] At 1900 hrs on 23 May General Franklyn received from BEF HQ the order that Arras, now partially encircled[11] on the north, west, east and north-east[12] was to be held at all costs. During the late evening a new instruction arrived: the entire battle group and the Arras garrison were to pull back behind the Canal Line.

This British *retreat* provoked a heated exchange of telegrams between Churchill and the French Minister-President. Weygand – as Reynaud reported – saw the withdrawal of FRANC Force as a threat to the carrying through of his Plan if it did not actually kill it off.[13]

Frequently later on, this British retreat came in for harsh criticism being allegedly not only contrary to the orders of Army Group 1 but above all premature.[14]

The whole problem had a military side: the pulling back of FRANC Force enlarged the gap behind the Canal Line between Army Group Blanchard and Army Group Bresson from 40 to 60 kilometres thus depriving the planned offensive of its most favourable departure point.

It must not be overlooked, however, that Arras was surrounded on three and a half sides by an enemy force far superior to the FRANC Force detachment, even if the Germans were not in immediate pursuit of the retreating British.[15] A successful Allied attack from Arras to the south could only have been achieved with adequate reinforcements which were not available. In such a situation it was surely better for the Battle Group to withdraw before it was finally engulfed in the pincers of the superior enemy force.

There is also a psychological-political aspect: on the one hand, the British retreat seems to have motivated General Weygand to consider the possibility of abandoning his plan. This is to be inferred from a telephone conversation he had shortly afterwards with Blanchard in which he argued that – if an offensive southwards had become unfeasible – a bridgehead should be set up to cover Dunkirk and other Channel ports.[16] On the other hand, this whole affair cast a long-lasting and malign shadow over the Anglo-French alliance at the highest level.[17] Yes, and the danger existed, precisely on account of their retreat from encirclement at Arras, that the British would be held solely responsible for the collapse of the Weygand Plan.

Once Arras had been evacuated and FRANC Force was behind the Canal Line, from then on the thinking was directed towards an alternative to the Weygand Plan, while not finally abandoning it. Henceforth, The Retreat remained a further heavy burden on the Anglo-French relationship.

4. The Instruction of the Army Commander–in Chief of 23 May 1940

A further, momentous decision had been taken at OKH on 23 May! The final phase of the great encircling battle as per the *Sichelschnitt* Plan, namely the final destruction of the enemy, seemed imminent. Firm, disciplined leadership was found to be increasingly necessary, keeping the great strategic aim of the offensive in mind, the more so in the short term as the left fast wing of Army Group A (4. Armee) had to meet up with the left wing of Army Group B, thus resolving various problems of organization at the right time. Did Brauchitsch, Commander-in-Chief of the Army not feel up to the task? Were a certain dissatisfaction with the less dynamic Rundstedt and sympathies for the more temperamental Bock the reason for his surprising decision to transfer 4. Armee to Army Group B? General Halder noted in his diary: 'The express will of the Army Commander-in-Chief to award to the *High Command of Army Group B* the unified leadership for th*e last act* of the encirclement will bring great difficulties which lie in the nature of the Officer Commanding B and his Staff...The urgent desire of the C-in-C Army seems to me to be *an evasion of responsibility*. He protests repeatedly that there is no option but to either restore harmony himself between the 'kraal' (*Afrikaans*) of procedures by both sides or harness them all under von Bock. The former, which seems to me to be the more natural and masculine, is too uncertain for him. He seems happy to eschew responsibility. By doing so he also relinquishes the honour of success.'[1]

Around midnight the new order from OKH, which the Chief of the Army General Staff, Halder, had refrained from signing as an expression of his dissenting opinion[2] arrived at the headquarters of Army Groups A and B. With effect from 2000 hrs on 24 May 1940, Army Group B was to assume tactical command of 4. Armee and all forces north of the line Huy–Dinant–Philippeville–Avesnes–Le Cateau–Bapaume–Albert–Amiens. The objective corresponded to the instruction of 22 May.

While *Army Group A* naturally considered this new order to be 'not a very auspicious one to receive at this point in time' and made their feelings distinctly clear to the Operations Division of the Army General Staff, Army Group B welcomed it. Bock wrote: 'Finally one hand is directing the battle through to its conclusion. Pity that it did not happen earlier, then much wastage of time would have been avoided'.[3] Army Group B took all necessary measures immediately for extending its area of jurisdiction. By midday on 24 May 'by means of one heavy and one medium radio installation' it had restored radio contact to OKH 4.[4]

5. The Luftwaffe

On the morning of 23 May the Luftwaffe had been able to provide the Army operations with little support on account of poor flying weather. Only after midday did conditions improve sufficiently for Air Fleet 2 to attack enemy movements behind the front and mostly towards the south in the sector Bruges–Roubaix. Effective attacks were also flown against enemy tanks and columns of lorries in the Orchies–Denain–Cambrai–Douai–Carvin areas.

Air Fleet 3 bombed principally troop assemblies at St. Omer–Arras–Somain–St. Amand–Seclin and also tanks and positions near Arras. 'In the Amiens–Creil–Château Thierry area railway tracks and trains were attacked successfully.'[5]

The German successes and the looming victory in Flanders motivated General von Richthofen, Commanding General of VIII Flying Korps to proclaim: 'Today we won the great battle in Flanders! The fighting in the north is *pure liquidation*. But everywhere has still to be fought for, because the enemy is fighting for his life. We can weaken the grit and determination of the enemy at various places in three to four days of constant action…then we shall have to overcome the last bitter resistance of the enemy at Dunkirk. For that purpose we shall require a strong force of fighter aircraft and one Stuka squadron at St. Pol which at the moment is not possible due to problems of supply.'[6]

At OKW, Command Division had already begun on 20 May the operational preparations for the second phase of the campaign ('Fall Rot'). Hitler's momentary impulsive jubilation on 20 May when Abbeville fell to the Germans seemed to have devolved meanwhile into a rather more sober assessment of the situation, and it had become clear at Arras what the enemy could achieve when he put his mind to it.

On 21 May, moreover, Hitler had suggested during a situation report by Grand Admiral Raeder, Commander-in-Chief of the German Navy that the war might last longer than at first expected. After the conclusion of the campaign in France, he would arrange for the centre of armaments effort to be transferred to U-boat building and the Ju-88 programme.[7] On the basis of his World War I experiences Col-General Keitel, probably supported by Jodl in this, were of the opinion that the territory of Flanders was not very suitable for panzer operations.[8] Field Marshal Göring attempted to influence a quickening of the pace.

The Luftwaffe Commander-in-Chief was in his headquarters aboard his special train near Polch (Eifel). It seems Göring was of the opinion that 'his' Luftwaffe was not being given a sufficient share in the great victory which was looming which would determine the 'destiny of the German nation for the next thousand years.'[9] In addition, he had an almost 'childish hatred' of the 'conservative-traditional' Army. On 23 May 1940 he rang Führer-HQ at Münstereifel and talked Hitler into believing that the decisive objective of the Luftwaffe was impending, namely the annihilation of the British Army in northern France. All the Army need do was occupy. He stressed his claim that the final eradication of the enemy must be left to the 'National Socialist Luftwaffe' or he, the Führer, might suffer a loss of prestige amongst the Army Generals. Göring may probably have found Hitler's weakest point, the aura of his person! This would be understandable if he had been 'inspired' by Göring's thinking though the High Command of the Wehrmacht was less impressed, for as Jodl put it, 'Göring's been talking really big again.'[10]

6. The Situation on 24 May (Map 6)

Army Group B

In the course of the morning ahead of 18. Armee, the Belgians abandoned the Canal du Gand; XXVI Armee Korps followed them at once and in the afternoon took Eecloo. Five thousand prisoners were brought in, an indication of the sinking morale of the enemy. In the evening 208. Infantry Division was forward of Eecloo on the Lys Canal and 256. Infantry Division in staggered order to its right rearwards around Lumbeke. To advance was therefore particularly difficult for this Korps because of the water obstacles and for this purpose it was necessary to erect bridges for the panzers and artillery. South of Deynze, IX Armee Korps fought successfully to set up bridgeheads across the Lys at Gotthem, Olsene, and Oesselghem, while 225. Infantry Division moved up into the region south-west of Ghent (Melle).[11]

Towards midday, the Army Commander-in-Chief visited Army Group Command B in Brussels. Bock noted: 'We are in agreement that at the seam between 4. Armee and 6. Armee we must push forward vigorously to the north-west, but the mass of the panzers at the enemy's back (Hoth and Kleist) must also advance.' Brauchitsch then proceeded to 6. Armee HQ where shortly after 1500 hrs Major-General Paulus (Commander of OKH 6) briefed him on the situation. In the subsequent discussion Brauchitsch recognized the difficulties in having the southern wing of Army Group B advance but emphasized the necessity of assisting the right wing of 4. Armee to go forward. He also concurred with the view of Reichenau and Bock that the right wing of 6. Armee should go forward in the general direction of Ypres. In that case, he went on, it could be decided later whether 6. Armee on the other side of the Lys should proceed on a generally westerly heading to the Wytschaet uplands,[12] or wheel north-west to the high ground at Roulers.

Meanwhile the 6. Armee divisions along the entire Front took the western bank of the Lys in the afternoon but the enemy made such a bitter fight of it that XI and IV Armee Korps came to a halt a few kilometres west of the Zulte–Wevelghem line. On the southern wing, XXVIII Armee Korps had only been able to set up bridgeheads at Hergnies and Mortagne.[13]

Army Group A

On the morning of 24 May the Chief of the Army General Staff confirmed his pleasure that: 'The situation is developing thoroughly satisfactorily even if the arrival of infantry units towards Arras is taking its time. Since there is currently no danger south of the Somme, I consider that to be not threatening. The enemy strength to resist is no longer rated so highly apart from local fighting. Things will therefore take their course; we must just be patient and allow them to ripen. For the first time, Group Kleist is reporting enemy air superiority'.[14] Halder even had General Mieth, Quartermaster-General for Command and Policy Questions at Army General Staff, enquire of 4. Armee what measures OKH should take to tie off the Flanders Pocket more quickly. He himself was of the opinion that 'if the high ground (north of Arras) is firmly in our grasp, consideration should be given to advancing the panzers over the Estaires–Cassel line to join the spearhead pushed forward by 6. Armee over the Lys in the direction of Roulers.'[15]

Even the morning report of AOK 4 to Army Group Command A contained nothing special which could give rise to concern; in general the night had passed quietly 'except for local skirmishing'. Fighting was still under way at Boulogne. At II. Armee Group at 0530 hrs 12. Infantry

Division had advanced 'despite especially bitter resistance of (Northern) Irish regiments' in order to broaden the bridgehead north of the Canal sector Pelves–Athies: they had fought their way forward as far as Gavrelle. 'With the exception of local reconnaissance' no contact had been made with the enemy coming up from the south.[16]

When Col-General von Kluge telephoned Army Group Command A at 0941 hrs, he informed them that signs had been detected of the enemy advancing from the south with a concentration of effort based on Amiens–Péronne. Possibly they might try an attack on Amiens with a weaker force, or it could be defensive measures. He had two requests to make: first, it was important to free motorized forces for the fighting on the northern wing of the Armee and allow 9. Infantry Division, as far as possible, to push westwards and attach it to 4. Armee, and not 9. Armee. Secondly, he wanted the new limit of the Armee to pass not through Amiens but preferably through Corbie 'only then would a unified leadership be possible.'[17]

Army Group Command replied: 'The measures introduced yesterday by 4. Armee will remain in force.'

At 1130 hrs the *Ia of 4. Armee gave Army Group Command* a further situation report stating: '6. Armee is advancing, (at) 0900 hrs the left-wing Division (269.) was fighting for the bridge over the canal at Valenciennes railway station. VIII. Army Korps has set up a bridgehead north of Bouchain and reached the Rieux–Bouchain road. Rearward elements are arriving. (The aim is) to advance over (the) line Orchies–Douai. Group Hoth is involved in fighting to the right towards St. Nicolas (north of Arras) and from the north against (the town). The (Group) is also moving towards Height 132 (Vimy)–Givenchy. Further left it has reached Bully–Hersin–Noeux les Mines–Verquin–Annezin–Chocques–Lillers. Group Kleist has taken a bridgehead at St. Omer. 2. Panzer Division is in action at Boulogne. According to Luftwaffe reports the bridges at La Bassée and Béthune have been demolished by explosives (and besides this) the enemy has been recognized making withdrawal movements from the Arras area.

'The Armee intends to let Group Hoth advance to the Canal in order to hold it for the eventuality of enemy attacks. Group von Kleist will take Cassel today. Forces have been deployed at Watten and Gravelines.'[18]

A short while later there arrived at 4. Armee HQ *a letter from General von Kleist* addressed to Col-General von Kluge personally, in which Kleist set out his current appreciation of the situation as regards the Group:

'On 23 May I was informed by yourself in the late afternoon as to my expected new task. There was also mention made of the troop estimates made by me.

'In order to prevent any misunderstanding, after further consideration of the situation I should like to set down in writing the vital points.

At the instant of relief, Group von Kleist (inclusive of XIV. Army Korps and the motorized Division) must be released from the Somme Front. That meanwhile my XIV Armee Korps and most of my motorized Division have been removed from my command jurisdiction I consider as a fairly short-term temporary solution.

'Boulogne and Calais will be a thorn in our flesh. The British will persist in attempting to erect a bridgehead protected by their Fleet. My Panzer Korps must be freed from there as soon as possible. The two SS-Divisions should suffice to surround the landing places.

'In order to advance in the direction mentioned by yourself, my whole Group subordinated to AOK 4 must be deployed, reinforced by 9. Panzer Division, (promised) by the Commander-in-Chief of the Army at my request as reinforcement for my weakened Panzer Korps.

'The Group von Kleist (the "Armee Group mot.") is not an ad hoc tactical outfit but a unit in its structure, composition and equipment designed for independent duties whose structure has been submitted to the Führer and approved by him.

'As the fighting of recent days in particular has further weakened my Panzer Division, it seems to me that the supply of at least one further Panzer Division (9. Panzer, *the Author*) and one motorized Division (SS-Verfügungs-Division: *the Author*) is desirable.'[19]

7. The Halt-Order of 24. May

On the whole this was the situation in the Army Group A sector of the front when Hitler arrived at the Charleville HQ with Jodl and Schmundt at 1130 hrs. Immediately, he had himself given a broad report on the fighting and the future intentions, acknowledging with satisfaction that

Rundstedt's measures coincided 'completely' with his own thinking. He was 'fully' in agreement with the opinion of the Commanding General of Army Group 'A' that the infantry must advance east of Arras, the fast troops 'on the other hand *could* halt on the line Lens–Bèthune–Aire–St-Omer–Gravelines which they had already reached in order to intercept the enemy being forced there by Army Group B.' This suggestion was probably accompanied by the worry that 'the weak Kleist force might be overrun by the retreating British.'[20]

Hitler underlined this by emphasizing that it was essential 'to spare the panzers for the coming operations.'[21] Furthermore a 'further tightening of the encirclement' would be most undesirable since it would restrict the activity of the Luftwaffe.

Since Rundstedt was to relinquish command over 4. Armee on this day, it remains uncertain whether he had uttered his intentions or his own desires at this time. At least one thing could not be denied: Hitler and Rundstedt were in accord in their assessment of the situation: this had repeatedly been the case in the previous few days.

To his great surprise, in the course of the discussions Hitler was made aware that 4. Armee, including all fast forces, was being transferred to Army Group B with effect from 2000 hrs on 24 May. As he expressed to Jodl, Hitler considered that this OKH order, of which neither he nor the Wehrmacht High Command had knowledge, was 'not only in a military sense, but also psychologically, wrong.'[22] That Brauchitsch and Halder had gone over his head, so it seemed, to make such a significant change to the relationship of command, outraged him and probably awoke in him new doubts as to the personal loyalty of the two officers. *He cancelled the order immediately.*

One thing led to another on 24 May: Hitler's agreement with Rundstedt in his assessment of the situation and Göring's warning of the previous day were probably the real cause. The new 'crisis of confidence'[23] (61a), however, provided the welcome motivation for the instruction which went out by telephone at 1231 hrs: 'By order of the Führer the advance is to be continued east of Arras with VIII and II Armee Korps in cooperation with the left wing of Army Group B to the north-west. The general *line Lens–Béthune–Aire–St. Omer–Gravelines* (Canal Line) is not to be crossed. It is more important on the western wing to close up all mobile forces and allow the enemy to run into the mentioned favourable defence line.'[24] Hitler therefore sanctioned what Rundstedt was proposing and declared that from now on he was determined to force through his military will regardless. He would show on the battlefield that he was not only nominally Commander-in-Chief of the Wehrmacht!

It was a characteristic of the entire conference at Charleville that no clarification was forthcoming as to how the operations were to be continued. The possibility of an enemy evacuation was not discussed nor even mentioned in passing. The conviction remained that the enemy would fight to the last round. The leading minds at OKW were of the opinion that '*the encircled enemy is not capable of unified action*'. Not until *Instruction No. 13* which Hitler signed that evening was the role of the Luftwaffe revealed: to break the resistance of the British in the Arras Pocket, prevent the British escaping over the Canal[25] and protect the southern flank of Army Group A at the Somme, meanwhile the German northern wing was to annihilate the enemy in a concentric attack, quickly capture and secure the Channel ports.[26]

As Hitler's Army adjutant Engel stated in his notes, at Charleville the Führer 'contrary to expectations left the decision to a large extent' to Rundstadt, took his leave of the Commanding General of Army Group A and after returning to Führer-HQ Felsennest arranged to have himself informed afresh on the situation.[27]

8. The Reception of the 'Halt-Order' in the Field

Hit worst by the surprising order was without doubt Col-General von Kluge. However much he favoured the closing-up of the fast troops, to the same degree he deprecated the unexpected new order. Kluge, and at this time probably Kleist too, took the view that it was more correct 'to keep going' and then at the first opportunity turn at 'Béthune to the Cassel–Dunkirk high ground.'[28] Only in that way could 'the enemy in the Flanders Pocket be totally wiped out' and the British prevented from 'embarking their forces'. Very probably had the advance continued, the panzers would have at least taken the positions on the Hazebrouck–Cassel uplands. From there it was only 45 kilometres to Menin, which had been occupied by 6. Armee since 25 May. In that case it seems more than doubtful that it would have been possible for all the enemy forces gathered south of the Lys to have got to the Channel ports in time to be evacuated.[29]

On 25 May Kluge discussed his ideas in a telephone call to Lt-General Sodenstern, Chief of the Armee Group A General Staff. In the afternoon the latter had rung AOK 4 to point out again that the panzers were to remain at the Canal. The Führer did not want this force to go east. Both he (Sodenstern) and Rundstedt considered the terrain eastwards of the Canal Line to be unsuitable for panzers 'therefore an advance that way was not desirable'. Brennecke (Chief of 4. Armee) indicated that his Commanding General (Kluge) 'would willingly have led the charge' especially since the Commander-in-Chief of the Army himself had propounded the view that everything was prepared for the advance to the east. Sodenstern gave it be understood that this instruction had been issued prior to the Führer-Order. In a telephone conversation with him between eleven and midnight, Kluge criticized the measures of Armee Group A. He said that the entire Panzer Arm had been paralyzed. What would happen now would be 'mere pinpricks'. The Armee could only <u>drill through</u> tomorrow 'underpowered'. At the very least he would like to have a panzer brigade at Lille. Sodenstern replied to the effect that the advance could not be authorized to cross the Canal because the Air Fleets were going to operate on the other side. However, he thought it might be possible to allow a panzer brigade to proceed to Lille (which finally ensued on the night of 25 May.) Kluge then regretted that at the moment all that was being accomplished 'was patchwork'. The enemy was defending stubbornly. Understandably, he wished to avoid unnecessary bloodshed but it was going on too long: we did not have much time. Halder, Chief of the Army General Staff said that 'in the view of the Führer the enemy would soon become demoralized'. The panzers had to be held back because we would soon be needing them. In conclusion, Kluge interpolated: 'If I had had freedom today' the panzers would already be on the Cassel high ground. Sodenstern retorted: 'The 24 hours delay has probably increased the fighting strength of the panzers.'[30]

XIX Armee Korps was on the left wing of the fast troops. While 2. Panzer Division was fighting at Boulogne and 10. Panzer Division at Calais, General Guderian wanted to let 1. Panzer Division proceed to

Dunkirk and also release SS-Leibstandarte *Adolf Hitler* (including Infantry Regiment *Grossdeutschland*) farther south on the Canal Front for an advance to Watten to lend the whole advance 'more vigour'. Whereas Guderian mentioned the 'Closing Up' Order of 23 May as little as did 'Panzermeyer' of SS-LAH, it would appear that the 'Halt-Order' of 24 May left them both 'speechless'. 'Not knowing the reasoning behind it, it was difficult to speak out against it,' the Commanding General of XIX Armee Korps declared later. In any case, Guderian approved an independent decision taken by the Commander of the Leibstandarte, SS-Obergruppenführer (Lt-Colonel) Sepp Dietrich who had gone forward over the Aa with a battalion contrary to the Order in order to take spot height 72 south of the village of Watten. Apparently he felt 'served up on a plate' standing at the western side of the Canal. In the early hours of 25 May XIX Armee Korps radioed to all its units: 'The Canal Line will be held. Boulogne and Calais will be taken. The Divisions are to use the pause in the forward movement to condition weapons, equipment, vehicles and panzers.'[31]

The Commanding General of XXXXI Armee Korps (south-east of St.-Omer) had requested Group Kleist on the morning of 24 May permission for an advance 'with a limited objective': namely authority to proceed to the eastern edge of the Forêt de Nieppe–heights just east of Hazebrouck–high ground around Cassel. General Reinhardt took the view that the Korps 'by remaining at the Canal d'Aire with weak forces at bridgeheads on the western bank did not do justice to either the special nature of the panzer as a weapon nor to the current conduct of the enemy.' He went on: 'It is certain that the enemy will use the last bridge at his disposal between Ghent and Dunkirk to bring up strong elements *northwards from the ring in order to embark them*. This can only be prevented by an energetic advance.' General von Kleist went along with this reasoning and finally approved it, ordering an advance as far as the line Merville–Hazebrouck–Cassel 'to thwart the building of a new enemy defensive front there from the start.'[32]

Reinhardt was intending to set off in the proposed direction at 1500 hrs when the 'Halt-Order' was issued at 1310 hrs. Without doubt that new instruction came as a great disappointment to the panzer crews: it caused much more disgust that the 'Closing-Up' Order of the day before.

At this time General Reinhardt was more convinced than ever that the enemy ahead of his Korps had 'no offensive intentions', and the purpose of all enemy measures was only 'to keep open the way to the coast'.[33]

XIV Armee Korps was occupying the Canal Line both sides of Béthune. The relevant entry in 3. Panzer Division War Diary reads: '… British columns flowing back deep inland to the north and north-west. The present enemy situation promises that *the best chance of success* is *immediate pursuit* of the retreating enemy. Enemy resistance is expected on the line Armentières–Estaires–Merville–Forêt de Nieppe–Hazebrouck. The emergency bridge at Robecq is being pulled down again…'[34] Meanwhile 4. Panzer Division came to the conclusion: 'By dusk the Division took over the sector from SS-Totenkopf Division and organized into a defence of the Canal. Our own battlefield reconnaissance never succeeded in getting northwards over the Canal on account of enemy snipers and heavy weapons. The intentions of the enemy were therefore never recognized.'[35]

Col-General von Bock, Commanding General of Army Group B, made it clear repeatedly how important he considered a swift advance by the panzers eastwards to be in order to relieve his Army Group from the heavy fighting in which it was involved.[36] Relying on the witnesses quoted here, there can be no doubt that the 'Halt-Order' came in for much abuse in the field. It was accepted quite generally that this 'wrong decision was attributable to Hitler alone'. Yes, but probably not until much later was the agreement of Hitler with Rundstedt known at OKH.

9. The Counter-Measure of OKH of 24 May

After Hitler's departure, Colonel Blumentritt, 1a of Armee Group A, notified first of all OKH (Colonel von Greiffenberg) of the new decisions by telephone. The Chief of the Army General Staff probably received a full account of the Charleville discussion around 1530 hrs. He noted in his diary: 'Führer orders that the new border (between Army Groups A and B) will not come into effect today. He will speak with the Commanding General (Brauchitsch). At 1800 hrs Halder telephoned Brauchitsch who had just arrived at the AOK 6 command post, and informed him of Hitler's decisions. Both agreed that Brauchitsch should pass the order at once to

Army Group B, Halder the same to Army Group A.[37] It was only towards evening that the newly worked-out OKH Instruction was received at the headquarters of Army Groups A and B in the following form:

1. OKH-Order of 23 May 1940 – Army General Staff – Op.Abt (1a) No. 3215/40 g.K. is annulled.
2. Intention OKH remains to encircle enemy in area Dunkirk–Estaires– Lille–Roubaix–Roulers–Ostend under cover of southern flank. OKH intends then to deploy Luftwaffe against this area.
3. The *right wing* and centre of *Army Group B* will resume the advance towards the line Ostend–Roubaix. Southern wing will roll up enemy border fortifications in direction of Lille.
4. Army Group A: The right wing of 4. Armee will continue the advance against the line Seclin–la Bassée–Béthune, the left wing will continue to hold the line Béthune–Aire–St. Omer–Gravelines.
5. The fortified area of the towns of Lille–Roubaix–Tourcoing is to be by-passed.
6. The dividing line between Army Group B and A on the advance is the line Valenciennes (West)–Orchies–Seclin (settled localities to B).[38]

At the same time, Col-General von Brauchitsch had another 'really unpleasant discussion' with *Hitler*, who reproached him forcefully for his high-handed proceeding. This was made worse by Göring's intrigues beforehand, in which he had reported to Wehrmacht High Command that 'an order of the OKH in no manner "urged" (see p.65) Army Group B but even "ordered it" to make available non-essential reserves.'

What provoked it may have been a mere trifle but nevertheless Hitler seized the opportunity to make the very sensitive Brauchitsch aware of his total dependency. The Army Commander-in-Chief had felt all along that he was no match for the 'brutal personality' and would have had the sensation on this occasion that Hitler 'had him by the throat'.[39] The irresolute manner in which he often delivered his reports at Führer-HQ conferences, and his weak arguments against the order, did not impress Hitler. On the contrary he reiterated in no uncertain terms his order of that midday. Furthermore, he made any fresh restructuring of the armies dependent on his personal approval.

After his talk with Hitler, Brauchitsch returned extremely depressed and disheartened to OKH (situated eight kilometres from the Führer-bunker in the forestry lodge of Herr von Haniel). He and General Halder were certainly deeply incensed at the 'Halt-Order' but what could they now do about it? That evening, Brauchitsch had neither the will nor the mental energy to make a new decision. Not so Halder! The unexpected decision had hit him hard, for in reality he ran the Army operations and rightly saw a threat to the successful conclusion of the first phase of the 'great concept'. Would it not be possible to supplement the 'Halt-Order' in such a way as to sweep along the Army Commander-in-Chief and Army Group A with it? The Chief of the Operations Division, Colonel von Greiffenberg and Chief of the Army General Staff Halder probably saw in the idea the only chance of realizing their operational intentions. On the same night, they issued the following signal to Army Groups A and B: 'In furtherance of the dispositions resulting from the OKH-Order of 24 May 40 authority is given to continue the advance to the line Dunkirk–Cassel–Estaires–Armentières–Ypres–Ostend. The area of operations for the Luftwaffe is narrowed accordingly.'[40]

Army Group Command B welcomed this instruction because it was in accord with their interpretation that it gave 4. Armee at least the chance of approaching the port of Dunkirk 'in order to tie down the constant movement of shipping traffic there'. Naturally it was to be lamented that the last act to complete the encirclement of the enemy was not placed in its hands.[41]

OKH had not ordered unequivocally that the advance was to be continued to Dunkirk – the business with the Order was too delicate for that – but rather it left the gate open. It made it possible for Army Group A to win back freedom of action in the OKH sense provided that it – as all representatives of the Army Group after the war emphasized expressly again and again – it was not in accord with Hitler's decision. Our sources, however, leave no doubt: when the new Order arrived at Charleville at 0045 hrs on 25 May, Colonel Blumentritt informed Col-General von Rundstedt and Lt-General Sodenstern immediately. Their decision was unanimous: *the Order was not to be passed to 4. Armee* because *'the Führer' had left 'the way in which the fighting was to be carried out to the discretion of the Army Group'*. Rundstedt considered it imperative 'to have the motorized groups close up first' if it was wanted to send them farther forward. He also pointed out that there was not going to be much time 'to come to a new agreement with the Luftwaffe necessary for when the Canal Line was crossed'.[42] If what he had said on the morning of 24 May corresponded more closely to his point of view, when 4. Armee was still under orders to attach to Army Group B, *now* his *clear will of leadership* found expression: based on Hitler's authority, he ignored an order of his superiors because it represented a flawed OKH assessment of the situation.

It was undoubtedly a remarkable way of acting which can perhaps only be understood if we refer to the War Diary entry for the same day which stated: 'The battle in northern France is nearing its conclusion. Crises can – apart from such of a purely local nature – no longer play their part. On the whole the mission of Army Group A can be viewed as fulfilled.' A General Staff Officer at AOK 4 noted in his diary on 24 May: '…The centre of effort of the Western Army is now being transferred to the Somme…The French Front in the south must not become established. We have to move south soon. The Flanders Pocket can be finished off co-laterally.'[43] That was nothing more than what General von Richthofen, Commanding General of VIII Flying Korps, had stated the day before: 'Today we won the great battle in Flanders! The fighting in the north is *pure liquidation'*.[44]

Everything indicates that, having achieved the breakthrough to the Canal Front, Rundstedt basically considered that the mission of his Army Group A had been fulfilled, as laid down in the instruction of 24 February 1940: '…to force the crossing of the Meuse … and penetrate in the direction of the estuary of the Somme.'[45]

Apparently, Rudstedt had only obeyed half-heartedly the OKH order of 22 May to veer north-north-east with the fast units in order to cooperate with Army Group B in destroying the enemy. On the one hand he was convinced, as were many officers, that sooner or later the pocket would be cleansed, and for that matter by Army Group B, while on the other hand he was deeply concerned about the difficulties of the second phase of the campaign, to which he devoted increasingly great attention. It therefore seemed to him more advisable to spare the valuable panzer units. Here – as become clear during the operational planning in the 1939 winter – how what the German generals thought and felt was deeply rooted in the concepts and experiences of World War I as regards *the assessment of the enemy*.

On the morning of 25 May Brauchitsch tried once more to convince Hitler to release the panzers; but he stood his ground firmly, pointing out that he had left the decision to Army Group A. They had declined to deploy the panzers which they required to be fully operational for the offensive to the south.[46] Halder wrote about this discussion: 'The day began with an unpleasant altercation between Brauchitsch and the Führer about the continuation of the encirclement. I myself had so arranged the battle that the conclusion would come about by having the enemy retreat according to plan to be confronted by the major frontal advance of Army Group A, which would overcome the beaten enemy and then get to work on him from the rear. The fast troops were the means to be used for the purpose. Now the political leadership is becoming involved and doesn't want to have the last decisive encirclement battle in the territory of the Flemings, but in northern France. In order to cloak this political intention it is being said that the territory of Flanders has got too much water and *per procurationem* is not suitable for panzers. The panzers and other fast vehicles must therefore come to a halt after reaching the line St. Omer–Béthune.

'Therefore we have a total volte-face. I wanted Army Group A as the *hammer*, and Army Group B as the *anvil*, now we have the reverse. Because B is facing a firmly entrenched enemy, that will be costly in blood and time. For the Luftwaffe, to which people have pinned their hopes, is dependent on the weather. Out of these differences in concept we have a tug-of-war which is harder on the nerves than the whole leadership thing. Despite all that we will win the battle.'[47]

Army Group Command A passed the strict instruction to AOK 4 once more at 1145 hrs: '*By order of the Führer* the eastern wing of 4. Armee will advance with VIII and II Armee Korps in a north-westerly direction, the *north-west wing* (Groups Hoth and von Kleist), will *halt* at the favourable *defensive line* Lens–Béthune–Aire–St. Omer–Gravelines and allow *the enemy to run up against it*. This line may be crossed only *on the express order of the Army Group. It is now imperative that the panzer units are spared for later major tasks.* Therefore, Boulogne and Calais are only to be encircled in the case that the fighting would lead to greater failures and breakdowns for the panzer arm.'[48]

a) The Allied Front on 24 May
Dr K. J. Müller

French Army Group 1 (GA 1) during its operational planning was always occupied with the preparations to carry out the order which General Weygand had issued on 22 May 1940 and which required Army Group 1 to break out to the south ('Weygand Plan').[1] Although in the opinion of the Generalissimo[2] the British retreat from Arras and surroundings had condemned their own plan to failure, General Blanchard, who had taken over the Army Group in a representative capacity following the death of General Billotte, contacted BEF headquarters[3] that morning in order to discuss the planned attack. The previous day Lord Gort and Blanchard had discussed the participation of the British divisions. Blanchard had now received agreement that BEF forces would support the operations. Details of this offensive were set out in General Instruction No.40 of Army Group 1.[4] General René Altmayer, Commanding General, French V Army Corps, was appointed to the lead the attack. Two assault groups were to be made ready: one east of the Canal du Nord towards Péronne (25th DIM and the two British divisions), and a second one west of the Canal towards Bapaume (2nd and 5th DINA). It was also envisaged giving the protection of the right flank to the CC and maintaining a further division in reserve.

On 26 May a limited attack would expand the front to Arras and create bridgeheads on the southern bank of the Scarpe. The main attack was planned for 27 May.

Without doubt therefore on the morning of 24 May the planning for an attack based on Weygand's thinking was going ahead. Absent from the leadership of Army Group 1 was active initiative and determination. On the one hand Blanchard probably did not have the authority of his predecessor (he had not yet been confirmed as Commander of the Army Group), on the other hand Weygand did not insist unconditionally and decisively in his telegram of the afternoon of 24 May that it should be carried out but left the final decision to the Army Group.[5] Additionally, for all his loyalty, it was undeniable that Lord Gort was sceptical with regard to the competence of Army Group 1 and the breakthrough to the south.[6]

Finally, it is fruitless to try to assess the degree of determination or indecisiveness of the Armee commanders involved, for on the afternoon of 24 May events occurred on the Belgian Front which changed the entire situation of Army Group 1 from the ground up.

How did things look on the individual sectors of the front?

In the foreground of the Allied Western Front, *Boulogne and Calais* were now fully encircled.

The Germans had appeared off Boulogne on 22 May, the day after the town was encircled lock, stock and barrel. On 20 May, 20th Guards Brigade had been disembarked there in the strength of two Battalions.[7] In the course of 23 May the British Admiralty sent six destroyers which provided the defenders with gunnery support and later carried out the evacuation under RAF protection: this was terminated on 23 May at 2130 hrs.[8] On 25 May Boulogne was finally *in German hands*.

British troop reinforcements disembarked at Calais on 22 and 23 May.[9] Two cruisers and several destroyers also provided the troops ashore with supporting fire. The embarkation ordered on 24 May countermanded the following day.[10] Only a few wounded were transported out. The brave garrison under Brigadier Nicholson fought on until the evening of 26 May.

At the Aa Line there had been fighting the previous evening. The 24 May counted as the first day of the 'Battle on the Aa', on this thinly occupied, improvised front line. Between Gravelines and the sea several German attacks were beaten off. Their main thrust of the concentrated on the Gravelines sector,[11] but even here all positions were held.

Between Gravelines and Watten the defenders were forced back at St. Nicolas and Bistade but German units crossed the Aa. The French Front (Infantry Regiment 137, 18th GCRA and DCA/402 RA) was pushed aside as a result south-east to the line Capellebrouck–Pont l'Abêsse and contact lost to the units at Gravelines and Watten but a penetration of the front was prevented.

This, and the fact that as a welcome reinforcement XVI Armee Corps under General Fagalde arrived with the first units of 68. Infantry Division brought back from Belgium, gave rise at Dunkirk to a suppressed optimism, the bulk of the Division being given the order to take over the defence of Dunkirk forthwith. Admiral Abrial sent a confident telegram to the French GQG.[12]

All was quiet that day at Watten: Battle Group Forêt held as far as Cassel. Independent of it, MACForce operated there and at Cassel together with the 1st Light Armoured Reconnaissance Brigade which had arrived that morning, built a defensive position for protection against the Germans, who had crossed the Canal Line between St. Omer and Forèt de Nieppe. In this sector up to the area around Aire the situation was developing in a disquieting manner. The Germans, who had pushed forward across the Canal the previous day, captured the Forêt de Nieppe and the Forêt de Clairmarais. As long as the divisions released in the east had not yet arrived, the situation here was fairly precarious for the Allies.

Also in the sector of POL Force, between Thiennes and Robecq on the Aire Canal, gaps existed in the defensive Front through which German elements (SS-Verfügungs Division) felt their way forward to St. Venant. North-west of it, British detachments were forced to pull back at Morbecke.

Left of this sector, south of Hinges, between Béthune and La Bassée, the Groupement Mariot (reconnaissance unit) and Battle Group Tarrit (remnants of 1st DINA) held the front. Here all attacks were beaten off.

In this situation, BEF headquarters took in hand an adjustment of the command arrangement on the Western Front. At 0300 hrs on the following day (25 May 1940) the improvised 'Forces' were transferred in from the Divisions (2nd, 44th, 48th) brought up from the east and III Army Corps was assigned the task of leading the operations on the Western Front.[13] This adjustment was then soon revoked and the three Divisions placed under the command of Major-General Eastwood while III Army Corps was assigned to lead the attack to the south agreed for 26 May between Gort and Blanchard: for this purpose 5th and 50th Divisions and the 1st Tank Army Brigade (4th/7th Royal Tank Regiment) were to stand by at readiness.

In the course of the day GQG placed 48th Division (minus one brigade) to defend Cassel, Wormhoudt, Bergues, and Hazebrouck. South of Hazebrouck now stood 44th Division with troops from POL Force; at St. Venant–Robecq–La Bassée was 2nd Division with 25 Brigade from POL Force. Between La Bassée and Raches 135 Brigade of 46th Division was deployed. Some French units also fought in this sector. At Arras 5th Division was engaged in fighting a rearguard action: by the end of the day the Germans captured the high ground north of the town.

Therefore the Western Front on 24 May had been subjected to comprehensive new groupings and a change in the command structure, while the front line had been taken over by the three Divisions coming up from the Eastern Front. The favourable factor here was the fact that as far as the uncertain situation in the St. Omer–Aire sector, the front here was not in serious danger.

On the other hand, decisive change had occurred on the *Belgian Front*.[14] Belgian troops stood alongside the BEF Divisions between Menin and the Canal de la Mandel with IV Army Corps (1st and 3rd DI); from there to Deynze with VII Armee Corps (8th DI and 2nd DChA); between Deynze and the Canal de Gand at Bruges with VI Army Corps (4th 5th and 2nd DI); this latter adjoined V Army Corps (6th and 17th DI) as far as Oostwinkel. The Belgian CC held the half-curve of the northern Flanders coast opposite the island of Zeeland. There were five divisions of Army reserves (9th, 10th, 16th, 18th DI, 1st DChA).[15] The northern wing of the Belgian Army had just carried out its withdrawal from the Scheldt to the Canal de Dérivation.

After midday on 24 May, IV Army Corps sector began to receive ever-strengthening artillery fire, and at 1500 hrs the German attack developed either side of Courtrai, their breakthrough east and west of the town being achieved a short while afterwards. 9th and 10th DI were thrown into the gap. The Belgian High Command made the effort to maintain contact with BEF units and for that purpose used 10th DI to lengthen the right wing but could do nothing to prevent the general spread of the breakthrough.

Although all was quiet on the British Front, the reports from the Belgian Front received that evening at II Army Corps (General Brooke) caused great concern. Even though the Lys provided a certain degree of protection for the flank, any further advance by the Germans would present a major threat to the BEF left flank. General Brooke noted in his personal diary[16]: 'I hope the report is false. But I am very nervous, for if my flank were to be exposed, I have no reserves available.' Towards 0200 hrs, however, it was clear to Brooke that the German advance was 'the beginning of an offensive which aimed to penetrate our rearward territory and link up with the panzer divisions.'[17]

Thus on 24 May on the Eastern Front, this event threatened to be fatal for the BEF and all of Army Group 1.

10. The German operations on 25 May

After the left, inner encirclement wing of the German advance had had to go over to the defensive as ordered, the success for which they strove in the Flanders Pocket depended basically on *three* factors:

a) that the Army Group B divisions on the northern wing succeeded in surrounding and wiping out the enemy in a concentric pincer movements south of Bruges and beyond. The nineteen German divisions fighting here faced eight Belgian, and the remnants of another thirteen Belgian divisions, eight French and seven British divisions (and seven brigades). In staggered formation to the rear were elements and remnants of another five British and twenty-one French divisions. The front south of Courtrai was especially strong and had the added protection of the French fortifications;
b) that the *right wing of 4. Armee* (east of Arras) came forward;
c) and finally that the *Luftwaffe* – with the mass of its units – could be deployed effectively against the encircled enemy.

a) In the course of 25 May, the Belgians gathered together and launched against the XXVI Armee Korps (18. Armee) Front surprising, heavy attacks supported by artillery. At some places (north-west of Ghent) they advanced to the eastern bank of the Lys. Not until the evening could their incursions be sealed off. At 0800 hrs IX Armee Korps attacked pushing towards Thourout but came forwards only laboriously. Only 56. Infantry Division found a soft spot north of Deynze, took the town and pressed onwards for Vynckt where as a result of heavy enemy artillery fire they remained short of the high ground south and south-east of Thielt. The bridgeheads of 216. Infantry Division at Gotthem and Oesselghem (south of Deynze) could not be expanded.[1]

While the right wing of *6. Armee* (XI Armee Korps) was forced by heavy enemy artillery to veer temporarily north-west (Meulebeke), the left wing (XXVII Armee Korps), as Col-General von Bock noted, 'came not a single step forwards' in the area Bruille–Odomez–Condé. The only way to make a forward thrust from here would seem to be if the French evacuated the sector faster under pressure from east and west. In any case, it seemed to Army Group Command B pointless to continue the attack here with concentration of effort since in the centre of the front IV Armee Korps – attack direction Wytschaete – *crossed the Roulers–Menin road* in the evening and reached Gheluwe with its vanguard.[2]

The result of the day's fighting caused Army Group Command to move the centre of effort of its attack to the inner wings of 18. Armee and 6. Armee corresponding to their 'original intentions'.

b) The operations of VIII and II Armee Korps (right wing of *4. Armee*) with the aim of cutting off the enemy forces in the Valenciennes, Pallue, Douai, Carvin, and Lille sack was not particularly successful. The attack of VIII Armee Korps south-west of Valenciennes met strong resistance and advanced only 'with dogged steps': here elements of First French Army even went on the counter-attack. II Armee Korps farther left (north-east of Arras) received the order at midday; 'The Korps is to *reach and hold* with its left wing (12. Infantry Division) the Canal between Hantay and La Bassée... (It) will advance *en masse* today between railway line Oignies (north-east of Henin–Lietard)–Lille and the Canal Hantay–Lille with strong echelon to the right and secure the Canal to the north *facing Lille*. 11. Infantry Division will be put under its command. Blocking the chain of lakes between Etrun and Pallue with sufficient forces is furthermore the task of II Armee Korps.' At 1530 hrs General Brennecke was able to inform Army Group Command A that the advance of the Korps had made good progress. He had pushed ahead via Lens to the La Bassée Canal and had echeloned right facing Douai. He was now advancing north-east in the direction of Seclin 'in order to give VIII Armee Korps a chance to draw breath' and close the pocket.[3]

In the combined evening/daily bulletin AOK 4 reported: '…At 1800 hrs on 25 May the right wing of the Armee reached the following line against bitter resistance:

- VIII Armee Korps is basically as previously, little progress west of Bouchain.
- II Armee Korps: with advanced elements against enemy falling back Canal east La Bassée. Main body of Korps right echelon rearwards. Group Hoth, La Bassée Canal from La Bassèe to Fierrière (south-west St. Venant):
- Group Kleist: with battle outpost bridgeheads east of the Canal sector La Ferrière–Gravelines behind which the Group von Kleist has set up to defend with forces from SS-Verfügungs Division, 8. Panzer Division, 6. Panzer Division, SS-Leibstandarte *Adolf Hitler* and 1. Panzer Division.'[4,5]

The enemy defended stubbornly ahead of VIII Armee Korps 'in extended field emplacements supported by heavy artillery'. Only in front of II Armee Korps was delaying resistance offered in the effort to avoid contact. Little enemy activity was noted ahead of the Groups Hoth and Kleist.

Air reconnaissance had registered movement northwards in the area Courtrai–Lille. The enemy apparently had no intention to break through to the west. OKH had the impression that no decisive opposition was being prepared on the southern Front.

The intention of the Armee for the 26 May was as before: to defend the Canal Line Gravelines–Béthune with the left wing, and for the Infantry Korps to take the Canal Front Lille–La Bassée–Béthune.

c) On the strengthened periphery, on the 25 May the *Luftwaffe* was to be deployed against the Flanders Pocket in order to finish off the last enemy resistance and prevent an escape to the British Isles. The VIII Flying Korps War Diary (Close Combat) reads: 'KG (Bomber Squadron) 77 and Stuka Squadron 1 supported the Army in defending against enemy attacks at Amiens. Fighter units were successful in delivering heavy attacks against two British tank regiments…Furthermore enemy columns were attacked by KG 77 in the area Aumale–Montdidier–Amiens.' To the south at the Somme they also had to protect the German defensive Front proceeding under construction slowly.

Repeated Stuka attacks (StG 77) were continued against shipping targets at Calais. Probably RAF fighters responded but with less success because German fighter protection had meanwhile become better organized. The German Luftwaffe was deployed individually as follows:

'*Air Fleet 2* (I and IV Flying Korps) supported the Army with rolling attacks against roads, railway stations and yards, columns and recognized positions in the area *Thourout–Roulers–Thielt* immediately behind the enemy Front.

'The *port installations at Zeebrugge, Blankenberghe, Ostend, Nieuport and Dunkirk* were attacked repeatedly with great effect to the port installations attacked. One destroyer, a merchant ship, and a patrol boat were sunk off the ports attacked and English Channel. One small troop transport was seriously damaged.

'At *Dunkirk and in the area south of the line Thielt–Deynze,* heavy, wellsited enemy AA guns.

'On the night of 24 May *a special operation* was carried out against the ports of Blankenberghe, Ostend and Nieuport (9. Flying Division).

'*Air Fleet 3* (II, V and VIII Flying Korps) In the area *Cassel–Bailleul–Carvin–Secklin–Ypres* bomber formations bombed important military targets especially troop aggregations and columns on roads and in inhabited places. Five enemy tanks were destroyed at Wavre. As in previous days troops assemblies and movements, and some railway installations in the area south-west of the line Abbeville-Noyon were attacked with effect.

'The woodlands east of Oise near Compiègne were flattened where military preparation areas were suspected.

'In air attacks on the ports of *Calais and Dieppe* destruction was inflicted on installations. In the English Channel a troop transport was bombed and probably sunk, one destroyer and a merchant ship damaged.

'The airfields at *Meaux and Romorantin* were bombed. Several aircraft on the ground were destroyed.

'At Lille, Estaires, Lens, Dunkirk, Calais, Dieppe, Marle, Creil, and Meaux, German aircraft were attacked by enemy fighters, especially heavily at Lille and Lens.

'Heavy enemy AA guns were confirmed in the area around Lille and at Dunkirk. (For the first time the enemy used AA munitions with yellow-greenish explosive cloud at Salbris, La Ferté and Chaumont.'

All in all, however, the operations of 25 May did not have the desired result.

a. The Allied fighting of 25 and 26 May

1. The determining event of this day, 25 May 1940, was the unstoppable spread of the German breakthrough on both sides of Courtrai. It was not recognized in all clarity at French Army Group and Army levels because they were concentrating on the planned preparations to attack south. At 0700 hrs the Chief of the Imperial General Staff, General Dill, appeared at BEF headquarters[1] where he was joined later by General Blanchard and his Chief of Staff. The French Commander-in-Chief renewed his agreement to send two French divisions and about 200 tanks to support the two British divisions which would lead the attack under General Sir Ronald Adam.

The fact of these conferences and the planning is not as such conclusive proof that Blanchard, who had been confirmed officially as Commander-in-Chief of Army Group 1 that day, was actually ready to realize the Weygand Plan whole-heartedly. The Generalissimo had already left the decision on the necessary measures up to him the day before.[2] Although Blanchard set in train the preparations for the attack to the south, at the same time he sent Commandant Fauvelle from his Staff to see Weygand, and at 1100 hrs in Paris Fauvelle delivered his report and stated that the situation at Army Group was giving more than mere cause for concern. The French Army was short of ammunition, the British were apparently toying with the idea of shipping out, and from the attitude of the Belgians they feared the worst.[3] Weygand concluded that under these circumstances it would be more expedient to set up a bridgehead surrounding Dunkirk than launch an offensive to the south.[4]

Despite the preparations for the offensive, Blanchard was not making very energetic efforts (although Weygand had given him full powers to see it through) and on the contrary referred back to the Generalissimo. One cannot reject out of hand that Blanchard and Army Group Command were no longer thinking of carrying out the offensive, the plans and preparations indicate it, but Fauvelle's mission shows that Army Group Command at this moment neither had the necessary initiative nor determination which the situation demanded. Sir John Dill also had the impression that Blanchard (like Gort) saw the attack of Army Group Besson to the north to unite the two parts as the more important operation.[5]

By sending Fauvelle, Army Group Command wanted Weygand either to order the offensive to proceed or state expressly that the decisive thrust could not come from the north.

Whatever the response, Blanchard was not using the freedom of action he had been given by Weygand to act swiftly and energetically. In any case circumstances had now intervened to influence events decisively in another respect: the spread of the German breakthrough from both sides of Courtrai.

On the Belgian Front, 1st and 3rd Belgian Divisions were practically out of action; 10th Infantry Division in reserve had been thrown into the battle, 6th Division split apart. At the Mandel Canal 9th Infantry Division attempted to seal off the front to the south. On its left wing was 8th Infantry Division at the Lys. The setting up of a bridgehead by the Germans on the north bank of the Mandel Canal could not be prevented. In the VI Armee Korps sector, the Germans broke through on the west bank of the Canal de Dérivation opposite Belgian 4th Division and erected a small bridgehead.

In the course of the day the Belgians were unable to halt the German incursions, on the contrary these were expanded. At Courtrai the breach was 25 kilometres wide and 6–8 kilometres deep; on both sides of Deynze (4th Division) 5 kilometres broad and 3 kilometres deep. The Belgian preventive fronts were still holding but had no depth.

This situation with the Belgians provoked portentous reactions at BEF headquarters. Above all, Lord Gort saw from Belgian calls for help and on the basis of reports by his own liaison officers that he had to act. BEF II Army Corps was the unit most immediately threatened.[6] Its Commanding General had already recognized this fact during the night. At 0200 hrs the report came in that the German incursion had widened. Brooke decided that it implied a new German offensive against the Allied eastern flank which would end with Army Group 1 being surrounded. Doubting the ability of the Belgians to hold the breakthrough,[7] he started setting up a Front at the Ypres-Comines Canal to protect his left flank. Initially he did not find it easy to convince Gort of the danger to the flank.[8] At Allied High Command HQ (GQG) at this time preparations for the South Offensive were the important matter. Therefore, Brooke received *one brigade* as reinforcements for the approximately 14 kilometre-long front between Ypres and Comines.

At 0530 hrs, 12th Lancers had received the order to operate reconnaissance on the left flank of II Army Corps in the foreground of the Ypres–Comines Canal,[9] a fact of which II Army Corps was not advised. Brooke had sent a machine-gun battalion there himself. In the course of the day, Belgian 4th Division captured some important German documents (*6. Armee orders which the liaison officer at OKH to 6 Armee, Lt-Colonel Kinzel, had lost*) from which it was known that 6.Army was to attack the Ypres–Comines Front from the breach at Courtrai while making a diversionary feint east of Lille.[10] Provided with this evidence, Gort could not longer listen with deaf ears to the urgings of General Brooke, *for now the great danger which threatened the entire left flank of the whole BEF was obvious.* Under these circumstances, at 1800 hrs Gort saw that he had no option but to ignore the instructions of the French High Command and the British Government to attack to the south,[11] *and on his own initiative and responsibility abandoned the planned offensive.* At 1830 hrs Gort received the following message from the British Liaison Mission at Belgian HQ:[12] 'German attack…today forced Belgians back to Gheluwe. Gaps exists between Gheluwe and and Lys which the Belgians cannot close. Last reserves already deployed.'

At 1945hrs the report arrived stating that the Belgians had no troops west of the line Gheluwe–Zonnebeke and they felt great disquiet about the gap between Gheluwe and the Lys.[13]

Because Gort had rejected the Southern Offensive, he now had at his disposal the two divisions (5th and 50th) which had been planned for this operation and could now be used to protect his flank. He saw that the only chance of saving the BEF lay in withdrawing it at once to Dunkirk, the last port still open. The way there could only be kept open, however, if II Army Corps covered the withdrawal flank and kept the enemy within limits to the east. Therefore a GQG-Order attached 5th Division to II Army Corps as reinforcements and to build up the Ypres-Comines Front. It arrived during the night. Next morning a brigade from 50th Division was placed at the disposal of II Army Corps, the remainder of the Division on the same evening of 26 May.[14]

On the basis of Gort's decision, which he communicated immediately to General Blanchard, from now on Army Group 1 had to call off the Southern Offensive. The new situation was expressed in operational Instruction No.30 of 25 May (2030 hrs).[15] Instead, Army Group 1 was ordered to pull back in stages behind the Lys where a limited bridgehead was to be built along the Waterline Canal de l'Aa–Lys–Canal de Dérivation providing cover for Dunkirk: another retreat was not yet in the offing. The Belgian Army had to clear up the incursions in their Front. To protect the northern flank, French 2nd DLM was transferred into the region east of Ypres by Special Order No.22 for detachment to the Cavalry Corps. In the west, the Aa Canal Line had to be held.

While the greatest danger to the Allied armies threatened from the east, the situation on the Western Front was in general less critical; in many sectors quiet even prevailed.

In the northern sector (Dunkirk defensive region) the front line north and south of Bourbourg was reinforced by two artillery units[16] attached to 21st Division d'Infanterie. North of Gravelines all attacks were beaten off. At 0900 hrs 137th Regiment d'Infanterie, which had been beaten back south of Gravelines, returned to the counter-attack in battalion strength. It laid the front line as far as the Gravelines–Bourbourg–Canal de la Haute Colme railway line and occupied more favourable defensive positions. The front was therefore held and stabilized both sides of Gravelines and the proof supplied (despite a retreat by the British detachment the same day) that the offensive spirit of the French troops remained unbroken.

South of Bourbourg all was quiet save for reconnaissance activity, but fighting occurred in the Watten sector. The German attack at 1400 hrs was preceded by heavy artillery fire, and the town was lost. In the evening after limited incursions, some of the dominant upland features (Mt. de Watten) fell to the Germans, but in this sector there was no crisis. Therefore the start to building the inner defensive line around Dunkirk,[17] where the first units of 68th Division d'Infanterie arriving from Belgium had set up, was not delayed. This was all the more important because it created the preconditions for the later defence of Dunkirk.

The other sectors of the front were now occupied by British troops as far as Raches: 48th Division at Wormhoudt (144 Brigade) and Cassel-Hazebrouck (145 Brigade); joined to the south with POL Force troops of 44th Division, followed by 25 Brigade of POL Force and 2nd Division between St. Venant–Robecq–La Bassée. From there to Raches 139 Brigade of 46th Division held with other formations.

This defensive line was reinforced on 25 May with whatever was available. Principally here the artillery was reorganized and some field fortifications installed. 1st and 2nd Light Armoured Reconnaissance Brigades[18] were allotted to 44th Division and 2nd Division respectively. These reinforcements and regroupings contributed substantially to delaying the German panzer thrust two days later.[19]

Southwards French troops (First French Army) held the front from Raches to the border positions. Here there was heavy fighting between Maulde and Condé. In the domain of 4th French Division d'Infanterie the Germans broke through between Bouchain and Roeulx as far as Mastaing.

On the morning of 26 May Lord Gort informed the War Office of the decision he had taken the previous day under the pressure of events. Soon afterwards, he and his Chief of Staff met with General Blanchard. The three generals then agreed the details of the proposed retreat (Order No.33 of Army Group 1).[20] The movements would begin on the night of 26 May and be carried out as follows:

First Night (26 May)
French: Rearguard at the Scarpe: the main body on the line Pont à Vendin–Thumeries–Pont à Marcq–Bourghelles.
British: Rearguard in the border fortifications: the main body on the line Sainghin–Annappes–Marcq–Warneton.

Second Night (27 May)
French: Rearguard at the Deule: the main body at the Lys.
British: Rearguards to vacate the border fortifications at midnight on 27 May for the line Warneton–Wambrechies–Deule near Lille; main body at the Lys. Fighting forces at the La Bassée Canal as far as Robecq to remain in their positions both nights.

Third Night (28 May)

French and British; Rearguards and fighting force to retire from La Bassée Canal as far as Robecq to the Lys.

What happened after crossing the Lys was not agreed at this conference.[21] This omission was to lead later to serious difficulties.

In the course of the day there occurred an exchange of telegrams[22] between Gort and Eden, Secretary of State for War. In one of the first Notes, Eden stated that there could be a situation in which the security of the BEF would become the most urgent problem if the French really were not in a position to break through to the south. Then Gort should prepare the way to the coast and use the beach and all ports east of Gravelines for shipping troops out.[23] Corresponding plans were to be drawn up immediately.

Shortly after, Gort informed him that disquieting reports were being received from the Belgian Front. He summed up his assessment of the situation with this gloomy prediction: 'I must not conceal from you that a great part of the BEF and its equipment will inevitably be lost.'[24]

Eden replied that under the given circumstances, Gort had no option but to withdraw to the coast with the Allied armies. He authorized him expressly to do this and announced an immediate corresponding statement to the French High Command in order to coordinate the Allied movements.[25]

Meanwhile, Blanchard had gone to the Belgian General HQ (St. André-lez-Bruges). Because the Belgians had found it impossible to clean up the German incursions and close the gap in the front, they had asked the British HQ if the BEF could carry out a relief operation.[26] Towards midday they received a negative answer from the British HQ. For his part, Blanchard had received from the Belgian High Command a situation report which contained the sentence: '*Les limites de la résistance sont bien près d'être atteintes* (The limits of resistance are very close to being reached).'[27] Gort also received the report that no forces were available to close the breach east of Ypres.[28]

Meanwhile the Belgians had probably succeeded in holding the defensive line around Roulers on the right wing of the front at the Canal de la Mandel, but in the Deynze–Canal de la Mandel sector their defence collapsed entirely. 8th Infantry Division was wiped out, 2nd Division

DChA (Ardennes Rifles), attacked on both flanks, broke up. In the late evening a new position was occupied on the Ingelmunster–Thielt–Deynze railway line. (Various elements of 9th, 8th, 15th, and 16th Infantry Divisions and 2nd Ardennes Rifles). In the German V Armee Korps sector the canal was crossed at Balgerhock and the Belgian defenders forced back to the Meldegem Heights.

The Belgian Army was therefore not in position to stop the Germans, divert them from the breach or seal it: on the contrary, the Germans widened it. Furthermore, the Belgian Front had been lengthened because the troops on the Ingelmunster–Thielt–Deynze line had been pulled back which had led to the all the reserves having to be deployed.

On the BEF Front, meanwhile, the Commanding General of II Corps was making feverish efforts to stabilize his left flank and extend north. That morning 5th Division had occupied its sector and – in the middle – already had contact with the enemy; its left brigade went into position first of all. Since there was no kind of communcation with Belgian troops, Brooke received a brigade from 50th Division to cover Ypres. Additionally 4th Division put a brigade under his command to be held in immediate reserve for 50th Division which became involved in a harder defensive fight in the second half of the day. During the evening the remainder of 50th Division was placed under II Corps which was extending the defensive line fromYpres northwards.[29]

Besides the job of expanding the protection of the flanks between Comines and Ypres, the BEF also had to carry out the first stage of the retreat scheduled for the following morning to the Lys and the Dunkirk perimeter. This was especially complicated for II Corps since its right wing was in the far advanced Halluin–Roubaix bend. The success of the retreat depended on the coverage of the flank by 5th and 50th Divisions being guaranteed. One favourable factor for the withdrawal movement was that most of the BEF positions were in the belt of border fortifications not exposed to any serious enemy pressure.

In the sector of the SFF (Secteur Fortifié de Flandre) to Watten all remained quiet. At Watten, French troops in battalion strength attempted in counter-attacks at 0500 hrs and again at 1645 hrs to force back the Germans who had broken through the previous day and reached the high ground. The French became bogged down literally at the Mont de Watten and in the Aa lowlands and had to pull back to Lederzeele, a most unfavourable situation in the woodlands before Watten.

Behind the advanced position held by SFF on the line Gravelines–St. Pierre Brouke–north-east of St. Momelin, 48th Division (BEF) developed their positions at Bergues Ledringhem, Soex, Wormhoudt, and Cassel. Here there was no kind of significant fighting activity except for artillery fire.

Farther south between St. Venant and La Bassée, however, 2nd Division counter-attacked in an attempt to win back the bridgehead east of Aire and the Canal Line but ran up against violent resistance. Its right wing (6 Brigade) was forced back with severe losses. The fighting was concentrated on the St. Venant–Robecq–Merville sector. Advancing German units were stopped short of Merville, and the town, whose defenders had received artillery and other reinforcements during the night, was defended successfully. The 2nd Division beat off attacks at the Bois de Pacquent and set up a barrage ahead of Estaires. At Béthune the Germans could not be prevented from building a small bridgehead.

Heavy fighting broke out at Carvin and Oignies on the Canal de la Haute Deule, where 46th Division (BEF) were, together with French forces (two divisions, which in the course of the retreat were to take over the line up to La Bassée). German spearheads were advancing to Provin, Carvin and Oignies; 151 Brigade/50th Division, which had not yet arrived at the Ypres Front, took action and stabilized the situation again in company with 1st DINA (North African Infantry Division) supported by 1st and 3rd DLM. The Cavalry Corps artillery, which had been carefully organized in the days previous, also supplied useful assistance.[30]

In the course of the day General Command III Corps, which had become available following the cancellation of the Southern Offensive, was given the task of coordinating the defence of the Western Front. Major-General Wason was to assume command while Lt-General Adam would organize the defence of the Dunkirk perimeter. In the meantime and until 30/31 May the General Commando failed to establish sufficient connections to the individual divisions and battle groups because the divisional headquarters had changed position too frequently and the situation on the roads was chaotic. This was to have major drawbacks in the fighting in the West of the next few days as compared to the example of the successful coordination of the defence in the area of II Corps.

The course of the operations on 26 May showed that on the Western Front the fighting spirit of the Allied troops was by no means totally shaken. If, for the lack of manpower, no decisive counter-measures were possible to improve the overall general situation, within certain limits the positions, especially in the area of 44th and 46th Divisions, and in the SFF sector (inner line in front of Dunkirk), were expanded and on the whole held. A contributory factor was the Germans, who went over to the defence here!

II. The order of 26 May to resume (Map 8)

On the evening of 25 May, Army Group A issued Group Order No.6 which stated in extracts:

> '1. *Strong enemy forces* (probably important elements of the British, Belgian and First and Seventh French Armies) are surrounded between Army Group B and 4. Armee: attempts by them to break out to the south-west or south must be reckoned with. It is not out of the question that the enemy is basing his movements on a unified plan with the intention to break through *4. Armee* and its fast units *by an attack from the north and south* so as to restore the connection between his separated Army parts.
>
> 2. *4. Armee* will follow instructions received to destroy the encircled enemy to the north, which is to be accomplished as soon as possible by an attack from the east (Army Group B). The Somme sector from the sea to Corbie (not the town) is to be defended by XXXVIII Armee Korps being brought up with 57.and 9. Infantry Divisions.
>
> 3. *9. Armee* (HQ Bertincourt) in combination with 12. Armee will take over the sector Corbie (incl. town)–Fargnier (including town). Transfer command: 27 May, 1500 hrs. Up to this time AOK 4 is responsible for, and in command of, the area of AOK 9.'[1]

On the morning of 26 May, with resignation the Chief of the Army General Staff diaried: '…The panzer and motorized units stand as if rooted on the heights between Béthune and St. Omer by order of the All-Highest [Kaiser] and must not advance. In this way, clearing out the encirclement can take weeks. Very much to the loss of our prestige and our other intentions.' Halder observed 'in the course of the morning' a 'pronounced nervousness' on the part of the Commander-in-Chief of the Army which was understandable because '(having the enemy) run against a carefully held back and therefore powerful Front (Army Group B), while Army Group A is left stationary in a position where the enemy's rear invites an attack, is "completely incomprehensible".[2] Apparently Rundstedt was also having second thoughts; he drove over to Groups Hoth and Kleist in order to 'clarify the circumstances' and check for a possible move forward by the fast troops.

In fact, at the same time, Army Group Command A had come to a new assessment of the situation! The radio message picture had shown strong troop movements south of the Somme; furthermore there was constant radio traffic between these troops and the enemy group fighting around Lille–Douai–St. Amand. From Calais and other Channel ports messages were being received regarding landings of troops. These signals pointed to the possibility that the enemy was intending to restore contact between the northern and southern sections of his forces by concentric advances.[3]

The commanders of Army Group A did not consider the situation to be serious, and were more of the opinion that it was better 'to bring the hostilities in northern France to a conclusion as soon as possible in order to win freedom of action to the south:' Therefore, not until the morning of 26 May 1940 did Army Group A think it necessary to have the fast troops embark upon an advance across the Béthune–St. Omer–Gravelines line. It would appear they they informed Hitler immediately of their deliberations. Colonel Schmundt, Chief Adjutant to the Führer, and Lt-Colonel von Trescow (1a 2 – No.2 Chief Staff Officer of Army Group A), linked by military service and through their families, discussed the matter under the guise of routine service business. What better way could there be than to use this relationship to evoke a new order from the Commander-in-Chief of the Wehrmacht? In the Army Group A

War Diary this eloquent entry appears: '…These discussions (see above, the author) led finally to the Führer giving Group Kleist the go-ahead to the east.'[4] Hitler's decision was probably reinforced by the news that the German attack would not make decisive progress either on the northern wing (Army Group B) against a well prepared enemy Front, or on the right wing of 4. Armee (Infantry Division east of Arras); while six large transports had sailed from Dunkirk.

At 1330 hrs Brauchitsch was summoned to Hitler; an hour later he returned to OKH 'highly pleased'. The Führer had ordered the advance on Dunkirk from now on in order to stop 'the transport out of the enemy from there'.[5]

Wehrmacht High Command passed this message by telephone to Army Group A at 1330 hrs. Col-General von Rundstedt was at 4. Armee headquarters at this time. Here Col-General von Kluge had informed him of the situation and advised him amongst other things of the difficulties of supply caused particularly by the coming forwards of the rearward divisions and refugees. Over 100,000 people would starve if a major effort were not made to help them. Regarding the operations of his armies, Kluge made a renewed request to resume the advance eastwards with the panzers especially in view of the threat coming from the southward! Rundstedt then telephoned his Chief of the General Staff who passed to him the text of the Führer-Order just received.[6]

At 1530 hrs, OKH issued the order to resume:

a) Army Group A will advance as soon as possible with the panzers until arriving as near to Dunkirk as will guarantee artillery fire on its roads and railway installations and also prevent enemy troop shipments out by night.

b) Every favourable opportunity for a further advance to the east can be used but only for the purpose of enclosing Dunkirk. Infantry forces will advance south of Dunkirk to the point where the Bailleul–Cassel–Bergues road will be held securely within range of our artillery.

c) Two to three panzer divisions and the necessary motorized division are to proceed between Bailleul and Armentières for the purpose of joining hands with Army Group B advancing to Ypres from the east.

The fast forces here, providing contact has been made with 6. Armee, will come under the command of Army Group B. They are then to proceed from here in the direction of Ostend in order to prevent troops embarking at Ostend and to encircle the Belgian Army wing.

d) Approximately two panzer divisions are to advance from the region south of La Bassée via Seclin in the general direction of Tournai. This attack group will cut off the enemy still holding out south of Lille and restore contact with Army Group B west of Tournai. Army Group B will advance farther in the framework of its attack plan'[7]

The die had been cast! However, another sixteen hours had to pass until the German units could actually attack Dunkirk – if still with certain restrictions – and take the high ground at Cassel. The German troops, subject to reorganization, partially rested, now busy with repairs and reconditioning, had now to receive new orders, have their attack goals set out and get ready to move.

Meanwhile the German attack on the 4. Armee right wing had won little ground. Towards 1730 hrs VIII Armee Korps forced their way into Bouchain and extended somewhat the bridgeheads either side of town. II Armee Korps especially had run into very stiff resistance. 32. Infantry Division had occupied a bridgehead close to Carvin while 12. Infantry Division at Bauvin had had to beat off renewed attacks by French-Moroccan troops.[8]

Neither XXVII Armee Korps (18. Armee) nor XI Armee Korps (6. Armee) made the progress forwards for which Army Group B had hoped. Their attacks were unsuccessful for the enemy held his ground with resolution. At least the general line Denterghem–Meulebeke–Iseghem was won, but after a stiff fight. Good progress was made by IV Armee Korps which pushed forward to reach the Yser Canal from Zillebeke to Comines by evening and with 14. Infantry Division as cover on the flank reached halfway between Dadizeele–Passchendaele.

At 1240 hrs when aerial reports reached AOK 6 that the enemy was falling back from the area of St. Amand towards Orchies (it had been noticed the evening before that the enemy signals network had been shifted back), Col-General von Reichenau made the decision from now on to close off the northern and eastern Fronts of the fort area around

Lille, to enclose the British tightly both sides of the Kemmel 'massively up to the Raismes Wood' and at the same time 'with his right fist' strike the enemy group at Roulers. The idea here was to split the Belgian Army, meet up with the spearheads of Group Kleist heading for the Kemmel, and in this way at least seal the pocket north of Lille as quickly as possible. The commanding General of Army Group B declared himself in favour of this intention. *The Army Group's centre of effort was therefore wholly transferred to XI and IV Armee Korps.*[9]

CHAPTER V

The battle for Dunkirk, 27 May–4 June 1940 (Maps 7–14)

1. The Enemy Situation from 26 May

Following the two Situation Reports West numbered 329 at 1215 hrs and 330 at 2300 hrs of 26 May, the enemy scenario emerged in this form:

Encircled enemy Army Group 1.

After stubborn defensive fighting, the Belgians moved back from the Lys drainage canal to the west; they still held the heights around Thielt.

West of *Courtrai* the British gave up Menin and the surrounding area to the north and pulled back to the Yser Canal east of Wytschaete. Between Roubaix and St. Amand the unchanged border positions were defended by the French and some British battalions.

Between *Roubaix-Condé* and at the Scheldt- and Sensée Canal the enemy was still defending remorselessly; there were apparently some French divisions here from now on. In widening the bridgehead both sides of Bouchain the strong enemy resistance was broken with the help of low-level aircraft. Between Douai and Bauvin (6 kilometres west of La Bassée) the French occupied a position well set up for defence. At the La Bassée Canal between La Bassée and the coast, where until now only British troops had been seen, individual French troop elements were now appearing.

At Richebourg and to the south-east and north of Merville, strong artillery groups were arriving. East of St. Omer several battalions of the British 2nd Infantry Division were noticed which had been at the Lys a few days before. In the enclosed area the British 50th Motorised

Infantry Division and some battalions of the British Divisions 4.Wave, which had probably arrived very recently in France, were now thrown into the battle.

Calais was still being held: the British commandant had declined to cede it. An intercepted radio message by the British War Ministry to him to carry on the struggle contained the sentence *'Every hour you hold out is of the greatest help for the British Expeditionary Corps.'* At *Boulogne*, prisoners taken mainly by the French 21. Division d'Infanterie and elements of British 5th Motorized Infantry Division [50th Motorized Infantry Division] were brought in, totalling around 8,000 men. At *Dunkirk* on the morning of 26 May, 13 warships and 9 transports were observed: at 0730 hrs six transports of about 10,000 tons each had sailed.

Also, the previous night, transports were seen crossing the Channel. Such confirmation and the observation that movements northwards were occurring within the encirclement, furthermore that British units were being withdrawn from the Lys and the area around the La Bassée Canal, and finally the text of the order to the commandant of Calais made it probable *that the shipping out of the BEF had begun.* The Luftwaffe also reported that at Dunkirk, troops were being embarked *without their weapons and equipment.*

26 May on the Somme Front had 'passed quietly'. Only between Abbeville and Amiens had reconnaissance units felt their way forward. In the Péronne sector powerful French reconnaissance units supported by tanks had attacked the German bridgehead.[1]

2. Organization and missions for 27 May

In order to make a judgement on the concluding fighting for Dunkirk one must look first at the missions of the armies and groups for 27 May. The left, fast wing of 4. Armee with its panzers had been marking time for almost three days so given the enemy a chance of inestimable value for the British Army to escape. The question is rightly asked, however: what *options* existed after 26 May to close the encirclement at the right time to prevent a further flowing out of the enemy to the Channel ports, and finish them off?[2]

The Luftwaffe measures appear in a special chapter towards the end of the book. How should Operation *Gelb* have been finished?

In its Instruction of 26 May (1625 hrs), coinciding with Hitler's guide-lines, OKH had set down the assignments in general terms. According to these, three pockets were to be created as follows:

1. On the left wing of 4. Armee: here it was intended to advance into the area south of Dunkirk to artillery range, surround the town and prevent the embarkation of enemy troops. The infantry was to advance sufficiently far as was necessary for the artillery to maintain fire on the retreat roads Bailleul–Cassel–Bergues.
2. A further group had to proceed to the Ypres-Lille line south of St. Omer between Bailleul and Armentières in order to meet up with the Army Group B divisions (right wing IV Armee Korps) advancing from the east. After the two German Army wings had reunited, it was intended to place the panzers and fast units under the command of Army Group B with the objective of surrounding the Belgian right flank and at the same time prevent troops embarking at Ostend.
3. When Ostend and Dunkirk were in German hands and surrounded, the Allies would have no other recourse available for shipping out their troops. Finally, two panzer divisions from the La Bassée area were to advance via Seclin to Tournai in order to link up with Army Group B west of the town.

By doing this it was hoped to cut off the enemy assembled south of Lille (small pocket).[3,4]

In addition, at 2100 hrs AOK 4 issued the following detailed instructions:

1. *Enemy* is still holding out stubbornly before the Army northern Front. According to Luftwaffe reports rearward movements have been observed in a north-westerly direction. 6. Armee has reached the region west and north-west of Werwicq. On the Somme Front the enemy is making a renewed attempt to feel his way against the Armee.

2. *4. Armee* is to continue the advance to the north on the northern Front with II Armee Korps and Groups Hoth and von Kleist with the objective of restoring contact with 6. Armee and enclosing the enemy standing south-east of Lille. The Somme Line is to be held.

3. *Assignments* (see Wartime Reorganization AOK 4 of 26 May 1940, 1300 hrs).

   a) General Command VIII Armee Korps will tie down the enemy before our own Front by further attacks. The II Armee Korps protective force at the Sensée between Etrun and Pallue will be relieved by a reinforced Infantry Regiment and a Machine-gun Battalion by 27 May at 0600 hrs.

   b) General Command *II Armee Korps* will leave the Carvin bridgehead early on 27 May towards Lille for the ordered advance. Flank protection from the Canal de la Sensée to Pallue.

   c) *Group Hoth* will advance early on 27 May over the general line La Bassée–Béthune towards Lille (not town)–Armentières. Weak forces for own flank protection and with contact to Group Kleist will advance towards Estaires and build a bridgehead there. 3. Panzer Division and a 15-cm cannon battery is to come under the command of Group von Kleist and is to detach to it immediately.

   d) *Group von Kleist* will advance early on 27 May with centre of effort right of the Canal line crossing the Bailleul–Cassel line towards Poperinghe. A further group is to head towards Bergues. This group is to strive to arrive within artillery range of Dunkirk. The breaking down of resistance in the town itself is to be left in the first instance to the artillery and Luftwaffe. Group von Kleist will receive 3. Panzer Division and a 15-cm cannon battery under its command from Group Hoth and is to proceed in agreement with these. General Command XIV will again receive at 0900 hrs on 27 May Korps troops (but no subordinated Army troops) and is to incorporate these and also 13. Motorized Infantry Division. A decision is to follow regarding the Army troops deployed with XIV Armee Korps.

   e) *General Command I Armee Korps* will proceed on 27 May with 46. Infantry Division via Fontaine–Sains lez Marquion–Haucourt to the area Vitry en Artois–Neuvireuil–Fampouix–Chériey–Inchy en Artois–Etaing to arrive at the disposal of the Armee: 251. Infantry Division via Arras to the area Vimy–Candlain l'Abbé–Duisans–Arraç and southwards; 27. Infantry Division Magnicourty–Tinques–Avesnes le Comte and south-eastwards.

f) *General Command XXXIII Armee Korps* at 0900 hrs on 27 May will take over former sector of XIV Armee Korps with the units deployed there 2. Infantry Division (mot.), 9. and 57. Infantry Divisions, 9. Panzer Division (Armee reserve) and the Army troops. As to these Army troops a special order follows. *General Command XIV Armee Korps* and 13. Infantry Division (mot.) is placed under command of Group von Kleist and will be incorporated. 6. Division, formerly XL Armee Korps, will be attached and is to operate in agreement. Reconnaissance unit 4./H.21 of 9. Panzer Division temporarily with XIV Armee Korps will come under command of XXXVIII Armee Korps.

g) XL Armee Korps and V Armee Korps will hold the Somme sector and come under the command of AOK 9 at 1500 hrs on 27 May.

At 2300 hrs Army Group Command B issued the order for the advance on 27 May. While 18. Armee was to advance with the centre of effort on its southern wing in the direction of Thourout, reserves following up on the left wing of the Armee, 6. Armee received the task of securing towards the fortified area around Lille, to capture the high ground around Kemmel and with the centre of effort of its attacking wing to advance to the high ground south-eastwards of *Dixmuiden.*

These were the dispositions ordered, but everything depended upon whether 4. Armee could actually restore contact with Army Group B and together with it complete the encirclement. The fourth large Pocket around Bruges also gained in significance.[5]

3. The Capitulation of the Belgian Army on 27/28 May

In the morning hours of 27 May the German units from Gravelines to Carvin (Army Group A) finally resumed their advance and in a north-easterly direction. The Chief of the Army General Staff noted in his diary: '…up to midday (this advance) …in the Douai sack made slow progress, quicker forwards at Béthune while between Bailleul and the coast progress seems to be greater.' 6. Armee too was apparently winning territory towards Ypres. Gradually the enemy was collapsing, but not quickly. It has to be remembered that in the pocket 'four enemy armies were surrounded and that *they had no alternative but to defend themselves for as long as the ammunition lasted* and which was gradually running out.'[6]

Army Group A

At 0835 hrs General von Kleist advised the Commanding Officer of 4. Armee that General Guderian had informed him 'yesterday' that '*he could not go forward with the panzer divisions*' because these *were chaotic after the fighting at Boulogne and Calais*. At that he, Kleist, had ordered XIX Armee Korps to advance with a battle group at least one division strong. In the event on 27 May 'the Korps' set out for Wormhoudt made up of 20. Infantry Division (mot.), the Leibstandarte-SS *Adolf Hitler* and Infantry Regiment *Grossdeutschland*: by evening it had reached the area of Bourbourg south-west of Bollezeele. Here it was decided to continue the advance on 28 May with two panzer brigades as reinforcements. Meanwhile the mass of 1., 2., and 10. Panzer Divisions assembled in the area Lumbres–Ardres–Desvres.[7,8]

XXXXI Armee Korps (6., 8., 3. Panzer Divisions, SS-Verfügungs Division and 29. (mot.) (Reserve) Division crossed the Canal l'Aire–La Bassée at 0800 hrs as ordered so as to resume the offensive. At 0930 hrs Kleist reported to AOK 4 that his right wing was in action south-west of Merville and was standing at the Forêt de Nieppes; 8. and 6. Panzer Divisions were south-west of Hazebrouck and west of Cassel. He had the impression that 'it was going forwards well on the north wing'. At the request of Army Group B, after capturing the Kemmel, the Group's right wing would then advance on Dixmuiden.

It became obvious very quickly that the enemy was putting up a tremendous fight for every metre of ground. For him, everything depended upon the west and east flanks being propped up as long as possible until the main bodies of his units had come though the

Lille–Armentières–Bailleul–Bergues avenue of retreat into the Channel ports. In the evening report to Army Group A, OKH 4 was forced to admit that Group Kleist (line reached: Merville–Eecke–Cassel–West-Ledringhem–Bollezeele–Bourbourg–Ville–Gravelines) was facing a very strong enemy which, supported by artillery, had entrenched himself in the heights east of Hazebrouck and Cassel from where he was putting up a stubborn defence using old German field positions. In addition, the deployment of panzers was being made difficult by the nature of the terrain.[9]

As to the fighting that day, the XXXXI Armee Korps War Diary recorded: '…At midday the enemy resistance strengthened along the whole Front, heavy fighting erupted everywhere, in particular in every village and hamlet, yes, every house, denying the Korps the opportunity of gaining any ground worth mentioning to the east and north-east. The losses in men and materials are fairly substantial. The enemy fights grimly and holds his positions to the last; if he is shot to pieces in one position he turns up a short while later in another and resumes where he left off. The enemy artillery apparently has very good spotter positions in the area north-east of Merville and north-east of Cassel on the path of the strategic advance and our foremost lines (from two to four batteries have been recognized). From the fighting, which as previously emphasized has cost us heavy losses in personnel and equipment, the clear and short inference is that the battle against a stubbornly defending enemy in partially fortified field positions, especially in barricaded localities, is less suitable for panzers because they have too little infantry support and the panzers make too good a target for the numerous in-built anti-tank weapons…'[10]

The advance by Group Hoth (left: XIV Armee Korps; right: XXXIX Armee Korps) was also unsuccessful. Not until the afternoon did the enemy resistance fall off somewhat. XVI Armee Korps fought alongside SS-Totenkopf Division (left wing) on the line Zelobes–west of Lestrem, while 4. Panzer Division (right wing) reached Richebourg at 1830 hrs, its vanguard Fromelles-Touquet at 2300 hrs. At 0630 hrs on 28 May the spearheads of XIV Armee Korps had got to the Lille–Armentières road where they threatened the enemy's avenue of retreat.

XXXIX Armee Korps was not able to leave the Béthune–La Bassée bridgehead until after fighting off French tank attacks.

In the afternoon a fresh enemy counter-attack against the left wing from the north-west had to be beaten off before the Korps could give chase to the fleeing enemy. Advanced elements of 7. Panzer Division approached Fournes towards 2115 hrs: 5. Panzer Division, in staggered formation to the rear right hand side followed as far as Wavrin.[11]

By evening Group Hoth in conjunction with II Armee Korps on its right reached the line Marchiennes–Raches–Oignies–Camphin–Allennes–Foutnes–Vieille Chapelle. It could also be seen on this sector of the front that the enemy had used the pause for breath skilfully in order to support his flanks and reorganize for defence.

XXXIX Armee Korps noted: '…On 27 May – as envisaged – the enforced two days' standstill by the Korps on the southern bank of the Canal had the following effect:

1. The men in the field suffered substantial losses in the attack across the henceforth heavily defended La Bassée Canal;
2. It was not possible to make a timely and effective enough interception to halt the stream of Anglo-French troops fleeing from Lille to the west in the direction of the Channel…'[12]

At the same time, heavy enemy transport movements at sea left room for doubt no longer that the enemy was embarking his troops with the intention of bringing them back to the British Isles. At 1707 hrs AOK 4 pressed Army Group Command A for 'an urgent deployment of Air Fleet 2 against Ostend and the other Channel ports in order to stop any more embarkations.' In response Colonel Blumentritt advised that General Fied Marshal Göring had reportedly said that on his orders Dunkirk was going to be attacked in such a way that 'embarkations would no longer be possible.'[13]

General Brennecke depicted the situation in the Channel ports in the following way: 'Large ships sail up to the quay. Boards are lowered and the men run up them on to the ships. (All) their material remains behind.' He told the 1a General Staff Officer of Army Group A, 'We are not interested in having these people confronting us again newly equipped'. Ninety minutes later he drew the attention of the Army Group to the enemy sailings again saying that 'flat-trajectory fire' was needed.

As Colonel-General von Kluge informed General von Kleist shortly after midnight, the artillery (15-cm)[14] intended for the bombardment of Dunkirk would arrive shortly after 2100. Their operation had to be guaranteed to be speeded up as fast as possible. Open fire early tomorrow morning.[15]

Similar observations were also made by the Id General Staff Officer of AOK 4 on 27 May at '…1350 hrs'. Reports were piling up 'that the enemy' was embarking 'intensively' at Dunkirk. 'It is therefore clear that we have lost two days as the result of the OKW (i.e. Führer's) Order. Naturally we shall set the Luftwaffe against the embarkations. But their effect also has its limitations. Some of the enemy force will slip through our fingers…'[16]

On the Somme Front the French had meanwhile not remained inactive. From 1100 hrs they had launched heavy attacks against the bridgeheads at Abbeville and Amiens supported by tanks and artillery. In the evening General von Manstein, commanding XXXVIII Armee Korps, which had taken over the sector from XIV Armee Korps, requested permission to widen the existing bridgeheads 'to the line des la Bresle–Senarpont (12 kilometres north-west of Aumale)–Conty (20 kilometres south-west of Amiens) in order to strike at the opposing enemy forces' and to keep the Somme Front effectively open. For this purpose he also required 2. Infantry Division (mot.), 9. Panzer Division, artillery, and pioneers. However, after a conference with the General commanding Army Group A, Kluge told Manstein at 2043 hrs: 'Having regard to the greater operations, they do not permit the deployment of stronger forces to enlarge the bridgeheads at the moment.' The Somme positions were to be held for as long as possible. There were no indications that the enemy intended larger offensive operations on this sector of the front.[17]

Army Group B

At 1145 hrs AOK 18 reported to Army Group Command that XXVI Armee Korps was making good gains of territory. (In the evening its most forward elements had crossed the Maldegem–Knesselaer–Ondank–Thielt road.) The General commanding Army Group B noted in his diary: 'We are going forward on the whole attack Front. I'd like to see anyone do better! On the move and in action sixteen days without a pause on quite thin, broad Fronts – against an enemy fighting for his life.'[18]

The attack of XI Armee Korps (255., 30., and 19. Infantry Divisions) was operationally decisive on this day. While IV Armee Korps reached the Ypres Canal with heavy losses at 1500 hrs, XI Armee Korps broke through the enemy defensive front south of Thielt. This tore apart *the Belgian Army*. After ceaseless fighting while retreating – squeezed into a narrow area – they showed that they were not up to another battle. The last will to resist collapsed once it was clear that there was no prospect of any Allied support.

On the evening of 27 May 1940, the representative Chief of the Belgian Army General Staff, General Derousseaux, appeared at the XI Armee Korps command post (Oostrosebeeke) in order to request on behalf of his King the conditions for surrender. At 1000 hrs next morning (28 May) – he signed the instrument of unconditional surrender demanded by Hitler.[19]

The Army Group B War Diary recorded: 'The 22 Belgian divisions, which defended their country bravely and tenaciously using the numerous sectors and fortifications, were forced to capitulate, shattered by the incessant attacks of Army Group B.'[20]

Meanwhile, ahead of the left wing of 6. Armee (XXVII Armee Korps), the enemy had abandoned the fortified Front between Mouchin– Escautpont: he held his ground ahead of the Korps right wing. Sections of 253. Infantry Division advanced to Bersee; 217. Infantry Division via St. Amand to the west.

The concentric German attack against the enemy encircled in the Flanders Pocket therefore did not have the hoped-for success on 27 May. Despite the heaviest air support, still being handled individually, no important gains of ground were made on either the Eastern or Western Fronts. The newly reorganized enemy defences had held the field and delayed the German advance decisively. To judge by the accounts of German prisoners of war, especially on the Ypres Front the British had orders to 'hold to the last man'.[21,22] Undoubtedly the collapse of the Belgian Army was a great gain, but military success depended upon whether the Allies could be cut off from the Channel ports in time! That the enemy force in the Flanders Pocket would <u>not</u> go so far as to 'fight to the last round' was something of which the German commanders were aware at the latest by 27 May.

The question was, whether the attack from east and west, but especially *on the northern wing*, would be continued energetically and uncompromisingly enough in order to achieve the strategic objective of the offensive. What was probably disadvantageous here was that from 27 May, *the operational planning for the second phase of 'Rot' (the French campaign) was capturing the attention of the higher Staffs ever more intensively.* That day at 1130 hrs, the Chief of the Army General Staff arrived at Charleville in order to discuss the necessary measures with the Chief or No 1 Staff Officer respectively of the Armees.[23] The intention for the 28 May remained to continue the attack as ordered so as to restore the contact between 4. Armee and 6. Armee and *the first thing was to cut off the enemy group at Lille.*

4. The last phase of the Allied retreat

At 1000 hrs on 27 May the German attack began in the northern reaches of the Western Front. While it remained quiet in the Gravelines sector, the main thrust followed at Bourbourg. After a breakthrough between Bourbourg and Capellenbrouck, the rearwards units and artillery emplacements were overrun. The German thrust followed on the Cassel road as far as Looberghe on the Canal de la Haute Colme in a south-easterly direction.

The result of this breakthrough was that the Aa Front, the left wing of which had already been forced back, could not be held, especially since farther south the German attack began between Watten and Cassel from 0630 to 0700 hrs and quickly gained ground. The defensive positions also had to be pulled back under the heavy German pressure. The French leadership in the Secteur Fortifiée Française (SFF) attempted to organize the defence along the 'Line of the Villages' Looberghe–Zeggerscappel–Wormhoudt–Herzeele where working parties had been preparing positions for some days. Because the Germans were already advancing north of Drinchans for Pitgam, this line could also not be held. Therefore General Barthélemy, Commander of the Land Forces in the SFF area, gave the order at 1900 hrs[1] to break off the struggle on this line and for individual units to draw back behind the Canal de la Basse Colme east of Bergues. From now on the Dunkirk inner defensive line, on which 68th Division d'Infanterie had installed itself, therefore became the front.

The German advance of 27 May threw back the left flank of the SFF northwards to the line of the planned Dunkirk perimeter, and this caused a broad gap to open between the SFF and the BEF 48th Division in the neighbouring sector. The British Division, on the Bergues road–Wormhoudt–Cassel–Hazebrouck was involved in fighting which caused them heavy losses and forced them to give ground. Their positions at Ledringhem and Wormhoudt were outflanked, while Cassel, after the loss of the advanced positions at Zuytpeene and Bavinchove, came in for violent attacks all day long. The severely decimated garrison at Hazebrouck was almost encircled, and German panzers surfaced at Eecke, south-east of Cassel, and north of Hazebrouck at Caestre.[2]

Gaps had now opened between Bourbourg and Arneke–Ledringhem, between Ledringhem and Cassel, and between Cassel and Hazebrouck. This meant that the Allied armies' line of retreat was now under serious threat *from the north*. Any further push forward would have the effect of an encirclement. Therefore the Cassel garrison, defending itself by a series of counter-attacks, was reinforced during the evening by a squadron of 1 Light Armoured Reconnaissance Brigade, while the French Cavalry Corps[3] standing in the Strazeele area was ordered to counter-attack on the line Bailleul–Caestre, Bailleul–Hazebrouck with instructions to halt the Germans come what may.[4] The 1st Light Mechanized Division, together with British forces (44th Division, reinforced by the newly arrived 131 Brigade) succeeded in holding the line Eecke–Caestre–Strazeele–Vieux Berguin. 44th Division also defended the front between the Foret de Nieppes–Merville–Estaires. Between here and south of the Lys stood 3rd Light mechanized Division and the BEF 2nd Division.[5] Here a serious crisis arose. The right flank of this Division (6 Brigade) was broken up. German spearheads were advancing towards Merville and Lestrem. In the centre of 2nd Division either side of Béthune, 4 Brigade was forced back and almost wiped out. Units of 25 Brigade/50th Division standing north of the Lys erected a new defensive Front at the Canal de la Lawe from Lestrem via Vieille Chapelle to Neuve Chapelle together with French battle groups.

Between Béthune and La Bassée the left wing of 2nd Division after much ebb and flow of battle was forced to yield the Canal line and pull back in the evening from Laventie-Estaires to the north-north-east where it followed the general direction of withdrawal northwards behind the Lys. At nightfall the Division had only the strength of a brigade. The French troops in this sector, especially the battle group Vernillat, were also very hard hit and forced north towards Armentières.

Even if the sacrificial defensive battle of these Allied units[6] had not been capable of halting the German advance, undoubtedly they delayed it. That the BEF 2nd Division succeeded in resisting the Germans for a whole day was the result not least of the strengthening of the artillery and MG-units[7] and improvements to the positions. This temporary defensive success made possible at least in part the ensuing withdrawal movement of 24/25 May by the Allied armies.

As against that, between the line Festubert–Nieuve Chapelle, Laventie and the units of First French Army behind the line Carvin–Seclin there gaped a wide breach through which German panzers forced their way forwards to reach the Lille–Armentières road at Lomme in the early hours of 28 May. This brought them within the First Army withdrawal movement[8] and to a substantial extent they cut off its line of retreat. Only a narrow corridor east of the Lille–Armentières road was still open, and was used for their retreat by divisions of the BEF withdrawing from the southern part of the frontier positions. Parts of First French Army (12th Light Mechanized Division except Infanterieregiment 106, the divisional reconnaissance group GRDI and also the 32nd Division d'infanterie) all found their way behind the Lys in this sector.

On the Eastern Front the BEF 42nd, 1st, 3rd, and 4th Divisions held the border fortifications without coming under strong enemy pressure. They prepared the night retreat to the Lys.

Between Lille and Marquette, BEF 42nd Divison had to leave behind a rearguard of brigade strength at the Deule Canal. On the other hand, after releasing three battalions to 5th Division, 1st Division had to pull back across the Lys into the Dunkirk Perimeter to take over a defensive sector. 4th Division also ceded two brigades to 5th Division and went to the Lys with its last brigade while during the night 3rd Division marched close behind 4th and 5th Divisions northwards in order to lengthen the Ypres–Comines Front north of Boesingnhe the next day. These movements went according to plan during the night: 4th and 42nd Divisions had contact with the enemy.

Meanwhile on 27 May a fierce defensive battle raged on the Ypres–Comines Front in the 5th Division sector (143, 13, and 17 Brigades) and the fighting spilled over later along the fronts of 50th and 3rd Divisions.

On its left wing (143 Brigade) north of Comines, 5th Division was forced back; 13 Brigade also gave way to the strong German pressure between Houthem and Hollebeke and withdrew to the second defensive line east of the Warneton–St. Eloi road. Here they received three battalions of reinforcements[9] from 1st Division and in counter-attacks (at 1800 and 2000 hrs) at least succeeded in holding the front line from the estuary of the Korteeke river into the Canal west of Comines at St. Eloi (on the Warneton–Ypres road). The right wing of the division, strengthened during the course of the fighting by 10 Brigade from 4th Division, was forced back to the Warneton–Ypres road.

In the end the German force achieved neither a breakthrough nor a decisive gain of territory. In the course of the day additionally the front line was lengthened by 50th Division to Boesinghe. It did not prove possible to restore contact during the day between 5th and 50th Divisions, however, so that finally 11 Brigade had to be deployed to cover the seam at Wytschaete. Next morning, 3rd Division, which had been brought up during the night, took position on the left wing of 50th Division.

North of the British divisions the devastated 2nd DLM moved along with the continuing extension of the front line northwards and received the assignment to build a defensive front on the Yser from the sea to Knoke, south-west of Dixmuiden, in company with Belgian 60th Infantry Division recalled from the Belgian Front on 24 May, the first units of which arrived on the morning of 28 May.

Between the British Front and the Belgians, 12th Lancers and a detachment of 101st Army Field Company of the Royal Engineers operated between Zonnebeke and Roulers.

Therefore, on this day in the west, the BEF 2nd Division with French battle troops could not prevent the lines of retreat of First French Army being penetrated to a substantial degree in their sector but their resistance held off the German advance for decisive hours.

In the east, the reinforced BEF 5th Division prevented the thrust of German 6. Armee towards the line Poperinghe–Kemmel; at the same time the continuing expansion of the Ypres Front protected the Allied armies against being outflanked.

At the same time, however, the collapse of the Belgian Army occurred. VII Army Corps, split into two, found itself disbanding. Thielt had been lost; the Germans pushed forward to Sysseek, the way to Bruges was free. IV Army Corps held Roulers and Westroosebeeke, but east of Roulers and north-east of Thielt the whole area was open to the Germans. Even II Army Corps at the Canal de Gand à Bruges had to move out.

In this situation the King of Belgium sent Lord Gort a Note in which he announced that a cessation of the Belgian Army's resistance had to be expected very soon.[10] General Koeltz was also informed on his visit to the Belgian headquarters (1400 hrs) that the Belgian Front was close to collapse.[11] At 1700 hrs the Belgian High Command sent a *parlementaire* to the German lines to enquire terms, and at midnight the Belgian Army capitulated. The appropriate military mission advised the Allies of this portentous event.

Despite the 'forewarning' given by Belgian HQ to General Koeltz at 1400 hrs, the news of the Belgian capitulation was received at Allied HQ with great consternation, further proof of how little the highest Allied leadership was orientated to the developments at the front.[12]

The British, however, had come to terms with the idea since 25 May that sooner or later the Belgians would call it a day,[13] and therefore they were able to prepare counter-measures which at the last minute prevented the BEF and French Army Group 1 being dragged into the Belgian catastrophe.

From 28 to 29 May the Allied armies were to withdraw from the Lys to the Yser and the lines Poperinghe–Ypres and Poperinghe–Lizerne.[14] That day at 1000 hrs, Lord Gort and his Chief of Staff met with General Blanchard at Houtekerque in order to discuss the further retreat.[15] To the astonishment of the British, the French wanted to remain for the time being at the Lys. Blanchard had no orders from GQG about a future evacuation involving a further and final retreat, and General Prioux had reported to him[16] that the First French Army could not move out that evening and wanted to make a halt first of all in the canal rectangle between Armentières and Béthune. Blanchard shared all of the reservations held by Gort, who was of the opinion that with the German advance in the 'Monts de Flandres' region, everything still standing on 29 May south of the Poperinghe–Ypres line was lost.[17] The British then declared that 'with great regret' they had taken the decision, 'to withdraw the British troops even if First French Army did not take part in the evacuation.'[18]

This left the French with no choice but to fall in with the British retreat; Blanchard and Prioux accepted the decision on the afternoon of 28 May.[19] At 2200 hrs Blanchard sent a telegram[20] to GQG headquarters with the request to order the evacuation of the troops to be brought out and to organize the transportation. Against the advice of his hesitant divisional commanders, General de la Laurencie (III Army Corps) ordered the battle-weary and exhausted troops to pull out at 2300 hrs.

The elements of First French Army already at the Lys, and the units of the Cavalry Corps (without 2nd DLM) were to leave in three columns.[21] It was immediately clear that the encirclement of the mass of First French Army south of the Lys in the Lille region had already been accomplished. These units[22] fought on until 1 June, tying down six German divisions.[23]

Meanwhile the BEF II Corps had kept fighting on the eastern flank in order to hold the avenue of retreat open:[24] at once its right wing began to disengage to the Yser where, together with 3rd and 50th Divisions, it set up an interception line in front of the Yser line, recognized as the Poperinghe–Noordschoote line, through which the remainder of the units to the south could withdraw.[25]

I Army Corps was to have[26] pulled back to the line between Poperinghe and Proven, but a part of it went directly to the Dunkirk defensive line. It became particularly obvious on this critical day, 28 May, how defective the cooperation was between arme, corps and divisions. The leadership of III Army Corps on its western flank failed completely. The divisions attached to the corps operated independently, however, and fulfilled the task they had been set, namely to cover the retreat with units of the French Cavalry Corps.[27] At the same time their troops had had to be led back into the Dunkirk bridgehead but this could only be achieved with great difficulty and heavy casualties. Because the defensive area was fairly extended, gaps were unavoidable in its front line, and this favoured enemy infiltration and outflanking manoeuvres.

The 44th Division[28] in the Hazebrouck, Caestre, and Strazeele region and the Cassel garrison[29] (145 Brigade of 48th Division) were almost totally wiped out, or so weakened as to be no longer operational. On the other hand, 48th Division together with 42nd Division held their defensive fronts between Bergues, Soex, Rexpoede, Bambeque and the Yser line. The operations of II and III Corps enabled the remaining Allied troops to complete the penultimate stage of the retreat by the morning of 29 May.

The final stage of the retreat was carried out overnight until midday on 30 May. Troops manning the Poperinghe–Lizerne–Noordschoote barrage, and 42nd and 48th Divisions, withdrew into the Dunkirk bridgehead[30] in time to deny the German divisions the opportunity to break through the front or cut off the line of retreat. *Accordingly by midday on 30 May all Allied fighting forces were within the Dunkirk Perimeter.* Thus the Army Group 1 retreat ended. The aim now was to protect the evacuation with all available means.

Meanwhile the erection of the 'Dunkirk Perimeter' under Lt-General Adam was almost completed. Before 24 May he had had the British anti-aircraft artillery increased[31] and set up three corps sections: II Corps to the east in Belgian territory; I Corps on the Franco-Belgian border and III Corps to the west of I Corps as far as the Dunkirk–Bergues Canal. Provisions – and ammunition – compounds were introduced and for each corps a defensive sector, an assembly area and a beach sector for embarkation.

On 26 May the French leadership[32] in this defensive zone split the sectors for their troops: 68th Division d'Infanterie from the sea via the Ancient Canal de Mardyk to Bergues; and for the SFF from Bergues eastwards to the frontier.

On 27 May at the Cassel conference an attempt was made to coordinate the British and French measures in the setting up of the bridgehead but agreement could not be reached. The same day the advanced positions in the west and south-west were abandoned[33] so that now the inner defensive line became the main battle line.

On 28 May at Nieuport a crisis arose. On that day only a weak holding force was present when German troops appeared in the town at

1100 hrs.[34] They had set up a small bridgehead across the Yser, and II Corps ordered 4th Division to attend to it. 4th Division did not occupy its sector from Wulpen to the sea until the evening of 29 May and ultimately the combined defence by French 60th Division and 2nd DLM (Light Mechanized Division) was responsible not least for preventing the Germans advancing sooner and breaking into the Dunkirk bridgehead. The 60th Division front was broken up towards midday on 29 May and the Division itself practically annihilated. Only remnants (about 1000 men) managed to get through to the Canal de Loo where 2nd DLM was standing. This division and the 60th Division survivors withdrew next day into the bridgehead.[35] (See Map 12)

Once the last Allied troops to escape the Germans had arrived at the bridgehead on 30 May, the defensive ring around Dunkirk was held by the following units:[36] i) In the west from the sea via the Ancien Canal de Mardyk and Spyker to Bergues: French 68th Division (272 Half-Brigade, 225th and 341st Infantry Regiments). ii) From Bergues along the Canal des Chats and with weaker units at the Canal de la Basse Colme to the border: SFF (Secteur Fortifiée Française) consisting of: Regiments Z and Y and 137th Infantry Regiment). iii) From Uxem on the Canal des Chats to the sea (along the border); 112th Motorized Division with the units 92nd GRDI (divisional reconnaissance, 150th Infantry Regiment and 8th Zuaven). Because the coordination of British and French troops had not been achieved for the sector Canal de la Basse Colme from Bergues to the border,[37] this section was held by elements of GRDI and British I Corps (1st and 46th Divisions) independent of each other. The Belgian sector of the bridgehead was defended by troops of British II Corps:[38] 50th Division (150 and 151 Brigades); 3rd Division (7, 8, and 9 Brigade of Guards) and 4th Division (10, 11, and 12 Brigades).[39]

5. The Encirclement of the Dunkirk Bridgehead, 28–30 May (Maps 10–12)

The German 4. Armee was only able to make poor gains of territory on 28 May. Ahead of the right wing the enemy resistance was slowly abating, but not for Group Kleist. The enemy was only being forced back to the north-east one step at a time along the whole Front. The previous day the Group had received the order to advance 'with panzers towards Dunkirk'. It was wanted to deploy 9. Panzer Division because XIX Armee Korps was still required at Calais and Boulogne. 9. Panzer Division was not operational before the afternoon of 28 May. The order came down next day: 'XIX Armee Korps is to cover the flank of XXXXI Armee Korps towards Dunkirk.' The town itself was not to be attacked: this target was reserved for the Luftwaffe.[40]

At 1900, 1a General Staff Officer of 4. Armee reported to Army Group Command A on the situation. He stated that VIII Armee Korps (28., 8., 83., and 1. Divisions) and II Armee Korps (with 12. and 32. Infantry Divisions) had been withdrawn from the front and combined because 'the *ring around Lille* together with the left wing of Army Group B' was so tight that the Armee could leave these divisions out of the reckoning. 267. and 11. Infantry Divisions had reached the southern suburbs of the city while Group Hoth (4. and 7. Panzer., SS-Totenkopf and 5. Panzer Divisions) had taken the Lille–Bailleul road but come up against stiff resistance. The SS-Verfügungs Division (mot.) was still fighting in the Forêt de Nieppe, and 8. Panzer Division likewise, both sides of Hazebrouck. To support these attacks, 29. (Mot.) Division had gone forward. 6. Panzer Division had encircled Cassel, held stubbornly by the enemy, and elements had gone eastwards through the fortifications to the Belgian border (1345 hrs). The northern wing (XIX Armee Korps) had reached Wormhoudt; from here the front sprang back to Gravelines. Dunkirk would be taken under fire by a 15-cm cannon battery.[41]

The overall impression of the day at Army Group A was: 'After the King of Belgium and his Army surrendered this morning, the situation in north-west Belgium could be cleansed in a few days.' In the south, the enemy at the Somme had increased his pressure: partial attacks against the bridgeheads at Abbeville, Amiens and Péronne had been fought off: the enemy did not seem to have 'attacking intentions in earnest'.

At 2010 hrs OKH 4 issued to Group Hoth the order for 29 May: 'Objective: To prevent pulling back by the enemy from Lille over the Lys at and north-west of Armentières remains in force. Infantry to push ahead with strong artillery involvement between Armentières and Estaires passing east of Bailleul to the north in order to restore contact with section of 6. Armee (IV Armee Korps) fighting south of Ypres and so accelerate the collapse of the enemy.' A few hours later the order was issued to Group Kleist, their assignment – as on the previous day – was to advance to Poperinghe in order to prevent a new defensive line being set up to protect enemy flowing to the north. Contact with 6. Armee was to be sought.[42]

A peculiar fact about the operations on 28 May *was the slow progress forward by XIX Armee Korps* which had advanced to only 16–18 kilometres from Dunkirk. One of the decisive reasons for this was the belief of the commanding general that a panzer advance in polderland was tactically wrong (see Map 9). In this way the men would be sacrificed in vain: it would be more expedient 'to hold the position reached' and *let 18. Armee advancing from the east take effect.*

On the evening of the same day, Guderian instructed Colonel Zeitzler to the effect that the resumption of the operations on the northern wing (before Dunkirk) were 'undesirable' because they would claim 'unnecessary victims'. His panzer divisions were only up to 50 per cent of their authorized strength, and were 'urgently in need of repair', for in a short while the korps would be wanting them ready for other duties. The Commanding General of XIX Armee Korps took the opportunity to reiterate that a panzer attack 'in polderland fully softened by rain' was pointless. The troops had taken the high ground south of Dunkirk and the important Cassel–Dunkirk highways and in the high land at Crochte and Pitgam had favourable artillery positions from where they could fire at Dunkirk. Besides, 18. Armee was approaching Group Kleist from the east. These units with their infantry were much better suited to polderland than panzers, and it was they who should be closing the gap at the coast.[43]

According to the XIX Armee Korps War Diary, General von Kleist shared this opinion. All three XIX Armee Korps panzer divisions should be withdrawn. Additionally, the reported panzer defects made Kleist thoughtful. In conversation with Reinhardt he said that the korps need not butt head first, but had to conserve itself to be as fighting fit as possible for 'impending greater tasks'.[44]

As regards the fighting of 28 May the Commander-in-Chief of Army Group B observed: 'The British and French in the pocket at Dunkirk and Lille are making a bitter fight of it. The pressure of our panzer korps here is and remains weak ... my southern wing ... wheeled at Orchies to fight at Lille; II Armee Korps (right wing 4. Armee) ... is west of it, apparently at the same latitude. VIII and I Armee Korps (4. Armee), which were for days in the Valenciennes region and never came forward, are all of a sudden squeezed out. The *result* of this memorable non-uniformity of the *leadership* at the focal point of battle, *upheld with such great energy,* is, that everything now rests alone *on my tired-out, weak units*, and that *the British are continuing to leave Dunkirk*. Even the Luftwaffe is not stopping them.'[45]

At this point it seems appropriate to make a few observations about the countryside that was the venue for the battle from this point on.[46] The region of 'Maritime Flanders' is bordered to the south-west by the Boulogne foothills, to the south by the hilly forelands of the *Monts de Flandre* which rise to a height of 30 metres. To the east and north-east we find the typical Belgian landscape, the whole area being *a great flat triangle* whose base is the coast; its shorter leg running from Sangatte to St. Omer, and the longer leg from St. Omer to the Belgian coast at Ostend.

The landscape is criss-crossed by a *widely branching canal system*. The principal canals are once again two triangles: one with the coast as the base bordered by the Calais–St. Omer canal and the canalized Aa; the other, also with the coast as its base, has the Aa and the Colme Canal as its other sides.

Four canals run concentrically into the town of Dunkirk; the Canal de Bourbourg from the south-west; the Bergues Canal from the south; the Canal des Moëres from the south-east and the Canal de Dunkerque à Furnes (see Map 9) which runs parallel to the coast. Maritime Flanders is further characterized by the trinity of *sandy beaches*, a *belt of dunes,* and *meadowlands*.

Between Dunkirk and Nieuport-Ostend the sandy shore, almost 25 kilometres long, slopes down gently to the sea. Between this and the dunes, often 30 metres high, broad seaside promenades have been built at Malo, Bray Dunes, and La Panne. Inland beyond the dunes is the *polderland* with its multitude of small and large canals and countless drainage ditches. The individual meadows with outer ditches are framed by low pasture and bushes which obstruct the view across this terrain. The landscape here is very even and rarely provides much cover.

Between the canals of Bourbourg, de la Basse Colme, and de Dunkerque à Furnes lies the so-called Ringsloot, the fertile Terrain des Moëres, surrounded by the Canal des Chats and a large dam. A comprehensive system of compact ditches drains water through the Canal Major into the Canal des Moëres, thus relieving the area which lies below sea level. The Moëres extend across the border into Belgium.

The *traffic system* in 'Maritime Flanders' consists of railways, roads and canals. The roads, with small ditches either side, are built mostly on embankments above terrain-level. The general ground level lies from 0–3 metres above, but at some places up to 1 metre below, sea level; *therefore the area is relatively easy to flood.*

This traditional defence can be achieved in two ways. A slower – but less damaging for the fertile soil – flooding, can be brought about through raising the ground water by closing the locks and other outflows to the sea. The more radical way is to open the floodgates, breach the dams, and take similar measures in order to allow the sea fast access to the land. The *Admiral North* was empowered to initiate the flooding on 20 May 1940. There was some initial delay caused by technical difficulties and sabotage at certain places until flooding commenced on 23 May between Bergues and Ghyvelde. Shortly after, the Moëres and forelands of the Colme-Canal were under water. (For the extent of the flooding see Map 9). Because they were built raised above sea level, roads projected above the flooded land as did also some higher-lying localities such as Notre Dame des Neiges.

Even if the flooding was not completely successful, at least it indicated where the German advance was blocked, enabling the Allies to concentrate their defences on the other routes. Additionally, a certain psychological effect on the German leadership is not to be underestimated. Nevertheless, the flooding caused the defenders many disadvantages in the setting up of their positions.

After the capitulation of the Belgian Army the right wing of Army Group B (18. Armee and right wing 6. Armee) was quickly pushed forward 'through the Belgian prisoners flowing eastwards'. There was no time to lose. In his Armee directive for 28 May, Reichenau had even ordered all his forces to assemble for the advance to between Kemmel and Houthulster Wood in order to bear down on Dunkirk and there cut off the enemy from the Channel ports! Motorized advanced units of XXVI Armee Korps reached Dixmuiden in the afternoon together with other mobile units. On the western bank of the Yser, where all bridges were down, the French and British had already organized a new defensive position. At the Ypres Canal, IV Armee Korps came up against fierce Scottish troops and English Guards units. At the same time elements of XXVII Armee Korps entered Lille. The intention of Army Group B for 29 May was 'in cooperation with 4. Armee, to attack and destroy the enemy still holding out in the narrow strips from Dunkirk to Amentières.'[47]

Two days had now passed since the left wing of 4. Armee had resumed forward movement but all that had been achieved in this period was the small encirclement at Lille. In the meantime, most of the Allied Army had flowed back into the area north of Cassel–Poperinghe. In Situation Report West No.336 of 29 May 1940, prominence was given to the claim that the resistance of the encircled army group had been broken. 'With every appearance of disintegration', the British were retreating from the Yser Canal to the north-west. They were apparently striving to reach the harbour at Dunkirk. From the area north of Bailleul, long columns (estimated in length at 25 kilometres nose to tail, some alongside each other) were heading north while the weak enemy rearguard was scarcely able to offer unified resistance. In the surrounds of Cassel one enemy group was still defending stubbornly. The enemy had lost weapons, equipment, and tanks in quantities that could still not be estimated.

In the Abbeville–Amiens sector and at Aubigny the enemy had pushed forwards in places, some movements being supported by single tanks. Luftwaffe reconnaissance had failed to detect any aggregations of troops south of the Somme to the line Bauvais–Compiègne–Noyon.[48] Indicative of the uncertainty as to how many enemy troops were actually trapped in the encirclement was a note by Halder the same day. 'One ought to be "really tense" about "what is still inside" the 45 kilometres long and 30 kilometres wide pocket', he wrote in his diary.[49]

Regarding the operations on 29 May, Army Group Command A wrote that: The previous night had passed quietly. The fighting on the 4. Armee northern Front was approaching its end, but still stood although the enemy was still offering stubborn resistance. Therefore, during the day the Armee had only been able to win insignificant areas of land. The general impression was that the Allies in the pocket were fighting bravely and doggedly to win the time and space to evacuate their troops from Ostend and Dunkirk. Attempts to break through to the west or south-west were no longer to be expected. On the Somme (4. and 9. Armee) the enemy was probably intending to set up a defensive Front, for this purpose he was using primarily the rivers as anti-panzer obstacles. The attitude of the enemy when facing 12. and 16. Armees had been purely defensive.

This general situation in Flanders motivated Army Group Command A to conclude: '...(They) are making it all the more possible from now on for Army Group Command to turn its attentions to the major matter, the preparation for the new Operations, which the tactical fighting of 4. Armee in the north – actually still in close cooperation with Army Group B – to which AOK 4 has contact – can bring to its end.'[50]

Decisive for the further course of the fighting, above all for the fact that the panzers on the north wing of 4. Armee were withdrawn and relieved by infantry divisions, were the vehicle upkeep reports of the two panzer groups Kleist and Hoth.

These reports state that the effective strength of the panzer divisions was below 50 per cent. The extent to which panzers could be reconditioned or repaired in the next three days, provided all remained quiet, could not be judged. XIX Armee Korps (1. and 10. Panzer Divisions) were particularly hard hit. In contrast the condition of the motorized divisions was markedly better. The same evening Group Kleist reported that it could reckon on having 50 per cent of the non-operational panzers back in service within two days, and 60–70 per cent of the non-operational panzers back in service in four days from now. General Hoth reported to 4. Armee that his grenadier regiments had suffered heavy losses. Some regiments had only 400–500 men: in both 5. and 7. Panzer Divisions the number of units (*Abteilungen*) per brigade had been reduced from three to one. The situation at 3. and 4. Panzer Divisions was rather better, where they had 80 per cent.[51]

These reports caused the 4. Armee Chief of the General Staff to point out to the Army Group B Chief of the General Staff, General von Salmuth in conversation, that the panzers had to be spared. The *terrain* towards *Poperinghe* was almost *unsuitable for panzers*. Even OKH seemed, on reflection, to have concerns about the renewed readiness of the panzer units. The Army Commander-in-Chief gave 4. Armee the job on the evening of 29 May of working out to what extent infantry becoming free could replace operational panzer units so as to speed up their removal and put them in good order.[52]

Losses of 3. and 4. Panzer Divisions in the Campaign in Northern France (10 May–6 June 1940)

	3. Panzer Division		4. Panzer Division	
	III and	IV Regiments	III and	IV Regiments
Starting strength 10 May 1940	343	68	351	64
Total losses	82	16	77	16
Under repair troops front area	79	10	67	7
Battle-ready 8 June 1940	182	42	187	41
Battle-ready as % 10 May 1940	54%	67%	57%	64%

Status of Panzer Regiments of 5. and 7. Panzer Divisions at 1200 hrs, 25 May 1940

5. Panzer Division: non-operational 33% of which 8-10% could be repaired in a couple of days. The Division intends to reorganize 8. Panzer Brigade into 3 *Abteilungen*.

7. Panzer Division: The three *Abteilungen* of the Panzer Regiment have been converted into one *Abteilung* as a consequence of the fierce fighting in the last 14 days. Operational: 5 panzers Mk.IV, 50 panzers 38(t),[53] 31 panzers Mk II. A number of the non-operational panzers will presumably arrive in the next few days.[54]

The XXXIX Armee Korps War Diary of 24 May recorded: 'Status of the troops attached…losses each…Panzer Division…30% of the panzer material … the loss in weapons, particularly MGs … is high.'[55]

As respects the 4. Armee breakdowns and losses in panzers, the reports of the Chief Quartermaster and individual Korps show that the figures officially submitted were too high.

The losses/breakdowns in armoured vehicles with 4. Armee from 10 to 30 May 1940 totalled 131, amongst them: 28 Panzer Mk I; 22 Panzer Mk II; 11 Panzer Mk III; 13 Panzer Mk IV; 14 LTM 38;[56] 11 armoured reconnaissance vehicles. (light); 12 armoured reconnaissance vehicles (heavy).

The Senior Quartermaster also reported as a *special discovery*: 'The 3.7-cm anti-tank gun (Pak) proved ineffective on numerous occasions against the better armoured French and British tanks. For that reason substantial losses in Paks were caused by running down and crushing, or being abandoned.'[57]

According to the files placed at our disposal, on 10 May 1940 the Field Army had available 2,580 panzers (of all types). In the period 1.5 to 30.6 217 panzers were added and 683 removed. That means therefore that the total loss in panzers was 466 or 18-20%.[58]

XIV Armee Korps (9. Panzer Division and 13.(mot) Infantry Division) received orders on the evening of 28 May to relieve 1. and 2. Panzer Divisions in the Bollezeele–Rexpoede–Hondschoote and Audriege Fort Philippe area.

On 29 May towards 1400 hrs the sector of 1. Panzer Division and at 2000 hrs that of 2. Panzer Division were taken over by 9. Panzer Division while XIX Armee Korps assembled its units farther west (Ardres–Colembert); these were to restore their 'full operational status…with all means.' On the same day elements of 9. Panzer Division and 20.(mot) Infantry Division probably advanced and took Rexpoede (south-east of Bergues) around 2200 hrs but called a halt to the advance on the night of 30 May 'in order not to collide with German troops coming from the east.'[59]

XXXXI Armee Korps operating farther south was intending to capture the Belgian–French border in the central and right fields of conflict. While 8. Panzer Division had reached its target for the day by 1330 hrs – the heights north of Thieushouk – 29.(mot) Infantry Division headed for the Boeschepe–Berthen (border) and here met X Armee Korps (6. Armee).

6. Panzer Division (left wing of Korps) was to have mopped up the territory around Godewaersvelde but at 1330 hrs received orders to prepare to advance to the north where the enemy was attempting to escape

to the north-west via Poperinghe. Shortly before 1500 hrs the Division set out and forced through to Height 62 south-west of Poperinghe 'with minor engagements on the way', its spearhead advancing to the Watou–Poperinghe road. Cassel remained 'a nest of strong resistance' in British hands to the rear of the Division.

At the same time XXXXI Armee Korps had made a renewed request to Group Kleist 'for a speedy advance by its neighbour right side (3. Panzer Division) and the arrival of XIV Armee Korps (left neighbour) towards and across the Belgian-French border' which did not happen for reasons to be mentioned later.

Regarding the fighting by the Korps in the few days beforehand, the XXXXI Armee Korps War Diary contains this remarkable account:

'...After occupying the whole territory as far the as Belgian-French border, the opportunity arose to have a closer look at the hamlets, villages and fortified field positions defended by the enemy over the last three days. They had all been set up for a strong defence with much skill using all the most up-to-date methods. The same went for the fighting in the Forêt de Nieppes which has a stock of old trees and much undergrowth so that even in the most favourable case visibility is limited to no more than 10-15 metres. Here the SS-Verfügungs Division had to *fight its way forward step by step* literally. We saw houses with in-built guns, barricades made up of all imaginable objects including tanks, the cellar windows protected by sandbags and iron plating against which only flamethrowers and balled charges were effective. The enemy resistance nest at Hazebrouck still resembled a fort after being bombarded. In the cellars were over 100 enemy dead and wounded, over 100 prisoners were taken. These numbers speak for the strength of this nest and the doggedness with which the enemy fought...'[60]

Meanwhile XVI and XXXIX Armee Korps had received the order to halt: they were to remain where they were north-west of Lille and stay ready 'for further deployment'.[61]

Just how the fighting in the Flanders Pocket was proceeding can be seen from the 4. Armee Order of the Day of 29 May: 'The first phase of the war against the Western Powers has ended victoriously.'[62] Up to this point in time, the Allies had shipped out just 20 per cent of the final total of their evacuees![63]

For the attack on 30 May, 4. Armee issued the following order in which Group Hoth had the task of mopping up enemy forces in the area between Lys–Basse–Deul-Canal–Lille–La Bassée–Béthune–Aire, in the north-eastern part, working with men of 6. Armee. The north-western edge of Lille would remain occupied until the Armee gave approval to form up.

It was for Group Kleist on 30 May to prevent the enemy from breaking out to the west and south-west, and also mop up the situation ahead of the front while advancing. In particular they had to pacify the area Lys–border to 6. Armee–railway to Dunkirk–Gravelines Canal–St. Omer–Aire.[64]

According to the Army Group B War Diary entry of 29 May, the enemy was offering energetic resistance at the Yser, especially near Nieuport. Here an advance with a strong artillery contingent was planned for 30 May. IX Armee Korps was to advance farther to Dixmuiden, XI Armee Korps was to hold once it arrived at Bixschote, 255. Infantry Division was to follow here behind the right wing. At midday no enemy was seen in front of IV Armee Korps and the divisions therefore set off at a fast pace westwards in order to meet Panzer Group Kleist at Poperinghe and from there to the north encircle the enemy flank in front of XI Armee Korps.

At 1315 hrs 18. Armee reported having crossed the Yser and that the Armee Korps would attack in the direction of Furnes and Hondschoote. The entries in the War Diary on the operations of 29 May to trap the enemy in the Dunkirk Pocket are as follows:

1640 hrs, AOK 6: Kemmel taken at 1330 hrs. The forces then turned north-west in order to cut off the enemy at Poperinghe. Contact to Group Kleist has been restored. (This meant that also here the ring had been closed! Alas too late, for meanwhile the British with their last remnants had escaped from Poperinghe to the north!)

1645 hrs, AOK 4: Armentières conquered. 3 Panzer Division is on the line Meteren–Berthen, 6. Panzer Division is heading for Abele, 8. Panzer Division for Winnezeele, 9. Panzer Division is advancing on

Wormhoudt, 20. Infantry Division is standing south of Bergues where the enemy still has strong bases.

1900 hrs, AOK 6: The enemy is still holding out at the Yser Canal; at 1830 hrs Bailleul was taken, SS-Verfügungs-Division has reported that the area south-east of it is free of enemy.

2140 hrs,: XXVI Armee Korps is advancing on Nieuport in the direction of the dunes. At the Furnes Canal the British defence is still dour. We have crossed the Canal north of Dixmuiden and in doing so eliminated several enemy batteries.

2310 hrs, AOK 18: Whereas the British are defending stubbornly, the French seem to be softening. Two battalions and one battery defected closed up.

2400 hrs, AOK 6: At Lille, 3. Moroccan Division surrendered.

Army Group B believed 'the overall impression received of the enemy during the course of the day' indicated that the will to resist was abating. In places the beginnings of disintegration was becoming noticeable. All the same the enemy was still resisting. At 2100 hrs Army Group Command issued this order to its armies: '18. Armee remains advancing on Dunkirk. 6. Armee right wing will join this advance, the left wing is to mop up at Lille and in the area between Lille and Poperinghe against enemy resistance nests still holding out.'[65]

In order to guarantee the uniformity of overall command around Dunkirk, AOK 18 was ordered to take over the entire sector here on 30 May.[66]

On the morning of 30 May the Chief of the Army General Staff remarked that the Army Commander-in-Chief was 'annoyed' because from now on the errors of Wehrmacht High Command were making themselves felt (detour towards Laon and holding back the panzers and mechanized units at St. Omer). The neck of the sack enclosing the Allies had been closed more slowly than had been possible. The guilt for that lay above all with the panzers…Now we had to wait for bad flying weather to see how the absence of the Luftwaffe would allow 'countless thousands to sail off to England before our very eyes.'[67]

Col-General von Bock expressed it similarly. He wrote: 'At Dunkirk the British are pushing off, even from the open coast. When we finally get there, they will have all gone! The holding back of the panzer units by the supreme leadership looks like a serious mistake'.[68]

In addition, insofar as the ammunition situation allowed, the 4. Armee artillery (four 14-cm batteries and some light artillery) firing at Dunkirk lacked effect[69]

In order to liquidate the Dunkirk encirclement, the following German troops were in position for the attack on 30 May:

From the east: Army Group B with elements of 18. Armee (XXVI and IX Armee Korps) from Nieuport–Furnes–Dixmuiden, with elements of 6. Armee (XI and X Armee Korps) both sides of Noordschoote.

From the south: Army Group B with elements of 6. Armee (IV Armee Korps) north-east of Poperinghe: 18. and 61. Infantry Divisions brought up after: Army Group A with elements of 4. Armee (XIV Armee Korps) south of Bergues (with effect from 30 May the divisions of XXXXI Armee Korps were withdrawn from the pocket).

From the west: Army Group A with 9. Panzer Division (SS-Leibstandarte *Adolf Hitler* with 11. mot. Brigade attaching) from Gravelines–Bourbourgville.

In all, one reinforced panzer division, one motorized and seven infantry divisions.

On 30 May, Col-General von Bock admitted in his diary: '...the struggle is *hard*. The British are as tough as leather, and *my divisions* are exhausted. The right wing of 18. Armee is not going forwards. The northernmost attack wing is receiving fire from British warships. Bergues, the possession of which is essential for the capture of Dunkirk, has not yet been taken, contrary to earlier reports. Now finally Army Command is attaching XIV Korps but at the same time with the proviso that it may have to be released soon.'[70]

To judge by the 18. Armee War Diary, the fighting of 30 May before Dunkirk 'lacked any uniformity.' Korps and Division went ahead 'more or less by themselves in deciding what was called for as regards changing the direction of advance or attack, and withdrawing individual formations; and on the other hand interpreting the not quite clearly understood relationship of command between the Armee and the panzers and motorized units.'[71] The 4. Armee War Diary also gives evidence of this tendency.

At 1238 hrs Colonel Wuthmann, 1a of 4. Armee, informed the Chief of the Army Group B General Staff that the Armee had reached the line Frelinghien–Neuve Eglise–Poperinghe–road to Bergues–Bourbourgville Canal–Gravelines. It was not intending to advance farther, but was rather requesting that 6. Armee come up to the allocated dividing line (Deulemont–Neuve Eglise–Boeschepe–Herzeele–Bergues). Dunkirk was not being attacked by the Luftwaffe (poor flying weather!) and the evacuations going on there had to be stopped.

Shortly after, the 1a Staff Officer of 4. Armee informed Armee Group Command A by telephone that 'only four 15-cm cannon batteries of Group Kleist would be effective for Dunkirk' (naturally this was also a matter of ammunition supply! General von Sodenstern asked if it were not possible to advance on Dunkirk from the south; perhaps the fast troops could attack again through Bergues! Colonel Wuthmann replied *'then there would have to be a new advance made only by the fast units which would cause substantial losses.'* At that, Sodenstern decided *not to order this advance for the time being.*

At 1340 hrs Wuthmann telephoned Oberst Zeitzler, Chief of the Group Kleist General Staff, and told him, '...the Group must approach Dunkirk as closely as possible so that the town is within range of 10-cm artillery'.[72] He had the impression that nothing would happen today, nobody was interested in Dunkirk any more. However, 'the town and port had to be bombarded, the evacuation halted and a panic created.'[73]

When Army Group Command A gave permission for the attack on Dunkirk towards 1500 hrs – previously only the northern wing was allowed to approach to within artillery range,[74] the 1a Staff Officer of 4. Armee stated that 6. Armee (IV Armee Korps) had now apparently gone over to 'rest and recuperation'. While 4. Armee was standing on the line ordered, 18. Armee had just reached Nieuport–Furnes and Ypres. For the fast troops such an operation would result in heavy losses: the Armee was requesting strict orders regarding whether it should attack or not.[75]

When Col-General von Kluge and General Brennecke returned to the command post at 1500 hrs after a visit to the front (XXXVIII

Armee Korps, Somme), they were informed of the 'slow plod of things at Dunkirk'. The 4. Armee Commanding General took the initiative at once: he was determined to bring the fighting around Dunkirk to a quick conclusion. He ordered Group Kleist to attack both sides of Dunkirk, force a way through to the coast and then continue the pursuit to the east. Group Kleist responded by arguing that 'our own organization is not suited to such an attack.' Panzers could not be used for it. Colonel Wuthmann, leading the conversation replied that that was known. 'But on orders from on high, an end must finally be put to the embarkations at Dunkirk. Therefore Dunkirk must be by-passed by a thrust along the coast.' Kluge repeated the order and pointed to the indefensible situation at Abbeville. Therefore, 'the encirclement in Flanders must be liquidated at once. For that purpose, advance with all forces immediately to the coast east of Dunkirk. You are to tell the Divisional Commander that he is to be at the coast tonight without fail,'[76] Kluge said in conclusion.

At 1615 hrs Group Kleist reported that: '…20.(mot.) Infantry Division is now advancing on Bray Dunes in order to cut off the enemy's lines of retreat from Furnes.' The left wing was off Bergues and at Gravelines on the Canal and could not move forwards, having in its path the fortified Dunkirk bridgehead. They had reached Fort Mardyck and would now attempt to fire into the port with light artillery. *Since yesterday the heavy artillery was out of ammunition.* In the evening AOK 4 reported to Army Group A:

'Armee on 30 May with individual battle groups in action against tough, resolute enemy.; *Group HOTH*: After house-to-house fighting against Moroccans, XXXIX Armee Korps closed up with 5. Panzer Division and elements of 11. and 267. Infantry Divisions to arrive from the south, west and north-west at the Haubordin–Loos–Lille area.

Group von KLEIST, has reached…along the whole Front the dividing line agreed with 6. Armee, and at 1700 hrs together with 20.(mot) Infantry Division passed either side of Bergues to advance on the coast eastwards of Dunkirk. Cassel was taken. The enemy in Bergues is being tied down by the advance to the coast. Enemy attacks against the Abbeville bridgehead before the *southern Front* have resulted in a temporary pulling back of the main Front on the south-east wing. We are counter-attacking since 1430 hrs. The enemy has not been active today against the Amiens bridgehead. The enemy there appears to have gone over to the defence, is digging trenches and putting up obstacles....

Intention for 31 May 1940: Cleansing of situation around Dunkirk in agreement with 18. Armee. Regrouping of the now relieved Panzer, motorized and Infantry Divisions north of the Somme[77]...'

In general the picture of Dunkirk in the late evening of 30 May was as follows:

No success had been achieved anywhere to overcome the stubborn enemy resistance at the Canal line Nieuport–Furnes–Bergues–Brouckerque–Mardick.

XXVI Armee Korps (256. Infantry Division) was preparing near Nieuport to advance on 31 May, while the spearheads of IX Armee Korps (56. and 216. Infantry Divisions) had reached the Canal de la Basse Colme in the line Bulscamp–Houthem and intended to advance across the canal at 1100 hrs.

X Armee Korps (14. and 254. Infantry Divisions) – under the command of 18. Armee since 2300 hrs – had pushed up to the line Hondschoote–Warhem. Here the intention was to advance to the Canal line on the morning of 31 May, and cross the Canal in the afternoon to advance on Dunkirk. Meanwhile 18. and 61. Infantry Divisions had arrived at Wormhoudt in order to relieve 9. Panzer Division.

XIV Armee Korps had had no luck in its attempt to cross the Canal de la Basse Colme, and it was decided not to try again on 31 May. The infantry and artillery force was too weak, furthermore the terrain was unsuitable for panzers. The Korps wanted to concentrate its artillery on Dunkirk and hold the canal line reached until X Armee Korps arrived in order then to pull out its own fast units.[78] As the Army Group B War Diary makes clear, *the advance of XIV Armee Korps was halted primarily because a new assignment awaited it 'corresponding to Movement Instruction Red'.*

Army Group B 'regretted this extremely, since it meant that the decisively important renewed advance from the west' could not now take place.[79]

Not until the evening of 30 May did OKH put the tactical command 'over all the German troops attacking the French-British forces in the region of Dunkirk' into one hand. With effect from 0200 hrs on 31 May, AOK 18 took over command of the offensive to capture the town and port of Dunkirk.[80]

6. The Conquest of Dunkirk (Maps 12–14)

On the morning of 31 May the Chief of the Army General Staff wrote in his diary: '…The *sack around Dunkirk* has *shrunk* more. But the British, continuing to ship out from here under the most difficult circumstances, are defending desperately. They must be working very accurately to a plan of proceeding with all means at their disposal…On the *southern Front* the enemy is making very strenuous efforts to remove our bridgeheads. Until now with only limited local success…Our attacks (Dunkirk), which *as a result of deficient unified command* – AOK 18 had not been able to act in time – individually bouncing off a dogged enemy holding out behind his canals, have only had limited local advantages. An intercepted signal has let us know that tonight the enemy is going to do some more shipping out. It will be difficult to prevent that. The failure to close down the coast caused by the interference from above is now wreaking its revenge. The artillery is not as effective against the enemy as it should be because in sand dunes our shells neither ricochet nor hit sufficiently well (Führer suggests the flak double-detonator).'[81]

On 31 May the German attack against Dunkirk concentric on three sides only won ground step by step. While XXVI Armee Korps (right wing 18. Armee) and IX Armee Korps succeeded in making a 'flat bridgehead' at Nieuport and Furnes, X Armee Korps with 14. and 254. Infantry Divisions edged nearer the Canal de la Basse Colme. In the afternoon it was found that the enemy resistance was stronger than had been expected. 18. Armee therefore decided 'to order a planned unified Armee attack for 1100 hrs on 1 July in order to tie down the enemy on all sides and…make possible operations by our bomber aircraft'.[82]

For this purpose the following units were ready:

- 256. Infantry Division (XXVI Armee Korps) either side of Nieuport on the north- and west-bank of the Canal. Target: dunes north and north-west of Nieuport.
- IX Armee Korps with 56. Infantry Division and 216. Infantry Division east of the Canal between Furnes and the Belgian/French border. Target: Coast from La Panne to Zuydcoote Sanatorium.
- X Armee Korps with 14., 254., and 18. Infantry Divisions between Hondschoote and Bergues on ther Bergues Canal. Target: Coast of Zuydcoote to Dunkirk.
- XIV Armee Korps with 9. Rifle Brigade bordering fromBdergues to the west at the MArdick Canal. Target: west bank of the Dunkirk–Bergues Canal.

All the same, Group Kleist requested AOK 4 'that 9. Panzer Division confine itself to the artillery support of the neighbour's attack. An infantry attack in this sector with the available force seemed to it to be too difficult.'[83] The same day 18. Armee was told that *only the absolutely necessary forces were to be deployed* in order to break the resistance at Dunkirk. All others, especially *the fast units* (XIV Armee Korps) were to be *released* as soon as possible for the next operations ('Fall Rot').[84]

On the night of 1 June the enemy in the eastward sector pulled back to the border fortifications at Bray-Dunes. This helped XXVI and IX Armee Korps to come forward better although the air attack scheduled for 1100 hrs had to be postponed in order not to endanger German troops.

At 1500 hrs X Armee Korps reported that they had succeeded in advancing over the Canal de la Basse Colme; the enemy there was defending doggedly. 18. Infantry Division had already reached les Moëres (about one kilometre north-east of Bergues). In order to advance farther, the Korps requested a Stuka attack in the area north of the line Uxem–Valliere.

Meanwhile the left wing of the German advance had stalled: the *flooding* caused by the enemy was creating many difficulties for the men in the field. XIV Armee Korps had the impression, however, that enemy resistance and Spycker region was falling off a little.

According to the War Diary, 18. Armee made the decision not to continue the advance until 2 June with centre of effort on the coast and at Bergues since the Korps had had many problems coming forwards since the afternoon. In order to make the IX Korps' turn to the west easier, it received 2.Artillery Abtg. detached from XXVI Armee Korps which had meanwhile forced its way out from the coast. 'X Armee Korps received the order to take over the entire western sector with the elements already there and the artillery of XIV Armee Korps. 61. Division was ordered to advance west of Bergues.'[85]

Situation Report West No.342 of 1 June 1940, 2345 hrs stated that enemy rearguards, mostly French, had defended the Dunkirk bridgehead tenaciously. Reports 'from a very good source' hinted that the enemy was probably intending to embark his last elements on the night of 1 June.

A clear estimate of the enemy losses in personnel and materials in Flanders could not yet be made. *According to the statement of a British military attaché abroad, 50,000 British had escaped from the Flanders Pocket but without equipment!*[86]

It remained the intention for Army Group B (18. Armee) for 2 June to wipe out the enemy forces still present in the narrowed bridgehead. At night (2300 hrs–midnight) IV.Flying Korps was to operate against the reported sailings.[87]

On 2 June Bock entered in his diary: 'Drove to the Dunkirk Front to a regimental battle post, to General Command X and to the ...famous 18. Division at present advancing to Bergues. During peacetime, Dunkirk had developed stronger defences than we knew; several defensive lines one behind another with strong wire obstacles here and there and a whole host of concrete bunkers. The road used by the British for their retreat is indescribable. Enormous quantities of vehicles, guns, tanks and army equipment all heaped closely together and driven into each other. The British have attempted to set fire to whatever they could but in their haste this has only been possible here and there. Here lie the materials of an army, and the totality of its equipment and supplies which we poor devils can only gaze upon with envy. Despite that... the ring around Dunkirk is being drawn ever tighter ... the enemy is putting up a desperate defence.'[88]

Details of the fighting were described as follows in the 18. Armee War Diary on 2 June:

'0900 hrs: IX Armee Korps, to which 208. Division is being attached, is leading the attack against the border fortifications in the dunes of Bray-Dunes with much artillery and few infantry. X Armee Korps, to where the commanding general went this morning, has before it an enemy defending grimly, supported by many floodgates which make (the proceedings)…extremely difficult. 61. Division, brought up to the left wing, is to advance at midday from Brouckerque to Dunkirk from a generally south-westerly direction. In order not to weaken the fighting power of this Division…the elements of 9. Panzer Division still present are provisionally not yet being released. A proposal to that effect submitted to the Army Group will towards midday decide that all elements of XIV Armee Korps of 18. Armee committed in the struggle against Dunkirk will remain under its command until the conclusion of the fighting.

'As a key point in the Dunkirk sea fortifications, Bergues, which is still holding out ahead of the 18. Division Front, must be taken as soon as possible. To support this attack against this extremely powerful bulwark with its old fortifications and casemates (the Armee requests the)… operation of Stukas with Air Fleet 2…

'1230 hrs: Flying Korps has informed that Stuka formations will attack towards 1300 hrs.

'By virtue of the commitment of a pioneer company commander, immediately after the Stuka attack on Bergues, 18. Division succeeded in entering the town and took prisoner its garrison, which amounted to about a battalion.

1700 hrs: A new attack has been initiated for IX Korps because after local initial successes the Division had come to a standstill. The…56. Division has…heavy casualties, especially amongst officers…, so that the attack does not have the necessary vitality and drive to overcome the desperate resistance of the enemy.

'An attack planned for 1700 hrs by bomber aircraft against Dunkirk has been postponed by the Luftwaffe until 1900 hrs.

'The enemy seems to be withdrawing, or to have withdrawn, according to plan into a much narrower bridgehead position around Dunkirk so that the best prospects…of coming forward in the afternoon lie with X Armee Korps. Signs of the enemy disintegration and disbandment have become more evident in this withdrawal, the streets everywhere are blocked by abandoned vehicles, guns and tanks, strewn with discarded weapons, equipment and clothing.

'The flooding of the terrain fronting the bridgehead at Dunkirk continues to increase and is making the advance of the Division more difficult…

'2000 hrs: As a result of the evening situation the Armee is ordering the *continuation of the attack on Dunkirk for 3 June*, in which the assignment of the Korps remains unchanged and the Korps has been freed to keep its own timetable.

On the evening of 2 June, IX Korps stood on the line east side Bray-Dunes–Ghyvelde opposite fortified field positions. X Armee Korps has reached the line Holikouke–Galghoek–Boomkens–Valliéres with the eastward attack group, with the westerly attack group (61. Division) the Spycker region and north-west.

'Statements by French prisoners suggest that the enemy probably needs three more days for the shipping out of his forces. We therefore have to reckon with a continuation of his stubborn resistance, and correspondingly we require all our available forces for a speedy success.

'However, in the late evening came the order that almost *all the Army artillery* and pioneers are to be *withdrawn* during the night. *The prospects of taking Dunkirk quickly are therefore lessened.*'[89]
The further considerations taken on 2 June by Army Group Command B can be seen in its War Diary entries for the same day:

'The withdrawal of XIV Armee Korps from the Dunkirk operation which has become necessary in the interests of Project "Red" presents AOK 18 with a question as to whether under such circumstances it may not be advisable to abandon the attack altogether, narrow down the bridgehead as much as possible and create for the enemy an area difficult to supply using up many of his personnel.' As against that it would tie down relatively strong German forces, at least two divisions.

In any case, Army Group Command B saw itself forced to withdraw all the heavy Army artillery from the sector so that it could reach its new theatre of deployment in the framework of Project Red in time. Even then, Command B wanted to continue the attack 'with the forces[90] still present and available'.

The 3 June had to bring the decision! Col-General von Bock was of the opinion that from now on 'the Dunkirk business is coming to its end': as he saw it, 'We could have had that eight days earlier if the uniformity of leadership had been restored in time'.[91]

The operations on 3 June explained in extracts in War Diary–18 read:

'It is not possible to "continue" the Korps attack on Dunkirk in the intended manner if the Army troops are withdrawn. IX Armee Korps believes an attack is not possible without totally new replacement artillery so that it cannot "resume" until the morning of 4 June. X Korps will attack at 1100 hrs with the support of Luftwaffe bombers.'

The commander-in-chief emphasized again that 'the operations at Dunkirk must be brought to a conclusion as soon as possible in order to release all forces for the planned operation against France. The enemy scenario leaves the possibility very much open that the enemy will perhaps attempt to hold Dunkirk and use it to create a threat to the flank of the German Western Army which will bind strong forces for a considerable time.'

'In order to release the last elements of XIV Armee Korps as soon as possible, 251. Division has received the order to mobilize one regiment of captured vehicles to be placed at the disposal of 61. Division in the area around Bollezeele. This regiment is to be used primarily to prevent an attempt by the encircled forces at Dunkirk to break out to the west...

'1400 hrs: For the eventuality that today's attack by X Armee Korps does not bring about the collapse of the Dunkirk bridgehead positions, the Armee intends for the early afternoon of 4 June to combine IX and X Korps in a unified attack against Dunkirk in which IX Korps will have Malo les Bains as its target, X Korps the town and harbour of Dunkirk.' For this purpose...Luftwaffe bombers will be used again.

1520 hrs: The most forward elements of 18. Division have reached Dunkirk while 254. Division has succeeded in crossing the Canal les Moëres northwards. The arrival of 61. Division at the Canal de Bourbourg from the south-west will tighten the ring around Dunkirk. IX Armee Korps is still in the line reached on 2 June.

'1800 hrs: The Chief (of the Army General Staff, who has been forward with 14. Division) states that the Division has crossed the Canal des Chats at Holiekouke and is proceeding towards Leffrinckoucke. Because of the flooding, the Divisions can only use the road so that it will need longer for the development of stronger forces. Enemy resistance at Uxem and Leffrinckoucke seems to be totally collapsed.

'At the same time the Commanding General of X Armee Korps, returning from 6. Division, informed the Chief that the Division has set up bridgeheads over the Canal de Bourbourg at Pite Synthe and le Moulin de Spycker by which further advances can be made against Dunkirk.

'In the course of the evening AOK was informed by the Air Fleet that Stukas would not be available for the attack on 4 June and that only bomber units are operational. Because this means the loss of support immediately before the front of the attacking Division, Flak-Korps IV was requested to eliminate the involvement of enemy warships in the Armee attack and to protect our own area against enemy aircraft.

'2100 hrs: The korps have received instructions to lay harassment fire on the assumed embarkation places following the arrival of ten to fifteen enemy warships off Dunkirk apparently for the purpose of transporting out more enemy troops.

'No hostilities took place during the day in front of IX Armee Korps.

'In the framework of the regroupings for the attack on 4 June, the battle-worn 56. and 208. Divisions have been relieved and 216. Division strengthened by elements of 256. Division.

'Because of the success of X Armee Korps, the Armee can reckon with certainty on taking Dunkirk on 4 June. Accordingly, thinking about a joint start to the attack on 4 June can be discarded and the order was given that X Armee Korps had to remain in constant contact with the enemy and that IX Armee Korps should advance and attack as early as possible[92]...

'4 June 1940

'In the early hours of 4 June 1940 the enemy resistance began to slacken, enabling IX Armee Korps to advance early. The Korps quickly gained ground and at 0700 hrs 208. Division took Bray-Dunes.

'At 0940 hrs X Armee Korps reported taking the town and port of Dunkirk. At the same time the forward troops of IX Armee Korps reached Malo les Bains. With that the last enemy resistance ceased and the whole coast was in German hands.

'The number of prisoners taken was initially not possible to estimate and after a few days was given as 80,000[93]...'

After nine days uninterrupted hard fighting the attacking German units finally succeeded in taking Dunkirk! Both Halder and Bock confirmed it: 'Town and coast is in our hands! *French/British are gone!*'[94]

7. Planning and Execution of Operation *Dynamo*

When the last Allied troops reached the Dunkirk bridgehead on 30 May, the evacuation by sea had already been under way for five days.

On 19 May, a day before the German panzer spearheads had arrived at Abbeville on the Channel, the War Cabinet[1] entrusted Vice-Admiral Dover, Admiral Sir Bertram Ramsay, with the task of assembling ships for the eventuality that certain troops of Army Group 1 under threat would have to be brought out by sea from the Channel ports (Ostend, Dunkirk, Nieuport, Calais and Boulogne). It was conceived initially as a preventive measure to save small units of stragglers, though Gort had already reported that day[2] that a retreat by the BEF to Dunkirk might perhaps be unavoidable. On the other hand, at this time the Allies were still considering the idea that Army Group 1 might join up with the forces standing at the Somme and make a combined attack from north and south. Nevertheless, at a conference of the military offices involved at Dover on 20 May, there was talk of making preparations for a possible evacuation of 'very large forces' across the Channel. It was thought that 10,000 men could be brought out every 24 hours. At first, therefore, 30 ferries, 12 auxiliary ships and six small coastal steamers were readied. On 22 May additionally 40 'schuits' used by the fleeing Dutch were requisitioned and all vessels thought suitable were rounded up in British ports. Therefore the preparations for a possible evacuation of small units had been far exceeded and an operation of considerable size was now envisaged.

When, on 25 May, Gort had withdrawn his two divisions preparing for the offensive to the south in order to use them to plug the gap between the Belgian and BEF Fronts, it was clear that the Weygand Plan was no longer going to be realized. The day after, Churchill approved Gort's decision and informed the French Minister-President that a defensive position around Dunkirk could not be held for ever; therefore an evacuation had to be planned. Gort received the corresponding orders, but as it seems, *either* the French Government *or* the French High Command did not pass this important decision of the War Cabinet to the Commanding Officer at Dunkirk, (Admiral North), Admiral Abrial nor to General Blanchard, for neither received before the 28-29 May any such instructions.[3]

At 1857 hrs on 26 May, however, the British Admiralty issued the order '*Operation Dynamo is to commence!*'[4] and so began that evening the operation which would not end until 4 June, by when 350,000 Allied soldiers had been shipped out successfully.

At the outset even the greatest optimist would not have thought a success of that size feasible. At the beginning of *Dynamo* the figure of 45,000 men evacuated within two days was being reckoned possible. On the one hand, up to 26 May, 27,936 British personnel had been transported out from Dunkirk, Calais, and Boulogne; for already on 20 May Colonel G.H.P. Whitfield (Assistant Adjutant General) had received the task[5] of collecting up superfluous Staffs and other non-combatant units for shipping out. On the other hand, apart from Dunkirk, all Channel ports were no longer available although their use had been calculated into the planning at the start. In addition, German air attacks on 24 May against the town and port of Dunkirk had caused heavy damage – the system of water supply no long functioned – so that from that day onward even the supply for the BEF was greatly impeded.

On 26 May, the first night of Operation *Dynamo*, 4,247 men[6] were evacuated.

In the course of 27 May a large number of ships assembled at Sheerness sailed for the port and beaches of Dunkirk. On this second day, a disappointingly small number of 7,669 persons were brought out. The cause was the false report[7] that Dunkirk had fallen, as a result of which many ships were recalled before they had reached Dunkirk.

After the error had been discovered, more bad news arrived. The Senior Naval Officer (SNO) Dunkirk, Captain Tennant, in charge of the evacuation, reported that evening that the situation was very critical: any kind of craft capable of carrying personnel should be sent to the coast immediately because it 'is doubtful if we can keep the evacuation going longer than tomorrow evening'.[8] The situation on the land front was especially dangerous, German troops having appeared[9] on the weakly defended eastern side of the bridgehead, and it was by no means certain that Allied troops would be able to complete the last phase of the retreat.

Because of this situation, on 28 May the British Admiralty sent one cruiser, eight destroyers and 26 other ships, while destroyers from Portsmouth and the Western Approaches were also despatched to Dunkirk. This increased the tempo of the evacuation. 17,804 persons – almost three and a half times more than on the previous day – were brought out on 28 May; of these around one third were lifted directly off the beaches, where meanwhile around 20,000 men had gathered. The relatively quiet aerial situation was another factor in favour of the evacuation on this day.[10]

In contrast to the previous day, in which there had been twelve heavy air attacks, the activity of Luftwaffe bombers was concentrated against the Allied retreat on the perimeter rather than against the evacuation[11] while the RAF had increased substantially its constant string of operations. With brief pauses there were now up to two fighter squadrons over Dunkirk. The aircraft flew up to 321 missions and protected the embarkation points along the beaches three miles in either direction. Thus Captain Tennant could signal to England that evening: 'Fighter protection has been invaluable – bombing only sporadic.'[12,13]

On 29 May the total of evacuees was considerably higher as a result of the numbers of ships and other craft which were taking over the removal of men from the beaches. 20 destroyers, 20 steam and motor-powered minesweepers, numerous fishing boats and Dutch 'schuits' were employed. Though the number of those evacuated had greatly increased, so also had the losses: two destroyers were lost to German motor torpedo boat attacks, a passenger ship was mined and sunk, another destroyer and three passenger ships lost to aerial bombing. Five of the eleven ships at the Dunkirk mole were sunk. In all, apart from the three destroyers, 21 other ships went down.

On 29 May the Luftwaffe concentrated once more on the evacuation. Between midday and 2000 hrs bomber activity continued almost without a break. The RAF, which had a strength of forty aircraft in the area, was absent during two of the air raids.[14]

Despite these difficulties and losses, 47,310 men were evacuated on 29 May. This was due not only to the greater use of vessels but also the improving organisation on the beaches and in the port. The strip of sand dunes between Bray Dunes and La Panne was put under the command of British 'evacuation officers'. Naval personnel took over the handling of the small boats which ferried troops off the beaches. This markedly reduced the number of larger vessels suffering damage by grounding and drifting etc.

Most disconcerting was the fact that Sea Route Y came under fire from a German battery on the mole at Nieuport. After the French minefields had been partially swept the 55-mile long Route X was used: by night temporarily Route Z.[15] Meanwhile after the Aa-Line[16] had been given up and the front drawn back to the Ancien Canal de Mardyk, Route X also came under artillery fire. Because British bomber attacks against these German batteries were unsuccessful over the next few days, daylight evacuations had to be stopped from 1 June.

It is useful for an understanding of the development at this point to review two documents dated 29 May. That day the British Prime Minister sent[17] a Note each to the Minister for War and also to General Sir Edward Spears,[18] his personal representative to the Minister-President and Defence Minister Reynaud. In them can be read his concern for the continuing danger to the BEF, and also his satisfaction that already a larger number of troops had been saved than had originally been thought possible, which justified further hope.

These Notes also contained, however, certain statements which shed light on quite different problems involving the political background to the operation. Churchill wrote to the Minister for War and the Chief of the Imperial General Staff: 'It is of the greatest importance that the French should be involved in all evacuations taking place at Dunkirk...so that no, or the fewest possible, reproaches can be made against us'.[19] To

General Spears he added these sentences to be passed to Reynaud: 'We wish that as many French troops as possible take part in the evacuation, and the Admiralty has been instructed to give the French Navy all the support it requires. We do not know how many Allied troops will be forced to surrender, but we must bear this loss together as best we can and above all without reproaches which arise from the unavoidable confusion, pressures and distress.'[20]

Here we have a duality: on the one hand the great concern about the state of the coalition;[21] for political repercussions could follow if there were too great a disparity between the numbers of evacuated British and French troops respectively. Therefore, from now on Churchill urged constantly that the French[22] were to be much more involved in the evacuation. On the other hand, the fact that a disparity in the ratio of evacuated troops threatened to arise makes clear the extent to which inter-Allied coordination and therefore also cooperation in Operation *Dynamo* was lacking. In the opening phase of the evacuation, the cooperation with, and to some extent, antipathy towards each other and national self-interest amongst the members of the Alliance was visible and showed themselves not only in the planning of the operation but equally in the organization of the bridgehead.

Not until 29 May, by when the British had evacuated a total of 72,783 men, did the French troops of Army Group 1 receive the order to evacuate. By the time the French Navy had begun the task, almost another 24 hours had passed.

How did this discrepancy between the French and British planning come about? This question is all the more pressing when one recalls that the French began discussing the possibility of an evacuation on the same day as the British.

On 19 May(!), GQG, Headquarters of the Allied High Command,[23] requested the opinion of the French Admiralty as to whether the 'evacuation of certain units by sea' was possible, without giving any indication of the size of the operation being considered. Three hours later the Admiralty submitted a comprehensive study.[24] In paragraph 5 of the document the conclusion drawn was that such an operation under enemy pressure was equal to a catastrophe. On the other hand, supplying the fighting troops by sea was less problematical.

This discussion was then broken off abruptly because of the change in the High Command. The new Commander-in-Chief, General Weygand, re-submitted the request[25] to the French Admiralty on 20 May but amended its terms 'to study the possibility of evacuating troops on the Army left wing.' Admiral Darlan replied next day[26] by drawing attention to his opinion of 19 May: such an operation was very risky and only had any prospect of success if given sufficiently strong anti-aircraft artillery and fighter support. In any case it would be extremely difficult and protracted.

Next day Weygand flew into the Army Group 1 northern pocket. After his return he issued his orders for the so-called Weygand Plan for saving Army Group 1 by means of a land operation. That ended the possibility of any further discussion for the time being on an evacuation by sea. When the Weygand Plan had to be discarded, the Generalissimo, General Blanchard, proposed setting up a bridgehead surrounding a great area of Dunkirk and which would be defended long term. The idea was that later on this bridgehead, if the situation at the Somme improved, could be used *offensively*, the troops at the Somme being supplied by sea. This thinking no doubt recalled the Admiralty opinion of 19 May.[27] In operational Instruction No.30 of 25 May, Army Group 1 was ordered to set up a bridgehead of that kind.

While the BEF received the order to evacuate next day, the above-mentioned instruction to Army Group 1 for French troops remained in force officially until 29 May. That was ultimately the reason for the altercation between Blanchard and Gort at Houtekerque on 28 May.

On the basis of the intervention of Blanchard with Weygand (after the latter's talk with Gort), and the reports of General Koeltz and Admiral Auphan, who had been sent to discuss the possibility of evacuating French troops to Dover,[28] Weygand decided finally on shipping them out[29] although Admiral Abrial (Admiral North) had sent a telegram from Dunkirk that a '…withdrawal of all important units by sea … seemed unfeasible because of the destruction to the town and port by German air attacks'.[30]

At 0720 hrs on 29 May an order to that effect was issued by HQ Allied High Command to Army Group 1; at 0948 hrs the French Admiralty received the instruction to introduce the necessary measures and swiftly.[31]

Meanwhile a certain period of time was needed until these orders could be realized resulting in units of the French evacuation fleet, 'The Pas de Calais Flotilla' drifting in line here and there with the current between England and Dunkirk until 30 May.[32]

After the order was given to evacuate the French troops, from now on the mutual cooperation of the two Allies should have been guaranteed. Although the next few days brought growing numbers of evacuated troops, a serious deficit in coordination between the Allies became noticeable, and in its turn very dangerous misunderstandings and differences arose provoking a crisis of confidence.

On 30 May, 53,823 men were shipped out aboard 830 vessels of all kinds including fifteen French. High though this number was, the reports from Dunkirk led to London fearing the worst. Admiral Wake-Walker[33] reported that the defensive positions on 31 May could barely be held; and Lord Gort[34] on the same morning also confided his doubts that a further successful defence of the bridgehead[35] was possible. He added the urgent request to send all available ships without delay. . In response the Admiralty drew up special plans of action[36] in order to accelerate the evacuation process to the maximum. At the same time Gort received basic instructions[37] regarding the termination of the evacuation and the order to return to England when the British force was down to only Corps strength.

During the course of 31 May in an intermittent operation, 68,014 men were brought out from the port and beaches. The great number of small craft and boats played a significant role[38] providing primarily ferrying duties on the private owner's own initiative, larger vessels and ships having certain difficulties coming inshore to pick up men from the beaches. The protection of the signals connections between the individual evacuation terminals could now be improved even if they remained a source of constant irritation until *Dynamo* ended.[39] Thus up to 30 May between the evacuation terminals on the beaches at La Panne and Bray Dunes there had been no contact at all; the evacuation at Bray had suffered considerable delays because no sea transports of any kind had shown up.

The considerable success of the evacuation on 31 May was achieved only after a grim struggle against great difficulties despite many improvements in the organization. In the early hours a fresh breeze caused such a rolling surf that all beach traffic was called off for several hours. Furthermore, since some of the beaches lay in range of German artillery; Admiral Ramsay held back the larger ships and in their place sent in hundreds of smaller vessels. The 6,000 British troops waiting on the beach at La Panne had to march to Dunkirk through the deep sand of the dunes on account of the enemy artillery fire. On this day the Luftwaffe flew three major operations against the evacuation[40] besides smaller delaying raids nearly all day.

The German pressure in the eastern section of the bridgehead was increasing considerably and for a time at Nieuport the danger existed that the British defensive Front might be penetrated. Therefore here in the evening, 18 RAF Blenheims and 6 Albatross of the Naval Air Arm attacked and destroyed German readiness positions. Other RAF attacks were mounted against German convoys proceeding from the south and east towards Dunkirk.

On 30 May at a conference[41] in BEF HQ it had been decided that in the course of the evacuation the bridgehead should be shortened from east to west. Accordingly at nightfall, II Armee Corps began to move out. Apart from a weak British rearguard, the French 12th Division Motorized Infantry held the eastern side of the bridgehead; behind it stood mainly as a reserve the BEF 50. Division.

While the Royal Navy made the greatest efforts to speed up the evacuation and end it as quickly as possible, there were substantial disagreements between the French commander and the British in the bridgehead. On the morning of 31 May, Gort had discussed with Admiral Abrial the coordination of French and British troops.[42] He had informed him of his impending departure and mentioned as his successor the Commanding General of 1. Army Corps, Lt-General Barker. At 1530 hrs to Abrial's astonishment, Major-General Alexander introduced himself as the Commanding Officer of the last British troops.[43] An immediate difference of opinion arose between Abrial and Alexander. Alexander wanted his troops at the Dunkirk Front no longer than 24 hours more before shipping out the last units. He considered Abrial's plan to defend the bridgehead as long as possible impracticable. In his opinion the evacuation of all troops had to be concluded during the night of 1 June.

Since there was no agreement, each reported the matter to his own superiors,[44] and so this difference of opinion arrived at the highest level. On 31 May, Churchill discussed the problem in Paris with Reynaud and General Weygand at a meeting of the Supreme Inter-Allied War Council.[45] Between the question of bringing out the last British troops and the evacuation of the French units there was for Churchill the political issues surrounding the withdrawal of the last British and in the number of Frenchevacuated.

Alexander now received a telegram[46] from the Secretary of State for War ordering him to evacuate his troops as soon as possible in the ratio 50:50 with the French in order to terminate the operation during the night of 1 June. The General passed the information to Admiral Abrial on 1 June. The latter agreed to the British planning, but as it was impossible to evacuate the French troops by 1 June, they would have to form the rearguard by themselves, against the wishes of Churchill, who had intended it for the British.[47]

This arrangement more or less calmed the tensions at Dunkirk for the moment. At the higher level, however, the discussion continued not without irritation and in a tone of reproach, from now on concentrating on the date for ending the evacuation.[48] The mistrust of the French leaders directed towards the intentions of the British was expressed in the fear that the Royal Navy would break off Operation *Dynamo* after the last British troops had been brought out. Therefore the British went to lengths to calm the French on this issue while doing everything to avoid disagreements and clarify misunderstandings.

Above all, however, they made it clear to the French that too long a delay at Dunkirk could lead to a catastrophe. On 1 June, Churchill sent General Weygand a message in which he urged an end to the evacuation soon, since 'the crisis stage…has been reached from now on.'[49] The Chief of the Imperial General Staff went out of his way to explain to the French that the stated closing date in the War Office order to Alexander was not a formal order, but only a target to be aimed for. The British side emphasized that everything would be done to save as many as possible of the French troops left behind at Dunkirk.[50] Finally, General Alexander received from the Chief of the Imperial General Staff the concluding instruction: 'We are not setting you a definite day for ending the evacuation. You have to hold out as long as is necessary to evacuate the maximum number of French and British. From here it is impossible to judge the situation on the spot and locally. Remain in close cooperation with Admiral Abrial. You must act on your personal judgement.'[51] This order modified the one issued by the Secretary of State for War as regards the closing date for ending the evacuation and bringing out the British troops. That Alexander did not keep British troops in Dunkirk on the 50:50 basis until such time as the evacuation had run its course can be attributed to his having underestimated the ability of the French troops defending the bridgehead to resist; and he also probably underestimated how many of them there were.[52]

These differences and the not exactly edifying discussions both at the highest level and also in Dunkirk were to a large extent an outflowing of the differing concepts between British and French regarding the sense and purpose of the bridgehead at Dunkirk. The *French* saw their *most pressing task* as being to *defend the bridgehead,* while *the British* had *the evacuation closer to their heart.*

What made things more difficult was that irritation and mistrust, also to some extent undisguised suspicions,[53] created an unpleasant atmosphere. A crisis of confidence of this kind was the worst thing which could happen to a coalition in a military crisis.

On 1 June another 64,429 men were evacuated, about 17,348 of them from the beach. On the other hand very heavy Luftwaffe bombing[54] and the enduring artillery fire caused losses to ships so high as to almost equal the losses of all the previous week.[55] For this reason it was decided that ships would only come inshore by night. This would also enable a higher degree of reconnaissance and security.

In the early hours the last British troops had begun to gather on the beach after being relieved from their posts and crossing the eastern defensive line of the bridgehead now held entirely by French troops.[56] From 1700 hrs on 2 June the ships of the evacuation fleet arrived off Dunkirk again.[57] After midnight there was no British presence in the bridgehead, and up to 0300 hrs on 3 June some French units were also transported away overland. A number of ships with room for about 10,000 men had to sail empty between midnight and 0200 hrs since they could find no French troops on the beaches.[58] This was undoubtedly due to the defective cooperation: it led to a very lively exchange of telegrams between the British Admiralty, the French Navy Mission in London, and the French Admiralty.[59]

On 2 June the Germans launched their general offensive against the Dunkirk bridgehead.[60] While the front held in the eastern part of the bridgehead on the border and at the Canal des Chats, in the western part the village of Spycker was lost. Three small bases were set up at once in the area close to the Canal de Bourbourg and staffed with the last reserves.

The situation in the central sector became critical. A counter-attack at 0600 hrs in the area of Notre Dame des Neiges against the Canal de la Basse Colme did not interfere with the German preparations for the offensive. Bergues fell to the German attack at 1700 hrs, then the French lines at Goudekerque-Branche and Teteghem (southern edge) were forced back to the Canal des Chats.

Thus this part became the most endangered sector of the entire defensive line – and the enemy was nearest here to the town and port of Dunkirk. Accordingly the French commanders reinforced the front with units of the 32. and 68. Divisions, and another counter-attack was planned for 3 June.

Next morning at 0400 hrs, two battalions supported by tanks and artillery set out towards Notre Dame des Neiges: they succeeded in advancing for several kilometres until sighting the Canal de la Basse Colme but at 0900 hrs the beginning of the German offensive put a stop to it.

The German offensive concentrated its fighting principally around Teteghem and Coudekerque-Branche. Towards 1800 hrs the German thrust towards Teteghem was halted, but ultimately the defenders were forced to withdraw to the Dunkirk-Furnes Canal under cover of an artillery barrage put up by the SFF (Secteur Fortifiée Française) with the last of its reserve of ammunition.

After the loss of the stubbornly defended bases St. Georges and Fort Castelnau, fierce house-to-house fighting ensued at Coudekerque-Branche. Here the Groupe de Reconnaissance Mariot was added as reinforcements: the southern edge of Dunkirk had to be held at all costs so that the evacuation could be terminated during the night.

In the eastern sector the right wing of the defensive line fell back but the front held. In the western sector in bitter fighting the Germans pushed back the French lines to the Canal de Bourbourg, and at the south-west edge of Dunkirk and the junction of the Ancien Canal de Mardyck with the Canal de Bourbourg they built a few small bridgeheads.

On the whole on 3 June the French defenders succeeded, often with serious losses, in preventing the Germans forcing their way into the town and port of Dunkirk, and so created the necessary requirement for the final evacuation on the night of 3 June.

On the morning of 3 June the British commanders were of the opinion that the transports could not continue, assuming that the French troops were not in a position to hold the bridgehead any longer, especially since the British naval forces were exhausted and worn out.[61]

After talks with the Mission Navale Française à Londres (French Naval Mission in London, MNFL) which was urging that Operation *Dynamo* be continued,[62] Admiral Ramsay sent a telegram to Admiral Nord at 1108 hrs advising him that during the night of 3/4 June between 2030 hrs (on 3 June) and 0230 hrs (on 4 June) a last embarkation for about 14,000 men would be attempted. For the Admiral himself a British motor torpedo boat would be placed at his disposal at 2200hrs.[63] Accordingly at a conference of the commanders in the bridgehead, it was decided with Admiral Abrial that the evacuations would be terminated in the coming night.

The French commanders calculated that there would be about 50,000 men (12. mot. Division, 32., 60., 68. Divisions, SFF and EOCA 10 to 16.3.5.[64] Already at 0730 hrs on 2 June in Note No.1727/CB from Armee Corps XVI, details of the final clearance of the bridgehead had been laid down. The enemy would be disengaged in two stages: under the protection of a first rearguard all divisions and other units would hasten directly to the embarkation terminals[65] already nominated.

Behind the first rearguard a second rearguard would be set up on the line Batterie de Zuydcoote–Canal Dunkerque à Furnes–southern edge Dunkirk–Canal Dunkerque à Pte. Synthe-Fort Mardyk.

In the second phase of the retreat operation, the first rearguard would make their way to the embarkation terminals through the lines of the second rearguard. Finally – if possible – the retreat and embarkation of the second rearguard would follow.[66]

At nightfall the troops succeeded in disengaging from the enemy without further incident. From 2130 hrs the first rearguard veiled the operation under cover of normal aggressive activity. The divisional units formed up behind it and all moved off to the appointed embarkation points. The first ships of the evacuation fleet appeared towards 2230 hrs. At 2200 hrs units of 32nd Division with the exception of troops still fighting on the defensive ring arrived at the port and were evacuated at 0130 hrs. The various EOCAs had already been transported out. 68.Division appeared at 2230 hrs at the Jetée d'Embarquetage; on the other hand 12th Motorized Division did not arrive until 0300 hrs after a six-hour march from where they had been unloaded. The SFF units, hindered by roads blocked or in a state of destruction, arrived between 0200 and 0300 hrs.[67]

Because the operation had to be broken off according to plan at 0330 hrs, nearly all 12th Motorized Division and SFF troops remained behind,[68] and only around 800 men of 68th Division could be taken because the evacuation of the various EOACs and 32nd Division, who were transported out earlier, took up all the time. On the beach at Malo were the remnants of 60th Division who also waited in vain because no ship had been sent there at all on account of an error of organization.[69]

At 0805 hrs on 4 June the French Admiralty reported to General Weygand (Telegram No. 7718[70]) that no further attempts to evacuate were possible. The approximate number saved the previous night was in the region of 25,000 (exact figure was 26,175). After the ugly Anglo-French differences of the last few days, the telegram ended in conciliatory fashion with Admiral Abrial considering that the achievements of the British had been magnificent. Upon his arrival at Dover in company with Admirals Platon and Leclerc, and General Fagalde, Admiral Ramsay had suggested making one more evacuation attempt for the coming night. Abrial said this was impossible. At 1100 hrs the French Admiralty rejected any further attempt and at 1423 hrs the British Admiralty declared Operation *Dynamo* concluded officially.[71] 338,226 Allied troops had been brought out of Dunkirk; around 40,000 became German prisoners-of-war on 4 June.[72] (See German estimate p.153 this book)

STATISTIC No. 1

The British and Allied vessels participating in Operation *Dynamo*. The troop numbers evacuated by them and the British ships sunk or damaged.

Kind of Ship	Number	Troops Transported	Losses[a]		Damaged
AA-cruiser	1	1,865	0	0	1
Destroyers and torpedo boats	56	102,843	9	0	19
Sloops and courier-boats	6	1,436	0	0	1
Patrol boats	7	2,504	0	0	0
Gun-boats (monitors)	2	3,512	1	0	0
Corvettes	11	1,303	0	0	0
Large minesweepers	38	48,472	5	1	7
Trawlers	230	28,209	23	6	2
Special naval craft	3	4,408	0	0	0
Armed boarding vessels	3	4,848	1	0	2
MTB's	15	99	0	0	0
Dutch schuyts	40	22,698	1	3	0
Yachts	27	4,895	1	2	0
Passenger ships	45	87,810	9	0	8
Hospital ships	8	3,006	1	0	5
Freighters	13	5,790	3	0	0
Tugs	40	3,164	6	1	0
Landing craft	13	118	1	7	0
Lighters, motor-barges	48	4,726	4	8	0
Light craft[b]:					
Naval motor boats	12	96			
War Department pinnaces	8	579			
Private motor boats	203	5,031			
RNLI lifeboats	19	323			
Totals	**848**	**338,226**			

(a) Losses to enemy action 72, other causes 163, damaged 45.
(b) 7 to enemy action, other causes 135; damaged, unknown

Of light craft, certainly a larger number than this took part, details not available.

Notes on the above table:

1. Details were taken from Appendix L of Capt. Roskill's book *op. cit.*, p.603.
2. Ellis *op. cit.*, p.248 states that 765 British vessels were known officially. Churchill, *op. cit.*, pp.145–146 reports 693 British and 168 Allied ships.
3. Saunders gives the following (*op. cit.*, p.133); 228 ships of all kinds sunk, 45 seriously damaged. Churchill gives 243 ships sunk.

The disparity in the number of ships sunk is partially explained by the uncertainty regarding the numbers of small craft as well as that in counting the number of ships, the nationality has been based partly on the crews (Belgian or French ships with British crews) or also on the port of registration.

STATISTIC No. 2

Details of the Numbers of Troops Evacuated from Dunkirk

Date	From beaches	From the port	Total	Aggregate Total
27 May	0	7,669	7,669	7,669
28 May	5,930	11,847	17,804	25,473
29 May	13,752	33,558	47,310	72,783
30 May	29,512	24,311	53,823	126,606
31 May	22,942	45,072	68,014	194,620
1 June	7,348	47,081	64,429	259,049
2 June	6,695	19,561	26,256	285,305
3 June	1,870	24,876	26,746	312,051
4 June	622	25,553	26,175	338,226
Total	**98,671**	**239,555**	**338,226**	

Note: These figures are taken from Churchill, *op. cit.*, p.145 (the Admiralty files). The War Office compiled its own statistics which give a figure of 336,427 men.

In Vice-Admiral Sir Bertram Ramsay's *Despatches* the following numbers are given:

26 May	4,247
27 May	5,718
28 May	18,527
29 May	50,331
30 May	53,227
31 May	64,141
1 June	61,557
2 June	23,604
3 June	29,641
4 June	27,689
Total	**338,682**

For the French troops evacuated to England, the Ramsay figures are as follows:

Date	By French Vessel	By British Vessel	Total
29 May	655	0	655
30 May	5,444	3,272	8,616
31 May	4,032	10,842	14,874
1 June	2,765	32,248	35,013
2 June	905	15,144	16,049
3 June	4,235	15,568	19,803
4 June	2,349	24,640	26,989
5 June	140	956	1,096
Totals	**20,525**	**102,570**	**123,095**

According to the French Navy the following numbers were evacuated by French and Belgian ships or by ships with French crews: (the numbers are based on a 24-hour day beginning at 0800 hrs):

21 May	600
26 May	570
27 May	175
28 May	1,527
29 May	5,178
30 May	6,363
31 May	9,984
1 June	7,483
2 June	6,474
3 June	10,420
Total	**48,474**

(French ships evacuated 3,936 British troops to France.)

8. The German Luftwaffe operations against *Dynamo*, 26 May–2 June

We look first at the daily General Staff Ic-Situation Reports of the Luftwaffe High Command (OKL) from 26 May to 2 June which provide an impressive picture of the extent and targets of the continuing air attacks against enemy shipping:

26 May 1940
Air Fleet 2: I and IV Flying Korps

Port Installations:

1100–1402: Dunkirk, tank plant west of port with success. Several large tanks at west end of tank compound burning. Direct hit factory hall near tank plant. Wharf with success. Bombs hit wharf and shipping. One hit SC 250 bomb on one freighter (c.2000 t) lying at quay.

	Exits to street in localities east of wharf and south of tank plant. Hits.
1100–1348:	Dunkirk; wharves and one boiler plant hit. Fire and smoke observed.
1153–1633:	*Dunkirk.* Shunting yard in north-west part, wharves. In northern part hall with piece goods. Attack on one steamer at quay, near miss. South railway station and track system hits observed.
1858–2145:	*Harbour installation Ostend.* SC 250 asnd SC 50 (bombs) on the quay in western part of harbour. Fires at various places: on west quay of new fishing boat basin, in the naval depot and stationary trains on the track eastwards of main railway station. Dropped leaflets. *Harbour installation Zeebrugge.* Effect, three sticks SC 50 on building, street and railway installation. East of port one SC 250 on bend in road, 3 SC 250 close south locks, 2 SC 250 east of locks. Incendiaries dropped over Ostend and Zeebrugge. In Zeebrugge fires at several places. Total payload dropped: 12 SCV 250, 96 SC 50, and 864 B1 E1.
2300–0413:	Ostend and Zeebrugge: bombing attacks.[1]

Air Fleet 3: VIII Flying Korps

Estaires–Armentières–Baille

27 May 1940
Air Fleet 2: I and IV Flying Korps

Port Installations and shipping:

0345–0540:	Two destroyers 50 km west of Ostend, fell 10–15 metres from target.
	Two freighters west of Dunkirk, unsuccessful.
0345–0635:	Port and town Dunkirk.

0711: Hit on railway track system in north-west of port. Heavy fires burning in harbour.

Ostend harbour: big fire in harbour.

0733–1035: Wharves and town Nieuport, effect not observed on account of cloud.

0805–1018: Freighter and destroyer at Ostend, unsuccessful:

Railway tracks on south bridge, Ostend. 3 hits.

Lock at south bridge, Ostend, 4 hits.

0600–0807: Port Zeebrugge, several silos destroyed, one direct hit on mole. Several hits on railway buildings and track system. One SC500 on dam between mole and beach. Tank installations on the mole hit and set ablaze. Two hits on Leopold Canal lock.

1207: Zeebrugge and Dunkirk. Report on successes still awaited.

1059–1318: Ostend, wharves. 4 hits on town areas around harbour south of the large lock. Two hits south of Eerenlahe bridge, Bassin de Chasse crossing.

Merchant steamer (500 t) in roadstead Ostend.

1345–1609: Ostend. 4 hits on town exits in south-west and 4 hits in northern part Ostend. 3 hits on wharves in northern harbour and 6 hits on wharves east of lock into south harbour.

1412–1708: Port installation Nieuport. Direct hit on trans-shipment silo in harbour. Explosion observed. Stick of bombs across harbour quarter. Some bombs into fort. Hit on street junction north-east corner of town.

One ship (1000 t) hit by several SC 50 in the harbour. Three smaller ships also hit. Probable hit on lock.

1515–1745: Harbour installation Ostend. Several direct hits on canal lock. Sticks of bombs dropped by 11 aircraft across port installation. One stick of bombs in the naval depot, several hits in main railway station. Incendiaries in south part of island and northern part of town.

Ship of 3000 to 4000 t (looked like warship) west, without success.

1747–2107:   Port installation and trans-shipment silo at Nieuport. Effect not observed due to thick smoke.
Port and railway installations and lock at Ostend bombs with good effect.

1559–1830:   Mole and town Zeebrugge, hits on end of mole and town railway installations.

1539–1825:   Port installation Nieuport. All bombs fell on quay.

Air Fleet 3: (II and VIII Flying Korps)

Dunkirk: (extensive fires in city centre and northern suburbs, burning oil tanks.)
Zeebrugge.
Port installation and ships: from Ostend
Zeebrugge, mole, harbour railway hit, small steamer in canal east of Zeebrugge hit, Dunkirk most bombs hit targets, extensive fires;
especially heavily hit south-east and south-west part of port, oil compound, two locks, freight barges, oil refinery tank installations on north-west edge, wharves. One merchant ship (about 2000 t) hit amidships.
Convoy of four ships and one escort attacked in (English) Channel. Bombs fell close ahead of bow 1 ship and 1 destroyer. Mine effect probable.
One destroyer between Dover and Calais probable hit on after-deck by 500-kg bomb.[2]

28 May 1940
Air Fleet 2

Port installations, ships:

0354–0617:   Ostend, port installations, town and bridge between merchant harbour with success. 2 transports and one AA cruiser (destroyer?), success not observed. Port installations and naval air base, with success.

0600–0918: Nieuport, hit on lock installations, harbour installations (silos) and in the town.

1057–1151: Nieuport. Much smoke on island, harbour and lock installations, trans-shipment silo and north-east edge of port. Hits on town of Nieuport.

1100–1523: Ostend. Hit on drydock, wharf and rail track system, compound shed and lock. One cruiser south-east of Downs with success (1 SC 500 close by stern, 2 SC 500 10–20 metres from side of hull) one cruiser eastwards of Dover (1 SC 500/20 metres from side of hull) and one cruiser off Dover without success.

1327–1640: Port Installations Ostend and Nieuport.
Group of destroyers 15 km north-west Ostend: hit on one destroyer 2 SD 50 and hits on another destroyer 2 SD 50 amidships, 1 SC 250 in front of bow. Both destroyers steamed on making much smoke. On a third destroyer 3 SC 250 close portside, 1 SC 250 20 metres behind it, came to standstill between Nieuport and Dunkirk 100 metres west of coast. Damage could not be determined.

1335–1620: Transport (freighter) ca. 3000–4000 t west Nieuport with 16 SD 50. Stick of bombs in the ship.

1345–1620: Port installations Ostend.

1500–1810: Port and lock installations at Nieuport. Several hits on quayside and sheds, 40 to 50 hits on town Nieuport. 6 bombs dropped on warship proceeding off Nieuport.

1500–1822: One merchant ship (about 7000 t) between Ostend and Zeebrugge, about ten minutes after attack submerged up to upper deck. One armed steam-freighter north-east Dunkirk about 20 kilometres offshore. Explosion observed on forecastle. One armed merchant ship of 8000 to 10,000 t 50 kilometres north Ostend, two bombs fell immediately ahead of bow. Further observation not possible due scattered cloud and simultaneous attack by three Spitfires.

Air Fleet 3: VIII Flying Korps

Estaires–Poperinghe

One transport north-east Dunkirk hit astern. Transport remained stopped in water. (Afternoon, bad weather)

29 May 1940
Air Fleet 2

Port Installations and Targets at Sea

1532–2006: One medium transport 40 km west Ostend grazed with SC 250 astern

1540–1900: One transport (15,000–20,000 t) 20 km west Ostend, direct hit with SC 500, 1 SC 259 near side of hull. Hits exploding observed by 2 aircraft. Transport sank.

1645–2245: At Dunkirk:

One merchant ship direct hit SC 250 amidships, smoke broke out.

Three merchant ships each of 5000 t caught fire.

One ship 4000–5000 t damaged. One heavy cruiser at Dunkirk, stick of 16 SD 50 went across stern, one hit close to stern. Cruiser headed west, thick smoke developing, on zigzag course.

One transport (about 4000–6000 t) stick of 32 SD 50 across amidships. Explosion with heavy smoke observed.

Two transports (about 3000 t) with 32 SD 50. Effect not observed on account of cloud cover.

2240–0315 at Ostend:

One destroyer (probably 'Vertry'), hit with SC 250. Probably sunk.

Four warships, hits, one on fire. One destroyer, hit.

Five transports, of which one sunk, one on fire.

Large lock, several hits, gigantic gush water observed.

Two transports in repair yard sunk.

One large freighter sunk.

One large freighter set afire.

Two freighters in the Channel hit.

One lighter off the coast with SC 50 and machine-gun. Success not observed.

Four warships hit, probably three cruisers and one destroyer:

Three transports, one sunk, two burning.

Port installations Dunkirk, bomb aim good, explosions observed, probably from gasometers and tank plants.

Air Fleet 3

Morning: for VIII Flying Korps poor visibility (from midday) In port of Dunkirk. Ships:

Hit on two cruisers probable, direct hits on several transports, amidst three small ships, on

Two large transports, One large transport, burning,

One large transport burning, direct hit amidships,

One medium transport, burning, direct hit astern,

One small transport sunk,

One transport burning,

One transport, burning, direct hit astern.

Attacks on nine warships and 15 transports between Dunkirk and Ostend (embarkations) Results:

Of nine warships (including one large), 7 severely, two lightly damaged. Of fifteen transports (including one small ship), five severely, two lightly damaged, 3 sunk, five on fire.

30 May 1940
Air Fleets 2 and 3

The planned attack against the continuing embarkations of enemy troops in the area Furnes–Dunkirk–Grand

Fort Philippe was made almost impossible by totally unfavourable weather. Several operations could not be flown, only at daybreak was an attack carried out by weak forces against the port installations and the town of Dunkirk during which hits on the town and wharf were observed.

31 May 1940
Air Fleet 2

Troops, Traffic Connections, Positions

1215–1350:	Dune positions south-west of Nieuport: Hits troop and vehicle columns, MG nests and battery emplacements.
1430–1705:	Battery west of La Panne. Bombed across battery.
1440–1525:	Battle tanks south of Abbeville. 13 tanks and protection destroyed.
1530–1645:	Attacked troop aggregations in woodland north-east of Huppy. Effect not observed on account of denseness of woodland.
1710:	Hits between pontoons and roads also AA emplacements at Bray Dunes.
1715–1820:	Assemblies of troops and vehicles around Huppy with success. Probably hit command post at Trenil.
1730–1840:	Patches of woodland and edges of wood at Huppy. Bombs well aimed.
1815–2230:	Direct hit on AA emplacement near Dunkirk harbour.
1834–2203:	Large assembly of British troops in Dunkirk territory and the villages of Coxyde, Bray Dunes, Zuydcoote and north-west Dunkirk.
1835–2159:	Bombs on town and port installations near Dunkirk.
2005–2130:	Troops in Huppy area, Huppy town on fire.
2020–2215:	Columns of troops, ships and AA positions at Dunkirk. Hits on two ships and on roads and AA emplacements at Bray Dunes.

Port Installations and Ships

0200–0530: Bombed beaches north-west of Dunkirk. Results not seen due to darkness.

1430–1705: Small ships lying closely together off Dunkirk. Effect not observed. One large ship hit. Huge quantity smoke.

1540–1929: Four hits on transport, 8000–10,000 t. On fire, probably abandoned. One hit transport 3000–4000 t. Two hits close alongside transport 6000–8000 t.

1645–1929: Cruiser 5000–6000 t one or two SC 250 bombs, major fire. Transport about 15,000 t hit astern and two bombs close to hull portside. Effect not observed duie heavy fighter and AA defences.

1650–1915: Off Dunkirk, one merchant ship 8000–10,000 t, direct hit SC250, on fire and listing.
One merchant ship burning, one heavy cruiser west-north-west Dunkirk lying stopped in water.

1815–2230: Hits on two warships (probably cruisers) off Dunkirk. Strong smoke development. Hit vicinity transport.

1834–2203: 10 kilometres west Dunkirk, direct hit one SC 250 on transport 8000–19,000 t, another transport same size probably hit. One 3000 – transport hit by SC250 bomb. Several SC 250 near hull smaller transport.

1835–2159: Hit with two SC 250 on 4000–5000 t transport. Explosion and fire. Three other small boats hit. Listing. Several hits amongst gathering of fishing boats.

2330–0425: Harbour installations, beach north-east and against ships to the north-west. Result not observed on account of darkness.

Air Fleet 3

(VIII Flying Korps not operational on account of bad flying weather)

1 June 1940
Air Fleet 2

Troops, Traffic Connections, Positions

0527–0820: Hit on Dunkirk railway station.

0558–0728: Dive-bomber attack on troops embarking and assemblies of vehicles at La Panne, aerial battle developed with strong enemy forces (Spitfire).

Before midday: Columns of lorries around Huppy and Oisemont (south Abbeville) and AA positions south of Bray Dunes with good results.

Port Installations and Ships off Dunkirk

0527–0820: Ships off Dunkirk.

0947–1230: One hit SC 250 on transport (8000 t), hit SC 250 on transport (10,000 t) 20 km north Dunkirk. Ship sunk. Hit close starboard on merchant steamer (6000 t) and on another merchant steamer (3000 t). Damage probable. One steamer of 500 t crowded with soldiers, sunk.

Pre-midday: Two medium-size and two smaller transports, one destroyer and armed fishing boat with MG. Hits.

Pre-midday: One medium transport and one small ship sunk, two medium transports severely damaged (stern under water). Other hit on destroyer or cruiser and a small transport.

Afternoon: 3 transports one hit SC 250 each, other transports (4–5) damaged (listing, stationary in water). Also one transport hit astern with three SC 50. One light cruisers hit forecastle with two SC 250.

Afternoon: Enemy evacuation. One destroyer and two medium size transports damaged.

1600 hrs: One transport (6000–8000 t) about 5 km west harbour entrance hit amidships with SC 250. Effect not seen.

1603 hrs: One merchant ship (3000–4000 t) in fairway about 1 km west harbour entrance hit amidships with 1 SC250. Fire broke out and ship down by the stern.

1605 hrs: One steamer (2000–3000 t) and boats in between about 7 km west of harbour entrance bombed with two SC 250. Hit close amidships on hull side and between the boats. On account of AA defence effect not observed.

1607 hrs: One transport (6000 t) and boats about 800 metres north of the mole attacked with 12 SCV 250. Five impacts in immediate vicinity of ship, some between the boats. Effect not seen.

1729–2119 hrs: Transport (500 t) 3 direct hits SC 250 astern, several impacts of SC 250 and SC 50 close to hull side, 20 km south of Dover. Effect not seen on account of poor visibility.

1818–2005 hrs: One light cruiser, hit on forecastle near ship's side. Ship lay stopped, list seen.
One transport (5000 t), direct hit, one SC 250 on stern. 4 SC 250 fell between troops queuing on beach and ferry boats.

Air Fleet 3

(VIII.Flying Korps: Operation against Dunkirk with 'very good' result)

2 June 1940
Air Fleet 2

Troops, Traffic Connections, Positions

0818–1145: Artillery and flak positions east and south-east of Dunkirk. Hits in and near several positions. Battery fire abated. Large clouds of smoke up to 4000 metres above Dunkirk and Malo les Bains.

0815–1115: Troop assemblies and artillery emplacements north and south of the Dunkirk–Zuydcoote railway line, about 3 km east Dunkirk accuracy good. Hits on infantry positions both sides of Dunkirk–Zuydcoote road, about 5 km east of Dunkirk. Hits on AA position south of Dunkirk–Zuydcoote road about 4 km east of Dunkirk. Battery ceased firing.

0820–1052: Battery emplacement between Zuydcoote and Malo les Bains. Attack on Malo with outstanding fire- and explosive effect. Explosion of an ammunition dump with enormous explosive effect, immediately after attack smoke development rose to 500 metres. Direct hit of several bombs in the AA batteries on the eastern edge of Malo. 40% of bombload against dune terrain between Zuydcoote–Malo with good effects from impact, also road at Malo. Malo burning.

0825–1105: Artillery and AA positions in the area Dunkirk–Zuydcoote. Artillery emplacement on railway Malo–Termines–Roosendaal recognized and hit. Column on road Dunkirk–Furnes bombed with good effect. Artillery in the dunes bombed with good effect. Much smoke rising at Dunkirk and Malo.

0840–0955: Fort St Louis and Fort Vallières. Nearly all bombs fell within the forts. Reconnaissance reports 15 direct hits in Fort Vallières confirmed.

0850–1007: Villages Leffrinckoucke and Uxem. Batteries not observed, bombs dropped on villages and isolated farmsteads. Some fires confirmed.

0900–1200: Battery position north edge Tlegerveld near Dunkirk. Direct hit on battery position 500 metres north of Leffrinckoucke.

1225–1345: 9 hits on motorized columns and troop assemblies near Dunkirk.

1425–1540: Fortified installation around Bergues, bombs fell where aimed.

1740–1900: Columns, artillery positions and ships in Dunkirk area. Direct hit on marching column.

1842–2020: Forts St. Louis-Mardyck and on troops in the Dunkirk area. Direct hit on AA and artillery emplacements in northern part of Dunkirk and on columns at Roosendaal.

Port Installations and Ships off Dunkirk

0749–0824: Port installations and town Dunkirk as well as fortified installations and troop assemblies north-east of Dunkirk.

a) hit in fortified installation north-east of Dunkirk.

b) hit on troop assembly on beach at Malo les Bains.

c) direct hit on tank installation in harbour. Stabs of flame and towering smoke up to 1500 metres in height.

d) HE-bombs, flame-bombs and incendiaries on the quay and in the town. Total of bombs dropped: 318 SC 50, 284 SBE 50, 114 BSK and 18 Flam 250.

1000–1449: Ships off Dunkirk.

1. 1 cruiser and two aircraft each attacked with 2 SC 500 and 2 SC 250. Hits 5–10 metres from ship's side and 10–20 metres ahead of bow.

2. 1 destroyer direct hit on forecastle causing fire and smoke development.

3. 1 destroyer with 2 SC 250 hit bow and stern. Stopped after detonation.

4. 1 direct hit of merchant steamer (about 1000 t).

1230–1355: Dunkirk area. Attack on two freighters. Each received direct hit on forecastle.

1900–2025: AA, artillery emplacements and ships in Dunkirk harbour.

a) 1 transport 5000 t sunk.

1 transport 8000 t hit and burning.

1 warship hit amidships, lifeboats lowered.

b) Direct hit on 3 AA and 2 artillery positions.

c) Direct hit on two marching columns.

2025–2135: Columns and ships at Dunkirk. I guard boat sunk, 2 transports hit. Direct hit on artillery positions and columns.

3 June 1940
Air Fleets 2 and 3

In the afternoon most of the bomber and fighter units grouped up for an attack against French Air Force installations in and around Paris.

Columns, Positions, Traffic Connections

0810–0910: Dunkirk several direct hits on very large columns and on the Roosendaal–Malo road.[3]

In particular the following is worth noting regarding the Luftwaffe at Dunkirk:

On the afternoon of 26 May 1940, Col-General Milch went to Panzer Group Kleist to inform its commander that the Luftwaffe had the task of making a concentric attack against Dunkirk. Britain needed to be shown what it looked like when a town had been 'heavily' bombed. This would also act as a 'warning' bearing in mind the enemy air raids on Bonn. 'In reality this ought to be the fate of Calais,' but the Korps Guderian beat the Luftwaffe to it.[4]

The same day, the Chief of the Luftwaffe General Staff, Major-General Jeschonnek, confirmed once more at a situation conference at Führer-HQ what Göring had said on 23 May. In reply to Hitler's question he had declared that the Luftwaffe could carry out the promised destruction of the enemy. For this purpose the necessary bomber units (Air Fleet 2) would have to be brought into the 'Army Group B' area.[5]

The following day the Luftwaffe Commander-in-Chief landed by Fieseler Storch at Münstereifel, and in a 'renewed discussion with the Führer' he reported on the first visible 'successes' of his aviators at Dunkirk. Göring concluded his report with the words, '...They are only sending over fishing boats; I hope the Tommies are good swimmers...'[6]

At the time of writing (1958), the only fragments of the VIII Flying Korps War Diary so far made available describe the decisive days between 26 May and 3 June 1940 as follows: On 26 May units of the Flying Korps made running attacks on the area Estaires–Armentières–Bailleul–Poperinghe.

They also did so on the morning of 28 May, although bad flying weather ruled out operations in the afternoon.

When on 29 May 'all senior centres' were calling for 'VIII Flying Korps to resume attacking ships and boats at Dunkirk with which the British divisions are saving their bare lives;' the Commanding General of VIII Flying Korps held the opinion that with cloud cover at 100 metres and heavy anti-aircraft defence, 'our own losses will be greater than our successes against the enemy.' Not until midday did the weather improve: the Flying Korps immediately resumed rolling attacks against Dunkirk so that even Göring could 'calm his nerves'.[7]

On 31 May General von Richthofen was forced to admit that the situation was very unsatisfactory. The long distances and certain difficulties of logistics had made it impossible for VIII Flying Korps to build a 'sharply tuned' base for its efforts. He was of the opinion that if the Army had put its back into it, the pocket could have been finished off swiftly. He found it impossible to understand 'why nothing had been ordered in this direction'. Thus nothing was happening at the coast and time was being lost...

Later he established: it was too far for Stukas to fly, therefore only few missions could be flown. The airfields near the front were short of bombs and fuel; this was caused by the supply problems. Moreover, the operations by British Spitfires were creating noticeable disadvantages. German fighter aircraft had 'a grim fight of it' to protect the inferior Ju 87s. General von Richthofen had to admit the Luftwaffe was not able to prevent the British being ferried out 'so to speak at the last moment' after the Army had failed to attack 'in the right way'. Finally he arrived at the conclusion that 'A victory over Britain has been given away'.[8]

It is difficult to set out in any detail the *reasons for the apparent failure of the German Luftwaffe at Dunkirk*. The meagre sources presently available are inadequate to provide even approximate numbers and composition of the bomber forces. Nevertheless one must try to provide a general point of view why the Air Fleets were not able to carry through to the full extent the task set them by Göring:

1. The fact that Air Fleets 2 and 3 had *flown missions of all kinds since 10 May almost without a break*. Luftwaffe General Kesselring, chief of Air Fleet 2, wrote in his memoirs: '... The Luftwaffe

Commander-in-Chief must have known the effect of the almost three weeks … of sorties flown by my airmen to have known not to order operations which could barely have been achieved with fresh forces. I expressed this very clearly to Göring and pointed out that the *assignment* itself was not solvable even with the support of VIII Flying Korps …' In this connection Kesselring spoke of 'groggy' and '… overtired' units which had to keep on taking off'.[9] All in all, therefore, the Air Fleets had been weakened in personnel as in materials: many squadrons had only 50 per cent of their authorized operational strength!

2. The *unexpected* and *sudden assignment* reached most of the bomber units when they were still being deployed *to support the ground operations* and were *harnessed* to them. Even after 26 May only elements could attack Dunkirk as the priority. Again and again units were called upon for other tasks, protecting the southern flank (e.g. especially on the afternoon of 31 May!) and striking at the French traffic network.

3. Furthermore *in the short space of time given*, it was *not possible to bring everything forward lock, stock and barrel as required* for the priority assignment. The building up of the ground organisations had only just begun in Belgium. As a result attacks had to be flown from any base considered handy from Holland to the Swiss frontier. Frequently other weather conditions would prevail between the taking-off point and target area so that from the outset the possibilities of the operation were limited. For this reason it was scarcely possible to decide where to put down the focal points of effort. The *long-range units* could generally only take off once per day because the flight legs were too long. For example, two groups of KG 51 (from the Bavarian region) had to make a refuelling stop in the Rhine Valley on the way back (see Map 12).

4. On account of the standards of technology and training of the time, *the long-range units* were *not yet in a position* to attack targets in the port of Dunkirk by night with any accuracy (although harassment bombing raids by night were not affected). Bombing of installations and so forth was only effective in the daylight hours. The port of Ostend also came in for heavy aerial bombardment until 29 May probably on the assumption that enemy troops would also be evacuating from

there. As Feuchter observed in his volume *Geschichte des Luftkrieges*, the Luftwaffe leadership had taken too little account of the evidence 'that in the Spanish civil war air attacks on shipping targets in the port of Barcelona did not much interrupt enemy supply traffic. On the other hand it seems that the Luftwaffe overestimated the very favourable experiences with German air attacks against the supply ship traffic of the British after their landings at Namsos and Andalsnes, i.e. too little account was taken of the fact that the British supply ships had no, or only an inadequate air-umbrella of fighters, while at Dunkirk the British could deploy sufficient fighter aircraft for the protection of their shipping movements because it was easy for British fighters to reach Dunkirk from airfields on the south coast of England.'[10]

5. To some extent, the *close-range units*, their advanced fighter cover and ground organisations were so distant from the target area as to be close to their maximum radius of action and so the time available over Dunkirk as regards fuel was therefore often very limited (see Map 12).

6. The *supplying* of the *close-range bomber units* and fighter cover also had its troubles. Principally Ju-52 transport aircraft had been envisaged for the purpose. During the airborne-infantry landing operations in Holland, these had suffered considerable losses. Furthermore the routes of the advance (refuelling in the street!) were often clogged up by Army units while the railway system in Belgium was not yet back in action.[11]

7. Above all, the weather made the deployment of Air Fleets 2 ands 3 problematical. As may be noted from the example of interruptions recounted (at pages 169–170 this book), the attacks either limited or cancelled as a result of poor flying weather – on four days 'a weather pattern rare for this time of year' – including almost a calm at sea, greatly favoured the Allied retreat:[12]

Date	No Operation Flown	Allied Troops Evacuated (approx.)
28 May	VIII Flying Korps, afternoon	17,000
29 May	Both Air Fleets, morning	47,000
30 May	Both Air Fleets, morning *and* afternoon	53,000
31 May	Flying Korps, morning VIII Flying Korps, all day (afternoon, most of Air Fleet 2 in the area Abbeville, Péronne and south.	68,000

8. Furthermore, the bomber units were *withdrawn too prematurely* from the Flanders Pocket. The 2 June was practically the last day of the attack against the embarkations. On 3 June the Luftwaffe flew a major operation against the Paris region as a preparation for the second phase *Fall Rot*, yet on 3 and 4 June the Allies brought out more than 50,000 of their troops to the British Isles[13] (almost 14 per cent of the total number of troops evacuated).

9. Whereas the enemy losses in materials and equipment were enormous, relatively speaking *the losses in personnel were light*. Whereas the bulletin broadcast by the Wehrmacht High Command on 27 May that at Dunkirk 'the port installation was in flames', ignoring the propagandistic effect which had to be aimed for, the statement was incorrect. This can be seen from the fact that up to the last day, over 65 per cent of the Allied Army had been shipped out from the port of Dunkirk and the British also extended the invitation to the wide sandy beaches between Dunkirk and La Panne. This was not recognized by German aerial surveys particularly so because trans-shipments from the shore occurred mostly at night. Thus attacks were made frequently against tiny targets, were splintered and lost their effect. General Alan Brooke depicted this very impressively in his diaries:

> The beaches, which were crowded with men, were being plastered with bombs. A black cloud of smoke soon shrouded the whole beach and was punctuated by vivid flashes as new bombs burst and threw up jets of sand and what appeared like human bodies, but luckily turned out to be greatcoats and clothing abandoned by men who had embarked. When the bombers had safely departed I went down on to the beach, expecting to find a regular shambles. To my surprise, I found only a few men who had been seriously wounded. The bulk of them were smothered with sand which they were busy extracting from their ears, eyes, noses, necks and sleeves. The men had all flattened themselves out on the beach, and I presume that the effect of the bombs had been greatly damped down by sinking into the loose sands before bursting. It was indeed fortunate, or the casualties would have been much more serious.[14]

10. Decisive for the German failure, however, was also the British counter-effect. The previously reserved and rested Homeland Air Defences of the British meant that their Spitfire squadrons could now be thrown at full strength into the battle, particularly their machines based on the south-east coast of England which required only a short flight before arrival. The fighters were managed by an outstandingly functional direction system, and the prevailingly westerly weather was more favourable for British warplanes.

A specially developed warning system detected bomber formations approaching from Holland so early that these could be intercepted by two-seater fighters of the types Boulton Paul Defiant. Because the Luftwaffe had to fly mainly at the medium altitudes in order to reach the target, this brought them within range of the British anti-aircraft cruisers.

Occasionally the British raised and maintained an air-umbrella over the area of embarkations. For the first time in the campaign a temporary and locally limited air superiority came into force.[15]

On 25 May, an entry in the VIII Flying Korps War Diary recorded: 'Our units have to go forward because the RAF at Calais ... is superior. We have losses and the troops are calling for help...(They) are very shy of aircraft because they are "quite unaccustomed to being attacked from the air".[16] "Without air support, our troops do nothing." The same day, the 1d General Staff Officer of AOK 4 wrote: 'For two days the enemy has had air superiority over Group Kleist, and partly over Group Hoth. That is something new for us in this campaign and is possible because the British air base is "on the island itself", therefore very close, while our forces are basically still operating from German aerodromes...'[17]

CHAPTER VI

Summary

We have thoroughly described the struggle for Dunkirk. It is no longer the purpose of this research to depict the second part of the campaign, although the further development will be looked at briefly here.

On 5 June at the shortest notice the regrouped German divisions prepared for the next operation 'Rot' (Red) in order to finally overwhelm 'the forces remaining to the Allies in France.' This would occur in three phases, one following after the other: an attack either side of Rheims between Paris (city not included) and the Argonnes in a south-easterly direction, to crush the French Army in the area Paris–Belfort–Metz and collapse the Maginot Line by frontal thrust and encirclement.[1]

In rapid, concentrically led offensive blows, in the real French Campaign now beginning, the enemy, already decimated and strongly demoralized, would be first forced south and after that thrown east against his own defensive Front. On the same day (14 June) when Paris was occupied without a fight, Army Group C, (Col-General von Leeb) which had until then been held back on the southern wing of the German advance, became involved in the fighting. In the very shortest time its armies (1. Armee and 7. Armee) broke through the line of enemy fortifications previously thought impregnable. Meanwhile Italy, which had declared war on France on 10 June following the successes of the Germans, opened an offensive on the Alps Front which very soon came to grief.[2]

In a few days, the French were in a hopeless situation. On 17 June, the newly-formed government of Pétain finally saw no way out of the dilemma than to offer capitulation which was signed on 22 June 1940 in the woods at Compiègne.[3] In a hitherto unprecedented kind of military campaign, Germany forced a brave opponent to concede, which in World War I, despite the greatest efforts, it had not been able to do.

This made Hitler Lord of Central Europe. In the triumph of this astounding victory, the self-consciousness of the German people awakened. What was fatal, however, was that with it the healthy ability to estimate what was militarily possible – and not just Hitler! – was lost and the supreme leadership was not able to make any political use of it. Only too soon the great error of speculation was apparent: the British were not going to give in. On the contrary: they were determined to fight with all means available.

Since Hitler was not inclined to end the conflict by negotiation, he sought new solutions for achieving his far-reaching goals by force of arms. The era of more portentous, even fatal, decisions matured and after a desperate struggle he led Germany into the abyss against almost all the nations of the world.[4]

In retrospect, if we now look for the general *causes*, to which, despite everything, the undoubted German success in the West was indebted, besides the bold operational planning there are several other factors to consider:

Without doubt, the tactical surprise at the beginning of the offensive – increased by the application of new kinds of weapon – was *fully successful* despite the long waiting period in the winter of 1939. The enemy recognized too late the centre of effort of the German attack and thus lost the initiative from the outset, besides which his strategic advance to the Dyle met one of the most important preconditions for the success of the *Sichelschnitt* Plan.

The *achievement of the Luftwaffe*, which supported the troops on the ground by missions flown day and night, won superiority in the air and finally – with the exception of Dunkirk – air supremacy, is undisputed. The Army groups even spoke of an 'exemplary' cooperation between the two arms of the Wehrmacht which contributed in no small measure to the initial successes. Coupling together the tactical involvement of the Flying Korps with the panzers and fast units on the battlefield was decisive.[5] In addition, the *fighting spirit* and *readiness for operations* of the Army exceeded 'even the most optimistic expectations'. And not least *the leadership of the troops merits high recognition* for the extraordinary decisiveness and boldness with which action was often undertaken 'even into the Unknown'. Also undeniable is that a lack of fighting spirit, poor planning, and hapless leadership on the part of the enemy also contributed to the German victory.[6]

From now on we look at the *Dunkirk Incident* in order to answer individually the questions thrown up in the Foreword of our study.

As regards the disputed 'Halt-Order' of 24 May 1940, in the light of the sources available we may say: On this day, Hitler neither broadened Rundstedt's decision of 23 May[7] (namely to close up with his troops at the Canal Line), nor did he solely on his own initiative or even against the will of the Commander-in-Chief of Army Group A, issue this undoubtedly portentous instruction.[8] On the contrary, he gave the order *at Rundstedt's suggestion* and *in total agreement* with him. Additionally, Göring had assured him that he could clear out the Flanders Pocket with the Luftwaffe. Another motive was the new crisis of confidence between the OKH and Hitler, who wanted to show that in all circumstances he and no other – now and in the future – led the operations.

More significant, however, is the fact that Hitler left it up to Army Group Command A to decide when the fast units should advance again. When OKH offered them the chance of continuing the offensive towards Dunkirk on the night of 24 May they declined to act because the commanders considered that to move at that time was not expedient. Not until 26 May did Army Group Command A make a new assessment of the situation which finally motivated Hitler to leave the attack up to them – with certain limitations.[9]

Without any doubt, it was primarily *Rundstedt's decision that the German panzers would spend almost three days at rest short of Dunkirk, although Hitler as Commander-in-Chief of the Wehrmacht cannot be acquitted of responsibility for the 'Halt'.*[10]

The events of 24 May can scarcely be understood unless certain factors are recalled from the preceding period 1939/1940. Certainly unintentionally, *Army Group Command A had from that time on had won the special trust of Hitler to an increasing extent.* It began when the then Chief of the Army Group A General Staff, Lt-General von Manstein, influenced Hitler decisively to carry through 'the great solution' of the disputed operational plan *Sichelschnitt*. How certain points of view of Army Group A coincided surprisingly to a great extent with those of Hitler! The civilian and self-educated Leader found his 'conception' confirmed by the suggestions of the recognized genius of the General Staff.[11]

In the spring of 1940, after OKH had replaced Manstein with the rather more cautious General von Sodenstern and had issued the new strategic plan, *OKH A suddenly uttered misgivings about the too daring deployment of the panzers*. Memoranda and lectures convinced OKH that in the given circumstances it was more advisable *to use the infantry divisions for the mass breakthrough* and then follow up with the operational thrust of the panzers for fear that the latter would be susceptible otherwise to too many breakdowns. It could not be denied that Army Group Command A was now also opposed to the more than daring 'Plan'.

Furthermore, during the course of the live operations it became clear that both Rundstedt and Hitler viewed with concern the advance of the fast units westwards on account of the endangered (because lengthening) southern flank, and kept trying to get it to close up before advancing farther.

The *agreement* of the operational viewpoints between *Hitler and Army Group Command A* can also be seen from how everybody had the Staff at Charleville informed of Hitler's satisfaction at the measures taken by Rundstedt, of which he fully approved. He placed a quite special trust in the person and leadership of the Commander-in-Chief of Army Group A.

In contrast to that, *the relationship of trust* between *the Commander-in-Chief of the Wehrmacht and OKH* had been *shaken* in the autumn of 1939 when Col-General von Brauchitsch made a dramatic statement to Hitler trying to convince him of the need to postpone the offensive in the West for reasons of personnel and materials.[12] Hitler's threatening speech of 23 November 1939 'against all alarmists' and against the 'spirit of Zossen' (Army HQ) led to a temporary truce in view of the intensive planning for the offensive in the West, in particular Operation *Weserübung* (the invasion of Denmark and Norway) which was increasingly pre-occupying the Wehrmacht leadership.

The opposing points of view intensified when the divergent opinions on the operational management showed themselves during the campaign. The events of 18 May bear eloquent witness to this![13] Added to that,

Hitler was more *Fabius cunctator* than a cool-headed Commander-in-Chief weighing things up and taking pleasure in reaching a solution – basically he had 'fear of his own courage'. Nothing of that Moltke-type calm and mental balance could be seen in Hitler. Here too, as in the Norwegian campaign, he showed his lack of ability to handle suddenly arising difficulties. How different on the other hand were *Brauchitsch and Halder*, who never lost sight of the strategic goal of the offensive. They guided the operations mindful of the German superiority and corresponding to the principles of modern warfare of mobility. They knew and felt that the troops expected to know whether something had just the passing appearance of a crisis, or whether the situation at the front actually was giving cause for concern. Doubtless the facts stated here provide another key to understanding the whole Dunkirk Incident.

On what grounds did *Rundstedt and Hitler* give the famous '*Halt-Order*'? This is our reasoning:

1. The valuable panzers were kept back for the second phase of the campaign, whose forthcoming difficulties had been generally over-estimated. Hitler had a special affection for the Panzer Arm as the Polish campaign had shown. Later, in 1941 at Leningrad, for similar reasons he had the Panzer Group *Hoepner* stop simply because he feared that it would suffer too many breakdowns before its new assignment. The Staff officers of Army Group A, on the other hand, felt an unconcealed respect for the French, whose imminent collapse was not fully comprehensible to them remembering their experience of the French in World War I.
2. The knowledge that *the polders or fens of Flanders were unsuitable for panzer operations*, this being emphasized on a number of occasions in May 1940 in the Korps and Divisional War Diaries.
3. The persistent *concern about the southern flank*. Rundstedt, who often imagined himself in the enemy's shoes, found it incomprehensible to the last that the Allies had not launched a 'retour-offensive' of the Marshal Foch school against the flank's 220 kilometres length.
4. Göring's assurance that his Luftwaffe could wipe out the enemy trapped in the Flanders' Pocket helped create the conviction that the 'great victory' did not lie with the Army generals alone.

5. The belief that the enemy would *attack the German lines at the Canal Front*. Although air reconnaissance and the intelligence division Foreign Armies West had indicated in time the possibility of an evacuation, the highest level of Wehrmacht command came *very late to clear recognition* of the fact that contrary to expectations the enemy would not fight to the last round on the mainland, but could evacuate his troops to England. This resulted from the strongly-impregnated Continental thinking of the military leaders and Hitler.

6. Rundstedt's impression that the Army Group A assignment had been *in large measure fulfilled*. And finally:

7. The only political reason which can be proved is that of Hitler's intention to avoid having the decisive battle in *Flamenland* (Flemish-speaking Belgium) in order to spare its land and people for possible later annexation into the Reich as 'Gau Flandern'.[14]

Frequently in the earlier literature one finds the idea put forward that Hitler issued the 'Halt-Order' intentionally to give Britain 'a golden bridge' so that parts of the British Army could escape. A 'chivalrous' gesture of that kind would contribute[15] to a quicker peaceable understanding with Churchill. This contention belongs in the realm of numerous untrue postwar legends. In the decisive days, both Army and Luftwaffe had the unequivocal order to wipe out the enemy in the pocket as was expressed in Führer-Instruction No.13 of 24 May 1940 in terms which were impossible to misunderstand.[16] Such a gesture would also hardly correspond to Hitler's political conception. It has been pointed out correctly by various sources that on 1 September 1939 Germany had no carefully defined war plan which later had fateful consequences. Nevertheless, Hitler had definite ideas on how he would force Britain to concede in the event of war. One thing above all was *clear to him*: Once war was declared, Germany would no longer have any option of being able to 'buy its way out cheaply'. That left only 'a life-and-death struggle'[17]: the bridges were to be pulled down. He knew, and stated it to his closer circles, that the British were proud, brave, tough, capable of resisting and above all gifted in organization, and that they knew how to evaluate 'every new event'.

Great Britain the World Power, protected by a strong navy and a good air force, was the reality for Hitler. In his opinion, however, Britain had a decisive Achilles heel: at the moment when Britain was cut off from its imports it would be forced to capitulate. If, therefore, the German Army could capture better bases for the German Navy and Luftwaffe in Holland, Belgium and France, this would provide the necessary preconditions to force Britain to its knees. Hitler's first idea therefore was to break the British will to resist by comprehensive economic warfare. This concept is clear from his supplementary Instruction No.9 in which, at the end of May, Wehrmacht High Command laid down new guidelines for war policy against the enemy economy. A commentary by the Naval War Directorate (*Seekriegsleitung*) confirmed that the German war aim was to destroy the main enemy Britain. The way to achieve this lay only *in the destruction of its mainland ally France so as to starve the British Isles and defeat its economic fighting power;* Britain could only be defeated by the 'greatest economic war of all time'.

With the wealth of evidence before us we can prove today that in order to make Britain ready to sue for peace the only option ·for Hitler up until May 1940 was: to destroy the military strength of his enemy on the mainland (in this he placed the greatest hope in May–June 1940), or introduce comprehensive economic warfare. The possibility of landings in England were only seriously expressed *after the campaign.*[18]

Finally we asked: after 26 May 1940 why did he not close the ring in order to prevent the enemy shipping out? It cannot be denied that the Allies knew how to devote feverish activity to the valuable hours of the *'Halt' and consolidate their defensive positions* to the west, but above all to the east. On the Canal Front they reorganized and set up a delaying defence, if also not excessively strengthening it. The British were far more critical of their situation at the eastern Front because they expected the collapse of the Belgian Army at any moment. It was certainly a far-reaching decision of Lord Gort to deploy his two divisions (50th and 5th) held in reserve south of Ypres, in order to support his front there at the seam with the Belgians. By doing so he created the means for the mass of the Allied units to be fed down the narrow corridor which led into the port of salvation at Dunkirk. It may be stated with justification that the *Allied defensive struggle* was admirable and continued the great tradition which had so impressed the Germans in World War I. The brave defence of Boulogne and Calais must also be mentioned in this connection: it was by no means pointless, for it delayed the advance of XIX Armee Korps by important hours.[19]

In the final assessment, however, this was not decisive, rather it was a *further series of German errors of executive leadership.*

First of all, the *Flanders Pocket* was considered too early as an adjacent front, yes, probably also its real strategic significance misunderstood, in addition to which it remained a mystery to the last how many enemy troops were encircled inside it. German estimates of the time spoke of about 100,000 men. Further: from 27 May the higher Staffs became increasingly preoccupied with the operational *planning* for '*Rot*' and allowed their concentration to be diverted away from the Battle for Dunkirk.

With regard to Dunkirk, it was the principle which Rundstedt expounded after the war which had been too little observed: 'First one brings one operation to its conclusion before thinking about the next.'[20]

Thus it came about that the *fighting in Flanders was not continued with sufficient energy and resolution to its end.*

Furthermore it *would have been more expedient to have placed 4. Armee under Army Group B* after the breakthrough to the Channel coast as Brauchitsch had planned, and not tying it down after Hitler's intervention. Army Group A, more concerned from the outset with the view southwards, and *apparently had too much on its hands additionally with 71. Division*, could then have taken over the (offensive or defensive) watch on the Somme. A unified leadership under Col-General von Bock of all troops against the pocket would then have surely and more successfully guaranteed the taking of the town and port of Dunkirk. Certain flaws in organization, such as the coincidence of both Army Groups in so narrow an area, would then also have been avoided. It was also definitely an error to have compressed the encirclement by stages in the south (around Lille) instead of sealing it off first in the north – very close to Dunkirk – by a reinforced outer surrounding wing (Panzer Group Kleist!). Furthermore, the troops themselves *may have lost some of their initial drive.* After the continuous heavy fighting and enforced marches they felt the need to pause for breath. Instead they were set too early on the later major task so that, for the time being, the operations against Dunkirk were only carried out half-heartedly[21] and the materials not fully employed (XVI and XIX Armee Korps!) Before the real culminating point of the battle was reached, the fast units were being relieved! Finally, the Wehrmacht leadership overestimated the *possibilities of the effect and achievements of its own Luftwaffe*. For the first time its limitations became visible and its aura of 'invincibility' shaken,[22]

The errors and mistakes of the German leadership – *and not only the 'Halt-Order'!* – set out here in broad terms – were, alongside the Allied achievements – the decisive reasons why the *real strategic goal of Fall Gelb was not reached*: the mass of the British field army decamped to England and instead of a crushing victory only a 'common or garden victory' was achieved.

It would be going too far to conclude that Great Britain would have sued for peace had there been a German 'total victory', and that Germany therefore missed its great historic hour, perhaps even gave away the palms of victory, so near, for it is certain that even then, Churchill would have been unbending in continuing the struggle.[23] To that extent the whole 'Dunkirk Incident' should not be dramatized and overestimated for the further course of the war.[24]

The deeper significance of this first great highpoint of World War II, seen from the viewpoint of the British (in order to underline this only briefly), was that it had retrieved *the nucleus of its Army* (including later very significant Army commanders such as Lord Alexander and Montgomery), gathered valuable experience for *future amphibious operations* and, above all, through the success of Operation *Dynamo*, whose success was due to the exemplary cooperation of all three branches of service, won the confidence and trust in its own abilities which made it possible to withstand the difficult struggle to its successful conclusion.[25]

For Germany, Dunkirk, far more ominously than the 'Halt-Order' and its immediate consequences, brought about Hitler's intervention in operational military leadership. In the winter of 1939 the Commander-in-Chief of the Wehrmacht had made it clear to OKH in no uncertain terms his claim to political-military leadership when against all advice he set the date for the attack. Now Hitler forced upon OKH his will as military commander when he neutralized it in one of the most significant moments of the battle and delegated a decision of far-reaching import to a subordinate commander whose viewpoint happened to coincide with his own. Ultimately that was another step towards the later military leadership chaos. It completed an *inner disbandment of the command function*[26] when the real leadership instrument of the Army was systematically undermined, overshadowed and finally – with the most dreadful consequences – pushed aside.

Endnotes

I. Operational objectives and deployment

1. Re: the outbreak of war see H. Herzfeld, *Die moderne Welt 1789–1945* Vol II (1890–1945): Westermann, 2nd ed. 1957, pp.317ff (especially p.326: indications as to literature).
2. For the previous history of the Western campaign, now: H. A. Jacobsen, *Fall Gelb, Der Kampf um den deutschen Operationsplan zur Westoffensive 1940*, Wiesbaden 1957. See also: Général Koeltz, *Comment s'est joué notre destin*, Paris 1957.
3. Jacobsen, *ibid*, p.44ff, 141.
4. Text: *Dokumente zur Vorgeschichte des Westfeldzuges 1939/1940*, publ. by H. A. Jacobsen, Göttingen 1957, p.64ff.
5. Jacobsen, *ibid*, p.136, 298.
6. On the campaign in the West generally: K. von Tippelskirch, *Geschichte des Zweiten Weltkrieges*, Bonn 1956, 2nd ed.. p.66ff.
7. Documents (Jacobsen), *ibid.*, p.64ff.
8. Jacobsen, *Fall Gelb, ibid*, p.154ff, see also: W. Melzer, *Albert-Kanal und Eben Emael*, Heidelberg 1957 (there further indications of literature). Additionally H. A. Jacobsen, *Der deutsche Luftangriff auf Rotterdam*, 14 May 1940, in *Wehrw.Rsch.*, May 1958, p.260ff.
9. Jacobsen, *Fall Gelb, ibid*, p.244 (here further details): Letter No.14: (see also Letter 2a). The first more comprehensive foreign account of the German operations in the West most recently: T. Taylor, *The March of Conquest*, New York 1958. On the whole Taylor's study can be counted as the first successful attempt to portray the campaign in the West, even if the author has only been able to base his assessment on the secondary literature plus the Halder and Jodl diaries. Above all his more moderate judgment here makes better reading than his first work '*Sword and Swastika*', 1952.
10. Translator: Original text had 45 1/3.

II. The German operations, 10–21 May 1940
A survey (Maps 1–5)

1. The capitulation of the Netherlands and the advance to the Dyle (northern flank) 10–15 May 1940 (Maps 1, 2a, 2b, 2c)

1. See Jacobsen, *Fall Gelb*, p.138f.
2. *Ibid*, p.203ff.
3. 18. Armee, War Diary (citation KTB–18.), 10 May 1940.
4. *Ibid*.
5. *Ibid*.
6. Army Group B War Diary (hereafter KTB–B), 10 May 1940: see also sketches by Col-General F. von Bock (Bock Diary), 10 May 1940.
7. See F. A. von Metsch, *Die Geschichte der 22.Inf.Div. 1939–1945* (Podzun Verlag), Kiel 1952, pp.8-15: also *Algemeen overzicht van de strijd om en in de vesting Holland (zonder het oostfront) en de strijd tegen de luchtlandengstroepen rondom 's-Gravenhage Mei 1940, 's-Gravenhage 1954*, (official account by the Dutch General Staff).
8. 6.Armee War Diary (hereafter KTB–6.), 10 May 1940. Generally on the deployment of 6. Armee: H.A. Jacobsen, *Les operations de la 6e Armée allemande du 10 au 28 mai 1940*, in: *L'Armée – La Nation*, Brussels, May 1957, pp.10–20. For the special commando units see recently: P. Leverkuehn, *Der geheime Nachrichtendienst der deutschen Wehrmacht im Kriege*, Frankfurt 1957, p.82ff.
9. For the German airborne landings see: W. Melzer, *Albert-Kanal und Eben-Emael*, Heidelberg 1957 (*Die Wehrmacht im Kampf*, Vol.13) – (see also the literature cited there.)
10. KTB–B, 10 May 1940.
11. KTB–B and 18., 11 May 1940, see Halder diary, 11 May (citation Halder).
12. KTB–6., 11 May 1940; Melzer, *ibid*, p.70ff.
13. KTB–6. and B, 11 May 1940.
14. Bock diary, 11 May 1940.
15. Appendix to KTB–18., 12 May 1940.
16. Bock diary, 12 May 1940: notes of 1a of 9. Panzer Division, Bundesarchiv Koblenz (cite BA), H 32-9/2 (folios 1–9).
17. KTB–18., 12 May 1940.
18. *Ibid*.
19. Situation report No.250, ObdL (Luftwaffe) Ic No.9030/40, 12 May 1940.
20. Situation Report West, 12 May 1940 (No 301), 1145 hrs (BA, H 10-3/2).
21. KTB–18., 12 May 1940.
22. KTB–6., 12 May 1940, see also KTB–18. of same date.
23. KTB–6., 12 May 1940, compare with operation of French armoured forces: H. Hoth, *Das Schicksal der französischen Panzerwaffe im ersten Teil des Westfeldzuges 1940*, in: *Wehrkunde*, July 1958, p.367ff., especially p.370f.

24. Compare also: VIII Flying Korps KTB (hereafter KTB–VIII), 12 May 1940 *'Einsätze wieder zur Unterstützung der 6. Armee. Schwerpunkt XVI.AK...auf Truppenkolonnen, aud Ortseingänge...mot Verbände...'*.

25. KTB–B and 18., 13 May 1940; Situation Report West No. 303 of same date. Author's emphasis.

26. KTB–B and 18., 13 May 1940.

27. *Ibid.*

28. *Ibid.*

29. KTB–B and 6., 13 May 1940. The entry in KTB–VIII of that date reads: '... In the afternoon all Stuka and bomber units went to the defence of the Meuse around Sedan in the framework of an offensive led by II Flying Korps...'

30. Halder, 13 May 1940: Situation Report West No.303 and 304 of same date (Bundesarchiv *op, cit.*)

31. KTB–B and Bock diary, 13 May 1940.

32. KTB–B, 13 May 1940.

33. KTB–18., 13 May 1940: Army Group B telegram to AOK 18 No. 2427/40 g.Kdos.

34. KTB–18. and B, 14 May 1940. Emphasis by author.

35. For the 'German attack on Rotterdam' see recently, H. A. Jacobsen in *Wehrw.Rdschau*, May 1958, pp.257–284 (see the individually listed literature there). This *'Attempt at a Clarification'* was criticized in parts as being totally unobjective and irrelevant by Rotterdam newspapers (see e.g. *Nieuwe Rotterdamse Courant* of 30 June 1958, 1 July 1958 and 2 July 1958 by Lt-General (ret'd) Wilson, formerly on the Staff of the Rotterdam city commandant: also *De Rotterdamer* of 5 June 1958 the most sharply critical.) The author intends to return to this theme and take issue with the Dutch side on the points they raise in the framework of a later, larger investigation into the 'Rotterdam Problem'. Based on the available evidence there can be hardly any doubt that the *responsibility* for the planning and execution of the tragic bombing raid rests with AOK 18. The part played by the Luftwaffe cannot be determined for the lack of almost all source documentation of Luftwaffe High Command (OKL). See most recently, T. Taylor, *The March of Conquest*, New York 1958, p.200ff.

36. KTB XXXIX Armee Korps, 14 May 1940.

37. KTB–18. and B, 15 May 1940.

38. KTB–6. and B, 14/15 May 1940.

2. The Breakthrough on the Meuse Front (Southern Wing) 10–15 May 1940 (Maps 1–4)

1. See Wehrmacht reports in: *Entscheidung im Westen. Der Feldzug der sechs Wochen*, publ. H. Schäfer, J., Cologne 1940, pp.10ff (OKW Reports, 10–15 May 1940).

2. Army Group A War Diary (hereafter KTB–A) of 9 May 1940. XXXXI Armee Korps War Diary (hereafter KTB XXXXI AK), April 1940: Pzr.Gr.Kleist War Diary (extract), 9 May 1940 (hereafter KTB Kleist); see H. Guderian, *Erinnerungen eines Soldaten,* Heidelberg 1951, p.87ff.

3. KTB–A, 10 May 1940; Halder of same date.

4. 4. Armee War Diary (hereafter KTB–4.) 10 May 1940.

5. KTB–A, 10 May 1940.

6. KTB–A, 11 May 1940., see also Halder, same date.

7. KTB–A, 11 May 1940.

8. KTB–A, 11 May 1940.

9. KTB–4., 12 May 1940, see also Hoth *op.cit*, p.372ff.

10. Translator's Note: see p.18 where third sub-group 'Treffen' is *XIV Armee Korps*.

11. KTB–A, 12 May 1940.

12. *Ibid*. see Guderian, *op. cit.*, p.89ff, also H. Reinhardt, *Im Schatten Guderians*, in *Wehrkunde* 3 (1954), pp.333–341.

13. *Ibid*.

14. *Ibid*.

15. Guderian, *op. cit*. 90f.

16. KTB–4., 13 May 1940, also Hoth, *op. cit*. p.372f.

17. Bock diary, 13 May 1940: emphasis by the author: KTB–A, 13 May 1940; Halder, same date.

18. KTB–A, 13 May 1940.

19. KTB–A, 14 May 1940.

20. KTB–A, 14 May 1940; KTB Kleist XXXXI.AK same date.

21. KTB–A, 14 May 1940.

22. Instruction No.11, 14 May 1940 WFA/Abt.L.33 002/40, g.Kdos Chefs.

23. OKH, Army General Staff, Op.Abt. 3240/40 g.Kdos.; Halder diary 14 May 1940.

24. Situation Report West No.307 15 May 1940, 1145 hrs.

25. KTB–4., 15 May 1940.

26. *Ibid*: emphasis by author.

27. KTB–A, 15 May 1940: emphasis by author.

28. *Ibid*.

29. *Ibid*: Emphasis of the author, Guderian (*op.cit* p.96) reported in his memoirs that on 15 May, Panzer Group Kleist had ordered 'a halt to movements and limits on the bridgehead'. After a very lively conversion with his senior commander, Guderian succeeded in having Kleist restore freedom of movement after 24 hours.

30. KTB–A, 15 May 1940.

31. Based on work of the study group for the history of the Air War: *Der Einsatz der Luftwaffe in der ersten Phase des Westfeldzuges 1940*, 1956.

3. The Pursuit to the Scheldt and Advance to the Channel Coast 16–20 May 1940 (Maps 1, 4 and 5)

1. Halder, 16 May 1940: emphasis by author.

2. *Ibid,* emphasis by author.

3. KTB–4., 16 May 1940.

4. *Ibid*.

5. KTB–A, 16 May 1940, also Halderd, same date.

6. Ibid: see Guderian (*op.cit* p.98) who after making a renewed protest against the Panzer-Group Kleist 'stop-order' (17.5) was close to being relieved of his command since he was 'placing himself above the intentions of the higher leadership.'

7. KTB–A, 16 May 1940.

8. HGr.B No.2469/40, g.Kdos, 16 May 1940, 0240 hrs.

9. KTB–6., 16 May 1940; see also KTB–B, 16 May 1940.

10. KTB–B and –6., 15/16 May 1940; Halder's diary same dates, see also Jodl's diary, 15 May 1940.

11. Bock diary, 16 May 1940: KTB–B same date.

12. Halder, 17 May 1940: emphasis by author.

13. *Ibid*, emphasis by author.

14. Halder, *op. cit.*; author's emphasis.

15. KTB–A, 17 May 1940.

16. KTB–A, 17 May 1940.

17. *Ibid*, emphasis by author.

18. Appendix to KTB–A, 17 May 1940.

19. KTB–A, 17 May 1940.

20. KTB–B and –6., 17 May 1940.

21. Halder, 18 May 1940, KTB–A, same date.

22. *Ibid*, author's emphasis.

23. *Ibid*, author's emphasis.

24. Jodl diary, 18 May 1940.

25. KTB–4., 18 May 1940.

26. KTB–A, 18 May 1940. Author's emphasis.

27. Halder, 18 May 1940.

28. OKH, Army General Staff Op.Abt. (1a) No 20 117/40 g.Kdos at 1350 hrs; OKH Army General Staff Op.Abt. 1655 hrs; Halder 18 May 1940.

29. Halder *ibid*.

30. OKH, Army General Staff Op.Abt. (1a) No.20 112/40 g.Kdos, author's emphasis.

31. KTB–A and –4., 18 May 1940.

32. KTB–A, –4., 18 May 1940; Guderian *op. cit.*, p.99.

33. KTB–B and –6., 18 May 1940.

34. KTB–6., 18 May 1940.

35. Bock diary, 18 May 1940.

36. KTB–6., 20 May 1940.

37. KTB–B and –18., 17–20 May 1940.

38. KTB–Kleist, 20 May 1940; KTB–XXXXI Armee Korps same date: Guderian, *op. cit.* p.100.

39. Jodl diary of 19–20 May 1940.

40. *Ibid*, emphasis by author.

41. Halder, 19 May 1940

42. Halder, 20 May 1940.

4. The Crisis at Arras, 21 May 1940 (Maps 1, 4, and 5)

1. KTB–B, 21 May 1940; KTB–6. and –18., same date.
2. KTB–6., 21 May 1940.
3. KTB–B, 21 May 1940, see also Bock diary, 21 May 1940.
4. KTB–6., 21 May 1940.
5. KTB–B, 21 May 1940.
6. Halder, 21 May 1940, author's emphasis.
7. KTB–4., 21 May 1940.
8. Ibid.
9. Ibid.
10. KTB–XXXIX Armee Korps, 21 May 1940.
11. *Ibid*; see text p.66f.
12. *Ibid*; appendix to KTB.
13. KTB–4., 21 May 1940, see primarily: H. Teske, *Bewegungskrieg,* Heidelberg 1955, p.44ff.
14. *Ibid*, see KTB–A, 21 May 1940.

III. The Allied resistance to the German attack, 10–21 May 1940 (Map 2a)

1. Army Group 2 (Third, Fourth, and Fifth Armies) and Army Group 3 (Eighth Army and 45 Fortress Armee Corps) based from Rhinau to Col de la Fancille held the Maginot Line. Inside the fortifications were about 22 divisions of fortress troops. On this *et seq.* see Gamelin, *Servir,* Vol I: *Les Armées Françaises de 1940,* Paris 1947, p.310ff: Lt-Colonel Lugand, *Les forces en présence au 10 mai 1940,* in: *Revue d'Histoire de la Deuxième Guerre Mondiale,* Issue 10/11 1953/54, pp.5–48. Very informative from the German side: U. Liss, *Die deutsche Westoffensive von 1940 vom Standpunkt des Ic,* in *Wehrwissenschaftliche Rundschau,* Year 8, Vol 4 (1958), pp.208–19.
2. See Deployment (pp. 5-6)
3. *Ibid.*
4. *Ibid.*
5. *Ibid.*
6. See Ellis, *The War in France and Flanders, 1939–1940,* London 1953, p.42. Present were the King of Belgium, General van Overstraeten (his military adviser), Defence Minister Daladier, the French Generals Georges, Billotte and Champon (Chief of the French Military Mission at Belgian HQ), General Pownall (Chief of BEF Staff) and Brigadier Swayne (Lord Gort's representative at General Georges HQ.
7. For strengths see Deployment (pp. 5-6). The Belgian operational plan envisaged that the territory south of the Meuse and east of Liège was to be secured by cavalry and the Ardennes mountain infantry. The bulk of the Belgian fighting force was to remain at the Albert Canal. Four divisions had to hold the Belgian sector of the Dyle Line between Louvain and Namur. The idea was that they

should offer delaying resistance east of Liège and at the Albert Canal to gain time for the Allies to occupy the Dyle Line.

8. Nucleus of the Dutch defences was Fortress Holland, its northern flank being the Ijssel Lake, the eastern flank secured by the Grebbe Line, the southern flank by the Waal. The enemy advance was to be delayed by the Ijssel Line in front of the Grebbe Line, and south of the Meuse the Peel Line.

9. See R. Villate, *L'entrée des Français en Belgique et en Hollande en Mai 1940*. In: *Revue d'Histoire de la Deuxième Guerre Mondiale*, 1953–54, issue 10–11, pp.60–76 and Ellis, *op. cit.* pp.23, 35–36. A.Goutard, *1940, La Guerre des Occasions perdues*, Paris, 1956, p.139.

10. Ellis, *op.cit*, p.23.

11. Now troop movements had to be made by day as well as night: since the beginning of the offensive the BEF had marched day and night under the protection of the RAF (Ellis, *op. cit.*, p,37). 7. Armee was to limit its operations to the Breda area. On 13 May it was ordered that the bulk should pull back to the west bank of the Scheldt to reinforce the northern flank of the Dyle position. Only a small bridgehead on the isthmus at Woermsdrecht was to be maintained on the other bank.

12. See P. Lyet, *La Bataille de France, Mai–Juin 1940*: Paris, 1947, pp.46–47.

13. On the 9. Armee left wing for example the occupation of the positions was often changed: in addition there was a mixing of infantry arriving and cavalry returning from the forefield. For the Ardennes breakthrough see the article by Fox and d'Ornano: *La Percée des Ardennes* in: *Revue d'Histoire de la Deuxième Guerre Mondiale*, Issue 10/11, 1953/54, pp.77–118.

14. Attacks had already been made against these bridges on 11 May.

15. On 14 May, Gamelin and Georges requested from Air Marshal Barratt the greatest possible involvement of the RAF.

16. On 14 May, 65 per cent of the bomber force sent failed to return: of 109 bombers in the Sedan area 64 were lost.

17. For this and what followed see the impressive representation in Goutard, *op. cit.*, pp.221, 243, 250ff, 254ff.

18. Ellis, *op. cit.*, p.59ff.

19. Certain difficulties developed as a result of poor coordination between the BEF and Belgian Armee in the retreat: see Ellis, *op. cit.*, p.66ff.

20. Cited per Goutard, *op. cit.*, p.280.

21. For the following see K. J. Müller, *Das Ende der Entente Cordiale, Eine Studie zur Entwicklung der englisch-französischen Beziehungen während des Westfeldzuges 1940.* Supplement 3 to the *Wehrwissenschaftlichen Rundschau*, Frankfurt 1956, *passim*.

22. Churchill, *The Second World War*, Vol.II, *Their Finest Hour*, London 1949, pp.42–43, see also Gamelin, *op.cit*, Vol III, p.210.

23. Per a note of 18 May 1940 to General Ismay (Churchill *op. cit.* pp.49–50) and in a note to the Chiefs of Staff, 27 May 1940 (Churchill, *op. cit.* p.78).

24. Ellis, *op. cit.*, pp.56–58, 60–61.

25. Thus the observation of Pétain at the beginning of June to the US ambassador, that the British had refused to deploy the RAF in order to use it and the Fleet as a negotiating trump in possible peace talks. See C. Hull, *The Memoirs of Cordell Hull*, New York 1948, pp.774 and 776, also Bullitts Report of 4 June 1940 in Langer: *Our Vichy Gamble*, New York 1947, p.19ff. Darlan justified this after the armistice in telegrams to the French Navy with *inter alia* the argument that Britain was responsible for the situation in which France found itself because the British aid during the campaign had been at best middling. (Telegram No.5146–50 and No.5159, 24 June 1940, published in Docteur, *La Vérité sur les Amiraux*, Paris 1949, pp.40–43.) See also pamphlets such as that by Jean Luchaire, *Les Anglais et Nous, L'action britannique contra La France*, Paris 1941.

26. See Charles de Gaulle, *Memoiren*, Vol I, *Der Ruf*, 1940–42., Berlin-Frankfurt 1955, pp.38–41, and Heinz Guderian, *Erinnerungen eines Soldaten*, Heidelberg, 1951, pp.98–99. De Gaulle's attack did not proceed for amongst other things inadequate artillery and infantry support. See Goutard, *op. cit.*, p.282: '*Encore un coup de poing énergique mais isolé.*'

27. Gamelin *op. cit.*, pp.3–4.

28. See also observation 26. On 19 May the CC was not ready to attack. Its tanks were distributed amongst the infantry units and could not be assembled in time. See Prioux, *Souvenirs de Guerre, 1939–1940*, Paris 1947, pp.90–95. See also the statements of the 2nd DLM commander: '*Mon impression est que, si j'avais ma DLM intacte, et surtout mes chars, je considérais comme très realisable d'attendre Cambrai. Mais je n'est que des éléments non blindés.*' (Quoted from Goutard, *op. cit.*, p.301.

29. See Ellis, *op. cit.* pp.87–97; Prioux, *op. cit.*, pp.100–102.

30. Both assault groups consisted of one tank and one infantry battalion, one battery of field artillery plus anti-tank guns and one company of motorcycle riflemen. Ellis, *op. cit.*, p.90.

31. The CIGS (arrival 20 May 1940 at 0800 hrs) had previously sent Gort the so-called 'Order A' of the War Cabinet which read: 'The Cabinet decided that the CIGS was to direct the C-in-C BEF to move southwards upon Amiens attacking all enemy forces encountered and to take station on the left of the French Army'. 2. The CIGS will inform General Billotte and the Belgian Command making it clear to the Belgians that their best chance is to move tonight between the BEF and the coast. 3. 'The War Office will inform General Georges in this sense.' (Quote from Ellis, *op. cit.*, p.83.) This was the reaction of the Cabinet to Pownall's telephoned situation report of 19 May. On 20 May after much effort Gort succeeded in convincing the CIGS of the impracticability of this order. He sent a telegram to this effect to the War Office (telegram, Ellis, *op. cit.*, p.106). Eden replied: 'All your immediate proposals approved, and we have full confidence in your discretion. Naturally Weygand will today concert the action of the three Allied Armies concerned. Dominating object must remain to ensure your power to retreat down your communications through Amiens, should this be enforced upon you. Pray keep us informed.' (Ellis, *op. cit.*, p.106)

32. See Ellis, *op. cit.,* p.104f (Report to Churchill by Sir John Dills).
33. See General van Overstraeten, *Albert I-Leopold III, Vingt Ans de Politique Militaire Belge 1920–1940,* Brussels 1950, p.3787ff. H. Pierlot, *La Conférence d'Ypres,* in: *Le Soir* of 12 July 1947. Jacques Weygand, *The Role of General Weygand, Conversations with his son,* London 1948, p.58ff.
34. Ellis, *op. cit.,* p.110.
35. See E. Wanty, *La Bataille de la Lys, vue dans un cadre élargi,* in: *L'Armée – La Nation,* No.5, 11th year, of 1 May 1956, pp.10–22.
36. Text at Ellis, *op.cit* p.111.
37. Protocol of the session at the Foreign Ministry: *Die Geheimakten des französischen Generalstabes,* Berlin, 1941, No.56.
38. See Ellis, *op. cit.,* pp.112–113, also M. Weygand, *op. cit.,* p.95.
39. For this and the following see further under the description of the operations during 23–25 May 1940.

IV. The decision to halt the German panzers, 22–26 May 1940 (Maps 5–8)

Sections 1-3

1. OKH Situation Report, 22 May 1940.
2. Situation Report West No.319, 21 May 1940, 1300 hrs (morning bulletin): see also Situation Report ObdL of 18 May 1940. These stated: 'After reconnaissance confirmed the morning picture, in particular, heavy traffic of motorized columns being observed from Dixmuiden and St. Omer to Dunkirk, leads to conclusion that the British intend to ship out at Dunkirk; especially with regard to the parking of 2,700 railway waggons observed at Dunkirk in the morning...'. See also Liss, U: *Dünkirchen gesehen mit den Augen des Ic,* in: *Wehrwiss.Rundschau,* June 1958, p.325ff, esp. 335–340.
3. OKH Situation Report, *ibid.*
4. KTB–A, 22 May 1940; Jodl diary, 21/22 May 1940. See also Halder diary 21/22 May 1940. In addition; Meier-Welcker, *op. cit.,* p.274f; Liddell Hart, *Jetzt dürfen sie reden, op. cit.,* p.227 (statement by Rundstedt): Ellis, *op. cit.,* p.87ff.
5. Jodl diary, 22 May 1940; KTB–A 22 May: Appendix to KTB–A, handwritten note by Keitel with 'The Führer's wishes.'
6. KTB–A 22.5, see also KTB–A, 18 May 1940.
7. Jodl diary, 22 May 1940.
8. KTB–4., 22 May 1940; telex by Army Group A to AOK 4, 22 May 1940 at 1700 hrs, received 1800 hrs. 'The Führer and Supreme Commander of the Wehrmacht lays decisive weight upon having the divisions brought up from rearward capturing territory as far west as possible at the earliest possible moment. The Armees must ensure that during the advance, the Divisions follow without great distances between each. Rest-days are only to occur in exceptional circumstances.'

9. KTB–A 22.5, KTB–4 22.5, KTB–XXXXI.AK 22 May 1940.
10. KTB–4. 22.5, 0912 hrs: KTB–A 22.5; Halder diary 22 May 1940.
11. KTB–4. *op.cit*; KTB–A *op. cit.*
12. Situation Report No 260, ObdL, Command Staff Ic, No.9766/40 (Luftwaffe), 23 May 1940.
13. KTB–4., 22 May 1945.
14. KTB XXXIX Armee Korps, 22 May 1945: Korps order for 22 May 1945; statement by Hoth to the author, July 1958. See H. Teske, *Bewegungskrieg*, Heidelberg 1958, p.44ff according to which the 1a of 12. Infantry Division advised the Commanding General of XXXIX Armee Korps on the night of 21 May that the division would take over the protection of the northern flank 'at the earliest from late afternoon' since 'the main body of the Division' was not expected here earlier than that!
15. KTB–4., 22 May 1945; KTB–VIII Flying Korps, 22 May 1940; Situation Report No 260, ObdL *op. cit* (Air Fleet 3); Ellis p.87f; Goutard *op. cit.*, p.303f.
16. KTB–4., 22 May 1945; *Goutard op. cit.*, p.304.
17. KTB–A, 22 May 1945.
18. See KTB XXXXI Armee Korps, 22 May 1940, especially KTB–PzGr Kleist, same date.
19. KTB–B, 6. and 18., 22 May 1940.
20. Situation Report No 260, ObdL *op. cit* 23 May 1940; KTB–VIII Flying Korps, 22 May 1940.
21. KTB–A and 4., 22 May 1940.
22. Army Order AOK 18 and AOK 6, 22 May 1940.
23. OKH, Army General Staff/Opl.Div. Ia, 23 May 1940, 0001 hrs, No.5848/40 g,Kdos. (see Jacobsen, Dokumente Bd. Westfeldzug, 1940); see Halder diary 22.5/23.5 1940; Meier-Welcker *op. cit.*, p.274f. (23) KTB–B and 18, 23 May 1940; Michiels, *op. cit.*, p.144f.
24. KTB–18., 23 May 1940
25. See KTB–B, 23 May 1940.
26. Halder diary, 23 May 1940.
27. *Ibid.*
28. *Ibid.*, Meier-Welcker, *op. cit.*, p.276.
29. Situation Report West No.324, 23 May 1940.
30. KTB–4., 23 May 1940, at 0045 hrs a telex from Kleist arrived at AOK 4: 'Fighting strength of five panzer divisions of which 50 per cent non-operational too weak for a 50-kilometre breadth. Availability of 9. Panzer Division requested.' At 0842 hrs the quoted telephone conversation ensued.
31. *Ibid*, author's emphasis.
32. Halder diary, 23 May 1940: Gyldenfeldt notes of same date; Meier-Welcker, *op. cit.* p.276f. Lt-General v. G. informed the latter on 25 May 1954: 'The numbers were actually seen as sufficient at Panzer Group because it had probably been overlooked that a large proportion of the panzers with damage would flow back

to the fighting troops within a short time after repair, a practice regarding which perhaps insufficient experience existed.' See also remarks on p.137 (this book).

33. KTB–A, 23 May 1940: Situation Report West No.261, 24 May 1940.

34. KTB–4., 23 May 1940; KTB–A, 23 May 1940; *ibid*, author's emphasis.

35. KTB–A, 23 May 1940: see Meier-Welcker, *op. cit.* p.276f.

36. Gen der Panzertruppen (ret'd) Kuntzen (formerly Commander, 8. Panzer Division), in a discussion at Bonn, 7.3.1958.

37. KTB–XIX Armee Korps, 23 May 1940 (see also Ellis, *op. cit.*, p.386). Here Guderian's criticism on the deployment of XIX Armee Korps by Group Kleist.

38. KTB–XXXXI Armee Korps, 23 May 1940, see Meier-Welcker, *op. cit.* p.277, footnote 11 (communication by Reinhardt to M.W, 2 May 1954.)

39. KTB–6., Panzer Division, 23 May 1940.

40. KTB–XXXXI Armee Korps, 23 May 1940.

41. Armee Order – AOK 4 –, 23 May 1940. Telephoned through at 2000 hrs.

42. Army Group instruction advised by telephone 2245 hrs to AOK 4, 23 May 1940 (appdx.KTB–4).

The Allied Measures of 23 May 1940
Dr K. J. Müller

1. For literature quoted hereunder see Chapter 3, chapter notes.

2. Impressed by the German panzer thrust, on 23 May General Brooke confided to his diary: 'Nothing but a miracle can save the BEF now.' Brooke, *op. cit., pp.113–114.

3. For the setting up of the individual 'Forces' and their deployment see Ellis, *op. cit.*, p.135ff.

4. Interception positions at Boeseghem, Steenbecq and Morbeque. Total Front of POL Force 40 km.

5. Between Forêt de Nieppe and St. Omer.

6. Elements of 21st French Infantry Division were fighting there.

7. See Armengaud *op. cit.*, p.132ff.

8. See Telegram No.975 (R 222), 23 May 1940, 2110 hrs, to the French Naval Mission, London (MNFL) with report of the Admiral, North.

9. Lord Gort, Despatches, in: Supplement to the *London Gazette*, 17 October 1941, p.5917.

10. North of it on the La Bassée-Aire Canal was only a thin veil of protection provided by POL Force units.

11. 1st DLM had lost Mt.St. Eloi and dug in again on the Neuvelle–St. Vaast–Souchez line; 3rd DLM had been forced north of Lens as far as the Lens–Pont á Vendin railway line. To the east of Arras the British 13th Brigade had been thrown back to Baileul: British troops were in the Baileul–Gavrelle–Plouvain sector, then on the Scarpe as far as Biache.

12. Gort, *op. cit., ibid.*
13. As a result of this withdrawal by FRANC Force, the right wing of First French Army was now in an unfavourable position. It stood now in a narrow arc on the Douai–Valenciennes–Condé–Maulde–Bourghelles line (Groupement TARDU – 5th DINA – 25th DIM – 4th DI – 15th DIM – 1st DIM – 2nd DINA – 32nd DI – 12th DIM).
14. Per Goutard, *op. cit.*, p.306.
15. 5. Panzer Division; 20. Motorized Division; 12. Infantry Division and 11. Rifle Brigade.
16. This is confirmed by telegram No.1730/3/OP, 23 May 1940 at 1635 hrs.
17. See K. J. Müller, *op. cit.*, p.11ff.

Sections 4-9

1. Halder diary, 23 May 1940: Meier-Welcker, *op. cit.*, p.279; Liddell Hart, *Jetzt dürfen sie reden*, *op. cit.*, p.236ff. (Here there is talk that the C-in-C had given the order so as to prevent a misunderstanding – meeting up of the two army groups – but this argument does not go to the core of the matter.)
2. This manner of proceeding corresponds in a certain sense to the 'common law right' of the great Moltke school. On the other hand HDv 92 (Handbook for General Staff Service in Wartime, 1 August 1939, Part 1, p.2(2) resp. p.14(4)) foresaw no circumstances in which the Chief of the General Staff would enter a dissenting opinion in the record. (See H.Z., February 1958, p.159f.)
3. Bock diary 24 May 1940; telephone conversation with OKH, 24 May 1940 at 01015 hrs, to Army Group B, Army General Staff, Op. Abt.(IIb) No. 5852/40 g.Kdos...KTB–B 24 May 1940. Furthermore Halder had stated on 17 May 1940 that in the course of an immediately following 'south-west operation' over the Somme towards Paris, 4. Armee should be detached to Army Group B: apparently Hitler rejected this plan. (See Halder diary 17/18 May 1940). Next Brauchitsch (in connection with the transfer of XVI Armee Korps from 6. Armee to 4. Armee) had mentioned to Bock in a telephone conversation 'that 4. Armee would if necessary turn inwards and detach to Army Group B' (see KTB–B of 19 May 1940.) Army Group Command A had since February 1940 never had to come to terms with the idea of relinquishing 4. Armee to Army Group B. (See Jacobsen, *op.cit*, pp.118, 130ff.)
4. Army Group B 1a No.2655/40 g.Kdos.; KTB–B, 24 May 1940.
5. ObdL, Luftwaffe High Command Ic, Situation Report No. 261.
6. Richthofen's notes, 23 May 1940. Emphasis by author.
7. Jodl diary, 20 May 1940; K. Klee, *Das Unternehmen Seelöwe*, Göttingen 1958, p.57f. Also: R. Wheatley, *Operation Sea Lion*, Oxford 1958, p.14f.
8. Liddell Hart, *Jetzt dürfen sie reden*, *op. cit.*, p.244; Nuremberg, Fall XII, Pr 6245 (Warlimont's testimony). Statement by Halder to the author, 21 January 1958.
9. Hitler's Order of the Day, 10 May 1940.

10. Notes, Engel, 23 May 1940; Statement by Halder to the author 21 January 1958: Statement by Gen. (ret'd) B. Schmidt of 18 June 1953: information from Fied Marshal (ret'd) Milch to the author 2 February 1958; information from Gen. of Infantry (ret'd) Stapf to the author, 31 January 1958; information from Gen. (ret'd) Kleikamp to the author, 3 March 1958 (following a statement by his friend Lt-Colonel von Tresckow). See also Kesselring, op. cit., p,78; also Liddell Hart, *Jetzt dürfen sie reden, op. cit.,* p.244; Nuremberg, Fall XII, Pr 6245 (Warlimont's testimony).

11. KTB–B, 6. and 18., 24 May 1940, see also Bock diary of same date (Documents Bd. Westfeldzug 1940).

12. *Ibid.*

13. KTB–6., 24 May 1940.

14. Halder diary, 24 May 1940.

15. *Ibid*; see also Meier-Welcker *op. cit.,* p.279f.

16. KTB–4., 24 May 1940.

17. *Ibid.*

18. *Ibid.*

19. Supplement to KTB–4., 24 May 1940.

20. Jodl diary, 24 May 1940; KTB–A same date; Bock diary, 29 May 1940; Meier-Welcker *op. cit.,* p.278f, footnote 17: the statement of Sodenstern quoted here from the summer of 1943 is refuted by the sources (see my explanation in the text, p.86ff). Emphasis by author. The literature hitherto reporting Hitler's talk at Charleville is to be treated with the greatest circumspection and especially that reported in: Liddell Hart, *Jetzt dürfen sie reden* p.229ff which contains many errors being based on memory. The details in J. F. C. Fuller, *Der Zweite Weltkrieg 1939–1945,* Vienna 1952, p.82ff also needs correction as do: K.Assmann, *Deutsche Schicksaljahre,* 1950, p.167ff: Görlitz, W. *Der Zweite Weltkrieg,* Vol 1, p.131; B. von Lossberg, *Im Wehrmachtführungstab,* 1949, p.81f., Nuremberg Fall XII Pr. 8584f (testimony of Blumentritt). The view of Ellis (*op. cit.,* p.350f) also based on Butler, *Grand Strategy,* p.190, f/n 1 and I. F. C. Fuller, *The Decisive Battles of the Western World and their Influence upon History,* Vol.III, 1956, p.400ff that on 24 May 1940 Hitler had simply confirmed and expanded Rundstedt's 'Closing-Up' Order from the morning is incorrect. Meier-Welcker *op. cit.,* p.278ff., p.290. see f/n 14 has already quite rightly drawn attention to it.

21. As is known, the panzers were always very close to Hitler's heart. In 1941 at the gates of Leningrad, he had Panzer Group Hoepner halt for similar reasons. (Statement by Blumentritt to the author.)

22. Jodl diary, 24 May 1940: Meier-Welcker, *op. cit.,* p,279; to all appearances Jodl was in agreement with the 'Halt-Order', contrary to his colleagues. (Statement by Warlimont to the author, 5 July 1958.)

23. Jodl, *op. cit.*: as it appears to me, H. Gackenholz in a discourse to the *Wehrkunde* section in Bonn (7.3.1958) evaluated the 'Halt-Order' too one-sidedly as a result of the new crisis of confidence. See to the contrary my statement at p.193ff this

book. Equally, in contrast to G., I am not of the opinion that after Charleville, Hitler was to a certain extent 'without an opinion' and what Rundstedt advocated was decisive for him. Such a way of looking at it disregards the entire pre-history of the 'Halt-Order' (see for example the two entries in KTB–A of 18 and 22 May 1940.) Furthermore Sodenstern's opinion (Meier-Welcker *op. cit.*, p.288 f/n 53) does not fit, namely that Hitler had come to Army Group A 'with the firm intention' to halt the panzers. See on the contrary the statement of Engels, *ibid*, 21 May 1954.

24. KTB–4., 24 May 1940 (not as Meier-Welcker, *op. cit.*, p.280, and Taylor, *op. cit.*, p.255 had to assume <evening!>, but early afternoon.) Author's emphasis. Ellis, *op. cit.*, p.139, writes: '…while Hitler was only too anxious to appear as the director of operations, Rundstedt saw that if he was to get his own way when it differed from the intentions of OKH he must make it appear that what he did was by 'the Führer's order''. This statement seems at least very questionable to me. Ellis (also Hoth in a communication to the author of July 1958) take too little account here of the accord in thinking between Hitler and Rundstedt and neglect completely the psychological moment of the 'unknown OKH' order (transferring 4. Armee to Army Group B!). Naturally this matter can never be clarified. I incline to the view that the 'Halt-Order' was an instruction by Hitler and not one declared by Rundstedt to be such, in order to realize his own intentions.

25. Translator's Note: also can be translated as 'Channel'.

26. Instruction No.13 WFA/Abt.L No 33 028/40 g.Kdos, 24 May 1940, see also Jodl diary same date, here the note: 'New guideline…1.) Destruction of the enemy north of the Somme and taking the coast…'

27. Engel, Notes, 27 May 1940.

28. Gyldenfeldt, Notes, 25 May 1940: see also Liddell Hart, *Military Review, op. cit.*, p.55.

29. Ellis (*op. cit.*, p.352) probably underestimates here the Stop Order to the German units. See on the other hand Taylor, *op. cit.*, p.255f.

30. KTB–4., 25 May 1940, see also statement of Blumentritt to Meier-Welcker of 4 March 1954, Brennecke to M-W of 15 April 1954 (M-W. *op. cit.* p.282 f/n 29.)

31. Guderian, *Erinnerungen eines Soldaten*, Heidelberg 1951 p.104f: Panzermeyer, *Grenadiers*, Munich 1956, p.26f: KTB–10. Panzer Division, 25 May 1940. What General von Thomas stated to Liddell Hart (*op. cit.*, p.55) is not supported in the sources.

32. KTB XXXXI Armee Korps 24 May 1940.

33. KTB–3. Panzer Division, 24 May 1940.

34. KTB–4. Panzer Division, 24 May 1940.

35. Bock diary, 24/26 May 1940.

36. Meier-Welcker, *op. cit.*, p.289f.; statement by Halder to the author, 25.1.1958.

37. Halder diary, 24 May 1940, see also KTB–6., 24 May 1940.

38. OKH. Army General Staff Op.Abt. (1a) No.3218/40 g.Kdos 24 May 1940 (see Jacobsen, Dokumente Bd. Westfeldzug 1940). Brauchitsch gave Bock to

understand on 26 May that he 'stood by the order now as before' (i.e. attachment of 4. Armee to Army Group B) but that this 'modification had not been possible to avoid'!) At the time, Bock had not been able to discover the real reason. (See Bock diary).

39. Jodl diary, 24 May 1940: Halder diary, same date: information from Halder to the author 21 January 1958.

40. Appendix to KTB–A, 25 May 1940: also KTB–A. The new instruction arrived at Army Group Command at 0045 hrs. KTB–B, 25 May 1940, arrived 0050 hrs: inf. From Halder to the author, 21 January 1958. See also Ellis, *op. cit.*, p.150. Emphasis by author. It was neither a 'revised previous' instruction nor 'a new one in preparation' as Meier-Welcke, *op. cit.*, f/n 25, had to assume. Rather the details in Ellis, *op. cit.*, are correct if short on completion.

41. KTB–B, 25 May 1940.

42. KTB–A, 25 May 1940; appendix to KTB–A, 25 May 1940, author's emphasis. In his memorandum from the year 1943 (see Meier-Welcke, *op. cit.*, p.281 f/n 25) Sodenstern maintains that 'enemy reports received in the course, 24.5 during the afternoon led to a different judgement of the situation. Army Group Command therefore decided to group the fast forces to attack to the north-east on 25 May 1940. Based on aerial reconnaissance results, Rundstedt came to the conclusion 'to continue the panzer advance'. He relayed this at once to OKH (24 May 1940). M-W was right to raise doubts about this version since he was unable to find any confirmation of it. From the files available to us today it may be considered certain that Sodenstern's statement on this point rests on an error. The attitude of Army Group Command A on the night, 24 May speaks against it, as do the events on the morning, 26 May (see text p.100ff). Also questionable is whether there actually was 'no complete agreement' between the Commanding General and the Chief of the Army Group A General Staff, as Sodenstern stated to M-W (*op. cit.*). Sodenstern was motivated here by the text of the mentioned entry in KTB–A, 25 May 1940 (morning). Everything points to the Chief of the Army Group A General Staff on 24/25 May 1940 sharing the opinion of his Commanding General. Infantry General (ret'd) Blumentritt (formerly 1a of Army Group A) informed the author on 11 July 1958 that Army Group A had 'probably' not forwarded the OKH instruction to AOK 4 because it was believed that OKH apparently 'did not know the full extent of the clearly given Führer-order to halt.' After a study in depth of the sources, the author cannot concur with this opinion. (See text p.99ff.)

43. Notes of Id, AOK 4, 25 May 1940.

44. See pp.76–77 (this book)

45. Jacobsen Dokumente Bd.2a, p.66.

46. Jodl diary, 25 May 1940. This observation of Jodl is no longer 'incomprehensible' as Meier-Welcker has established (*op. cit.*, p.283).

47. Halder diary, 25 May 1940.

48. KTB–A, Bock diary. KTB–4., KTB–Pz-Gr.Kleist, all 25 May 1940. Author's emphasis. When Hitler visited Army Group B on 1 June 1940, he is said to have opened his address with the words: '...You will probably have wondered why I halted the panzer divisions. I was concerned about the enemy attacks on the Somme Front. I could not allow them to suffer the slightest scratch there.' (Statement of Salmuth to the author, January 1958).

a) The Allied Front on 24 May
Dr K. J. Müller

1. See page 58 (this book).
2. This was expressed in a telegram sent by Minister-President Reynaud to the British Prime Minister on 24 May. It contained these three main points: a) a complaint about the British retreat at Arras; b) a demand for confirmation that Gort carried the responsibility for the collapse of the Weygand Plan; c) A demand that Gort should abide by the orders and instructions of the Allied High Command. See Reynaud: *La France a sauvé l'Europe*, Paris, 1947, Vol.II, pp.155–156: W. S. Churchill, *Der Zweite Weltkrieg*, Vol II, pp.93–94, Sir Edward Spears, *Assignment to Catastrophe*, Vol 1, *Prelude to Dunkirk*, July 1939–May 1940, London 1954, p.168. Ellis *op. cit.*, pp.141–142.
3. Meeting of 24 May at 1000 hrs; see Ellis, *op. cit.*, pp.141–142; Brooke, *op. cit.*, p.116; Gort, Despatches, *op. cit.*, *London Gazette*, 17 October 1941 p.5922.
4. General Wanty maintains (*op. cit.*, p.16), Blanchard had taken no decision but only sent Commandant Fauvelle into GQG. Reading Instruction No.40, however, shows that he was by no means inactive.
5. Already on 23 May, both generals were in agreement to begin the attack on 26 May (see also the orders of Georges and Weygand of 23/24 May). In contrast to Weygand and the GQG, Gort was of the opinion that the attack of Army Group I southwards could only be a kind of lunge, the main relieving offensive had to come from the standing Armee Frère (Army Group Besson) in the south on the Somme. Gort considered that the fighting strength of Army Group 1, especially First French Army, was no longer adequate. At GQG the weakness of Armee Frère, still in formation, was also known. Gort stood between two fires. He should have, and wanted to, take part in the breakout of the BEF to the south, but at the same time he saw himself forced to hold the Canal Line and secure his rearward lines of communication against the thrust of the German panzers. The War Office telegram of 23 May was less decisive in this question than that of the day before which contained the clear instruction to cooperate actively in the carrying through of the Weygand Plan. (Text at Ellis *op. cit.*, p.128).
6. Telegram No. 1730/3/OP, 24 May 1940, 1635 hrs. Besides the mention of a possible retreat at Dunkirk and building a bridgehead, this telegram contains

the observation that Blanchard was 'seul juge de l'opportunité de maintenir la contr'attaque.'

7. Ellis, *op. cit.*, p.153ff.

8. Roskill, Capt. *The War at Sea, 1939–1945*, Vol I, London 1954, pp.213–214 writes that many more troops could have been evacuated if they had waited for nightfall.

9. These were the 1st Queen Victoria's Rifles, the 30th Brigade and the 3rd Royal Tank Regiment. See Ellis, *op. cit.*, p.159ff.

10. See the signal sent to Brigadier Nicholson at Ellis, *op. cit.*, p.167: 25 May 1400 hrs: 'Defence of Calais to the utmost is of highest importance to our country as symbolizing our continued cooperation with France. The eyes of the Empire are upon the defence of Calais and H.M. Government are confident you and your gallant regiments will perform an exploit worthy of the British name.' 25 May towards midnight: 'Every hour you continue is of greatest help to the BEF. Government has therefore decided you must continue to fight. Have greatest admiration for your splendid stand.' See also the German enemy situation report, 26 May 1940 at 1215 hrs, printed in extract in U. Liss, *Dünkirchen gesehen mit den Augen des 1c,* in *Wehrwissenschaftlich Rundschau,* June 1958, p.355.

11. In the course of this day, USHER Force was withdrawn and transferred to Bergues.

12. Telegram No.987, 24 May, 2220 hrs.

13. Ellis, *op.cit*, p.139.

14. Good overall survey in Wanty, *op. cit.*, p. 15ff.

15. On average each division had three-quarters of its original fighting strength. 4th Division had only one regiment while two of the reserve divisions had practically lost all their artillery.

16. Brooke, *op. cit.*, p.117.

17. *Ibid.*, p.119.

10. The German operations on 25 May

1. KTB–B, 18. and 6., 25 May 1940.

2. KTB–6., 25 May 1940.

3. KTB–4., 25 May 1940.

4. *Ibid*

5. KTB–VIII Flying Korps, 25 May 1940; KTB–4., 24/25 May 1940, ObdL, Ic, situation report no.263.

a) The Allied fighting of 25 and 26 May

1. See his report to the Prime Minister in Ellis, *op. cit.*, pp.147–148, in which it is disclosed that at this point he did not view the attack to the south by Army Group 1 as the main operation, but rather the offensive of Army Group Besson (Armee Frère).

2. Telegram No.1730/3/OP, 24 May 1940, 1635 hrs.

3. For the discussions in Paris and the report of Commandant Fauvelle see Spears, *op. cit.*, pp.187–196.

4. See Telegram No.632A, 25 May 1940, 1645hrs (R226).

5. See Note 1 above.

6. For the following see Brooke, *op.cit*, pp.119–224.

7. See Brooke, *op.cit*, p.119.

8. Contact with enemy at 0945 hrs at Lenderlede.

9. Brooke, *op. cit.,* p.119.

10. See Brooke, *op.cit*, pp.120–121; Ellis *op. cit.*, p.148.

11. Gort, Despatches, *op.cit*, p.5923.

12. Ellis, *op. cit.*, p.148; Wanty, *op. cit.,* p.18, Brooke *op.cit*, p.148.

13. Ellis, *ibid*.

14. See Brooke, *op. cit.*, p.122, note 1.

15. Blanchard informed his intentions on 25 May at 2350 hrs (telegram No.304 517 S73) to HQ which approved them.

16. One group consisted of: 3 batteries of Artillery Regiment 35 and 2 batteries of Artillery Regiment 235. The other was composed of the third group of Artillery Regiment 35 and the fifth of Artillery Regiment 235.

17. It ran from the sea along the Ancien Canal de Mardyck, then along the Canal de la Haute Colme to Bergues, from there out to the Canal de la Basse Colme along to the border fortifications on the French-Belgian border.

18. The Brigade was regiment consisting of 5th Inniskilling Dragoon Guards, 15/19th Hussars and 4/7th Dragoon Guards.

19. See p.129ff.

20. See Ellis *op. cit.*, p.173 and Armengaud, *op. cit.* p.42.

21. See Ellis *op. cit.*, p.173, Blanchard's report in extracts to Weygand: 'The BEF, First Army and the Belgians will withdraw to the line Aa-Lys Canal de Dérivation: there will be no further retreat from there.'

22. Texts in extracts at Ellis, *op. cit.*, pp.173–174.

23. Gort was also promised a Canadian brigade for Dunkirk but this was retracted shortly afterwards.

24. Ellis, *op. cit.*,p.174. See also General Brooke's diary entry for 26 May (Brooke, *op.cit*, p.130), 'It is going to be a very hazardous enterprise and we shall be lucky if we save 25 per cent of the BEF.'

25. The British Liaison Mission reported immediately to the War Office that General Weygand, after receiving a memorandum corresponding to General Blanchard's order, 'had sent for Admiral Darlan to study re-embarkation' (Ellis, *op. cit.* p.174). However, neither Admiral Abrial at Dunkirk nor General Blanchard received a report before 29 May from the French High Command about an intended evacuation.

26. In the letter of General E. Wanty (*op. cit.*, p.18–20) the passivity of the BEF, which refused to come to the help of the Belgians, is bitterly criticized. Ellis *op.cit*,

p.176–177 is of the opinion that a British relief operation had not been possible because all units not in the front line had been on their way to the Ypres Front. The German columns seen by the BEF-Front striving northwards for the breach in the Belgian Front were not taken under fire by the BEF artillery in order to save ammunition from its very meagre stock. On the other hand, on 26 May the RAF flew three reconnaissance flights and 18 RAF bombers with fighter protection attacked German troop concentrations both sides of Courtrai at the Lys crossings. Independent observers will come to the conclusion that it would have been very difficult for those British troops defending the Ypres–Comines Front to have launched an attack to close the breach in the Belgian Front. They were much too weak, and in the next few days only managed to hold off the heavy German attacks against the Ypres–Comines Front after great efforts. On the other hand, the painful impression lingers that the Belgians were left in the lurch by their ally, an impression sponsored by a considerable body of political opinion, not to mention the moral consequences!

27. Wanty, *op. cit.*, p.,18.
28. Note from the Chief of the Belgian General Staff to Lord Gort, reproduced in extract in Ellis *op.cit*, p.176–177. A report also arrived at British HQ from Admiral Keyes, Chief of the British Mission to the Belgian King which contained the sentence: 'If enemy is not driven back in Courtrai salient the whole front may collapse.'
29. See Brooke, *op. cit.*, p.125ff.
30. See Ellis *op.cit*, p.176 and Armengaud, *op.cit*, p.42–43.

11. The order of 26 May to resume (Map 8)

1. Supplement KTB–4., 25 May 1940.
2. Halder diary, 26 May 1940; see Meier-Welcker, *op.cit*, p.283.
3. KTB–4., 26 May 1940.
4. *Ibid*, statement by Blumentritt to author, 25.1.1958: report by Engel to the author, April 1958.
5. Halder diary, 26 May 1940; see Meier-Welcker, *op.cit*, p.284.
6. KTB–4., 26 May 1940.
7. OKH, Army General Staff, op.Abt.(1A), 20133/40 g.Kdos 26 May 1940.
8. KTB–4., 26 May 1940.
9. KTB–B, 26 May 1940: KTB–18. and 6., 26 May 1940.

V. The battle for Dunkirk, 27 May–4 June 1940 (Maps 7–14)

Sections 1-3

1. Situation Reports West, Nos.329 and 330. See also U. Liss, *Dünkirchen gesehen mit den Augen des Ic*, in: *Wehrw.Rdsch.*, June 1958, p.335f.

2. The previous research on the Dunkirk Problem has paid far too little attention to this problem in my opinion. See Ellis, *op. cit.*, pp.183ff, 348ff.
3. See OKH-Instruction, 26 May 1940, p.121.
4. Armee Order No.6, 26 May 1940 (see Jacobsen, *Dokumente zum Westfeldzug 1940*). In the Panzer Group Kleist War diary of same date, it was noted in connection with the order of AOK-4: 'Do not attack Dunkirk, leave it to the Luftwaffe'!
5. KTB–B, 26 May 1940.
6. Halder diary, 27 May 1940.
7. KTB–4., 27 May 1940; Guderian, *op. cit.*, p.106: Panzermeyer, *op. cit.* p.27f.
8. KTB–4., 27 May 1940: KTB–XXXXI Armee Korps, also Army Group B, 27 May 1940.
9. KTB–4., 27 May 1940, also KTB–A same date.
10. KTB–XXXIX Armee Korps, 27 May 1940, also Ellis, *op. cit.*, p.387f; author's emphasis.
11. KTB–4., 27 May 1940, KTB–XXXIX Armee Korps, 27 May 1940.
12. KTB–XXXIX Armee Korps, 27 May 1940: Ellis, *op. cit.*, p.338; for operations of 32.Inf.Div see Schröder-Schultz-Naumann: *Die Geschichte der pommerschen 32.Inf. Div,, 1935–1945*, 1956, p.54ff.
13. Author's emphasis: KTB–4., 27 May 1940.
14. Translator's note: General Brennecke must have had in mind the battery (four guns) of 15-cm cannons mentioned in the AOK 4 detailed dispositions at 2100 on 26 May as being transferred to Group von Kleist. The purpose of the 'flat trajectory fire' would be to penetrate the transports at or below the waterline.
15. KTB–4., 27 May 1940, General Kleist wrote at 1348 hrs: 'It is a very bitter thing for our people to see the British embarking, and sailing past Gravelines and Calais!'
16. Notes of 4. Armee Id, 27 May 1940 (kindly placed at the disposal of the author). Author's emphasis.
17. KTB–A and –4., 27 May 1940. See particularly Manstein, *Verlorene Siege*, 1955, p.129ff; A. Buchner, *Der Kampf um den Brückenkopf Abbeville*, in *Wehrkunde*, September 1957, p.487ff.
18. Bock diary, 27 May 1940; (see Jacobsen, *Dokumente zum Westfeldzug 1940): see also* H. Breithaupt, *Die Geschichte der 30.Inf-Div., 1939–1945*, 1955, p.56ff.
19. KTB–6., KTB–B, 27 May 1940, see also Michiels, *op. cit.*, p.213ff; Goutard, *op. cit.*, p.321ff.: Van Overstraeten, *op. cit.*, p.703ff.
20. KTB–B, 28 May 1940.
21. Situation Report West, No 332, 27 May 1940, 2345 hrs.
22. Halder diary, 27 May 1940: KTB–A and B, 27 May 1940. The entries in KTB–A, 27 May to 31 May, and also in Halder's diary make clear that as a result of the new planning, the higher Staffs were becoming increasingly distracted from the battle in Flanders.
23. KTB–A, 27 May 1940.

4. The last phase of the Allied retreat

1. See Armengaud, *op.cit*, p.171.
2. See detail in Ellis, *op. cit.*, p.187.
3. The Cavalry Corps secured the crossings over the Lys for the retreat of First French Army.
4. See Prioux, *op. cit.*, pp.120–122; Armengaud, *op. cit.*, p.45.
5. 2nd Division BEF stood north of Merville to La Bassée. In the same sector was the French battle group Vernillat from Béthune to south-west of Wawrin at the Knie Deule–La Bassée Canal: north of Béthune as far as Lestrem was the battle group Tarrit (remnants of 1st DINA – North African Infantry Division – and smaller units. 7th GRDI (divisional reconnaissance group Mariot) was also at La Brassée.
6. Ellis *op. cit.*, p.189ff speaks constantly of BEF 2nd Division and never mentions the French units involved in the fighting. See on the contrary Armengaud, *op. cit.*, p.45ff and Prioux, *op.cit*, pp.124–125.
7. In the days preceding, 2nd Division had been reinforced by the following units: from GQG: 139th Army Field Regiment – 61st Medium Regiment – 6th Machine-Gun Battalion: from I Corps: 2nd (Manchester) Machine-Gun Battalion: from 50th Division: 74th Field Regiment; and elements of 1 Army Tank Brigade,
8. And additionally into the columns of 25th Artillery Regiment and the 8th Zuaven (12th Motorized Division). The First Army retreat was much delayed by powerful bombardments; see Prioux, *op.cit*, p.124.
9. See Ellis, *op. cit.*, p,194.
10. 27 May 1940, 1230 hrs: '*L'armée est trés découragée. Elle se bat sans arrêt depuis quatre jours sous un intense bombardement que la RAF n'a pu empêcher…Le moment approche rapidement ou elles (les troupes) seront hors d'état, de combattre. Le Roi va trouver se constraint de capitular pour éviter un debâcle.*' Wanty, *op. cit.*, p.20, Ellis *op. cit.*, p.198.
11. *Ibid.* 'Notre front est en train de s'effriter telle une corde que se casse après usure complète.'
12. On one hand between 21 and 25 May the Belgian Army had been four days without any instructions from Allied HQ; see Lt-General Nyssens: *Lord Gort avait raison*, in '*L'Armée – La Nation*, 1 May 1953), and on the other hand on 27 May at the conference in Cassel attended by Blanchard, Koeltz, Fagalde, Abrial, Prioux and Sir Ronald Adams, there was no Belgian representative present. These two facts show only too clearly the failure of the Allied leadership and its command apparatus.
13. See pp.111ff, 116ff. On 27 May Churchill desired (telegram at 0300 hrs to Sir Roger Keyes and Lord Gort), that the Belgians should sacrifice themselves for the Allied cause. See Churchill, *op.cit*, p.116.
14. See Prioux, *op. cit.*, p.129.
15. For this see in Churchill, *op. cit.*, Vol.II, pp.118–120, the partially published report of General Pownall, Lord Gort's Chief of Staff. See also Ellis, *op. cit.*, p.209.
16. Churchill, *op. cit.*, p.119.

17. *Ibid...* 'We agreed that we both...had received instructions which said the same thing. Now our Government had advanced the mission to the next logical step (which undoubtedly was advised to the French Government) while he (Blanchard) had not yet received the corresponding order. It was imperative to withdraw the troops from the Lys, we had not a moment to lose and ... to at least by this evening reach the line Ypres–Poperinghe–Cassel... We considered it improbable that we could get even 30 per cent of our troops out of there.'

18. Churchill, *op. cit.*, Vol.II, p.120.

19. Conference at Steenkerke (EOA, EOCA, remnants of 1st DIM).

20. See Goutard, *op. cit.*, p.52.

21. Armengaud, *op. cit.*, p.52. Easterly retreat route: (32nd DI): Nieuwe Kerk, Kemmel, Poperinghe, Kronbecque, Stavele, Bulskamp. Westerly retreat route: (Cavalry Corps): Bailleul, Boeschepe, Watou, Houtekerque, Rexpouede. Central retreat route: (12th DIM): Nieuwe Kerk, Westeutre, Poperinghe, Proven, Hondschoote, Ghyvelde.

22. These units were. 1st DIM, 2nd DINA, 15th and 25th DIM, 4th DI, also 1st and 110th Regiments of 1st DIM, 106th Regiment of 12th DIM and the GRDI.

23. Regarding break-out attempts by this unit especially from Haubordin towards Sequedin, see Armengaud, *op. cit.*, p.48.

24. II Army Corps had difficulties here in restoring the contact between 5th and 50th Divisions. This weak spot in the Armee Corps Front was not used by the Germans. The I Army Corps artillery placed with II Army Corps fired around 5,000 rounds of medium calibre within 36 hours during this defensive fighting. Brooke, *op. cit.*, p.139.

25. On the Poperinghe–Watou line, the Cavalry Corps, like the BEF II Corps, set up an interception line behind which the remnants of First French Army could withdraw. Armengaud, *op. cit.*, p.56.

26. On 28 May at 1400 hrs, I Corps received the order from BEF HQ to go to positions between Poperinghe and Proven. For this *et seq*, Ellis, *op. cit.*, p.204ff

27. Ellis, *op. cit.*, pp.209–210, Armengaud, *op. cit.*, pp.55–56; Prioux, *op. cit.*, p.131. The Cavalry Corps stood with two light mechanized divisions at Vieux–Berquin, Neuf–Berquin and Estaire. The line of the Flanders hills was held by the British 44th Division with the help of French tanks.

28. Retreat of 44th Division at 1000 hrs on 29 May. That night the remnants of the no longer operational 2nd Division reached the area of the Dunkirk bridgehead.

29. In its attempt to break out at about 0930 hrs on 29 May the brigade was virtually wiped out – 1,000 British troops were taken prisoner, at Cassel the death toll on the battlefield was between 3,000 and 4,000. (Oral statement by Col-General (ret'd) Zeitzler to Dr K. J. Müller.)

30. Lt. Ellis, *op. cit.*, p.225: of 42nd Division only 126 Brigade; of 2nd Division only a company made up of a few remnants of 5 Brigade. On 30 May, II Corps had the following strength: 3rd Division 13,000 men, 4th Division 12,000 men, 5th Division 2 brigades each with 600 men, 50th Division 2 brigades each with 1,200 men. Details from Brooke, *op.cit*, p.146.

31. For the following see Ellis, *op. cit.*, p.179.
32. Commander-in Chief of the bridgehead was 'Admiral North', Admiral Abrial. The land troops were under the command of the General Commanding French XVI Army Corps, General Fagalde.
33. See p.123f. this book.
34. See Ellis, *op. cit.*, pp.211–212 and Brooke, *op. cit.*, pp.140, 144.
35. See Armengaud, *op. cit.*, pp.175, 180ff.
36. See Armengaud, *op. cit.*, p.190ff. These units operated over 40 Hotchkiss and Somua type tanks from the Cavalry Corps stock.
37. See Armengaud, *op. cit.*, p.193ff.
38. Some of the BEF III Corps had already been evacuated, these men having assembled on the beach for shipping out.
39. 4. Division from the sea to Wulpen (not incl.town); 3. Division from Wulpen to Bulskamp (not incl.town); 50. Division from Bulskamp to the border.

Sections 5-6

1. KTB–Pz.Gr.Kleist, 27 May 1940 and 28 May 1940
2. KTB–4., 28 May 1940.
3. KTB–4., 28 May 1940, supplement. Emphasis by author.
4. KTB–XIX Armee Korps, 28 May 1940 (see Ellis, *op. cit.*, pp.206ff and 388f), emphasis by author. In his memoirs, Guderian does not say much about the conditions in the terrain. The generally fully preserved daily reports (from May 1940) end with his observation: '...by 28 May we had reached Wormhoudt and Bourbourgville. On 29 May 1. Panzer Division took Gravelines. The conclusion to the conquest of Dunkirk was achieved without our participation however ... relieved. It [conquest of Dunkirk. Author] might have taken substantially less time if the Supreme Command had not detained XIX Armee Korps repeatedly, thereby hampering its fast triumphant advance...' From the archives at our disposal it may be inferred that Dunkirk would certainly have been conquered earlier if XIX Armee Korps operating on the north wing had got through to the coast from south of the town freely. Apparently breakdowns and the terrain held back the Korps from making such an advance. There is no getting away from the criticism by Jacques Mordals, *Guderian sur l'Aa ou le veritable miracle de Dunkerque* in: *Revue de Défense Nationale* (August/September 1955, p.196ff) of Guderian's operations even if the author's theory that Guderian was responsible for the escape of the BEF goes somewhat too far.
5. KTB–XXXXI for 25 August: Reinhardt had reported to his commanding general that the damage to his fighting vehicles was 'considerable'! Emphasis by author.
6. Bock diary, 28 May 1940 (not all emphasis by the author).
7. Description of the landscape supplied by K. J. Müller.
8. KTB–B and 18., 28 May 1940.
9. Situation Report No.336, 29 May 1940.

10. Halder diary, 28 May 1940.

11. KTB–A, 29 May 1940, author's emphasis.

12. KTB–A, 29 May 1940.

13. *Ibid*, author's emphasis.

14. 'tsch' here means 'Czech',. i.e. medium Skoda-built tanks taken over by the Wehrmacht at the annexation of Czechoslovakia in March 1939 and reclassified as PzKpfw. 35(t).

15. KTB–5., 7.Pz.Div.; KTB–XVI Armee Korps, 29 May 1940 (outlines); 8 June 1940.

16. KTB–XXXIX Armee Korps, 24 May 1940 (see Ellis *op. cit.*, p.384f).

17. LTM 38 means the Czech CKD (later known as BMM)-built tank originally designated LT 38 and acquired by the Wehrmacht at the annexation of Czechoslovakia in March 1939. Re-designated LTM 38 (Mittlere = medium) by 1940, it was later reclassified as PzKpfw 38(t) in versions A, B, C and D later that year, being considered a superior panzer to both the Panzer Mk.I and II. See Alexander Lüdeke, *Panzer der Wehrmacht 1939–1945*, Motorbuch Verlag, 4th reprint 2010, pp.32–35. (Transl.)

18. KTB–4., 30 May 1940; KTB–XXXIX and XVI Armee Korps, 28 May 1940 (files). On 24 May 1940 at 1900 hrs, 10. Panzer Division reported to XIX Armee Korps, '...troops exhausted, need a few days rest. Losses in materials, vehicles and personnel one third, in panzers easily the half...' (KTB–10.Pz.Div., 24 May 1940).

19. Jacobsen, *Fall Gelb*, p.199.

20. KTB–4., 29 May 1940: notes of 1a Staff Officer of 9. Panzer Division same day.

21. KTB–XXXXI Armee Korps, 29 May 1940.

22. KTB–XXXIX and XVI Armee Korps, 29 May 1940.

23. Emphasis by author; KTB–4., 29 May 1940.

24. See Churchill, Vol.II, *op. cit.*, p.145.

25. KTB–4., 29 May 1940 (appendix).

26. KTB–B, 29 May 1940.

27. See Halder diary, also KTB–B and KTB–18., all for 29/39 May 1940.

28. Halder diary, 30 May 1940 (author's emphasis).

29. Bock diary, 30 May 1940 (see Jacobsen, *Dokumente zum Westfeldzug 1940*).

30. The German Army did not have a 14-cm gun in either world war. The 15-cm gun or 14.9-cm howitzer were the closest to this calibre. Alexander Lüdeke, *Deutsche Artillerie Geschütze 1933–1945*, Motorbuch Verlag, 2010. (Transl.)

31. Bock diary of 30 May 1940 (see Jacobsen, *Dokumente zum Westfeldzug 1940*), emphasis by author.

32. KTB–18., 30 May 1940, for the fighting near Dunkirk see also Hubatsch, W., *61. Infantry Division, op. cit.*, p.22ff.

33. The favoured Skoda-built ex-Czech 10.5-cm cannon sK 35(t) had a maximum range of 18 kilometres typical for German guns of this calibre; it reloaded at 8 rounds per minute. Lüdeke, *Deutsche Artillerie Geschütze, 1933-1945*, Motorbuch, pp.90–91. (Transl.)

34. KTB–4., 30 May 1940 (emphasis by author).

35. See OKH Instruction, 26 May 1940, p.121. (The favoured Rheinmetall 15-cm Kanone 39 had a maximum range of 24.8 kilometres and reloaded at two rounds per minute. Lüdeke, *ibid*, p.102. (Transl.)
36. KTB–4., 30 May 1940.
37. *Ibid.* emphasis by author.
38. *Ibid.* (Outline).
39. KTB, 30 May 1940.
40. KTB–B of 30 May 1940 (emphasis by author), see also Bock diary.
41. KTB–18., 30 May 1940; Army Group B 1a No.2762/40, gKdos of 30 May 1940, 1215 hrs.
42. Halder diary, 31 May 1940: author's emphasis.
43. KTB–18.and B, 31 May 1940.
44. KTB–4., 31 May 1940.
45. KTB–B and 18., 31 May 1940.
46. KTB–18. and B, 1 June 1940.
47. Situation Report West No 342 (OKH Army General Staff, Foreign Armies West).
48. KTB–B, 1 June 1940.
49. Bock diary, 2 June 1940.
50. KTB–18., 2 June 1940 (extract), author's emphasis.
51. KTB–B, 2 June 1940.
52. Bock diary, 3 June 1940.
53. KTB–18., 3 June 1940 (extract).
54. KTB–18. and B, 4 June 1940.
55. KTB–B; Bock diary, Halder diary of 4 June 1940.

7. Planning and Execution of Operation *Dynamo*

1. See the following: Churchill, *op. cit.*, pp.77ff; Saunders, 'L'Evacuation par Dunkerque', in *Revue d'Histoire de la Deuxième Guerre Mondiale*, No. 10/11 1953, pp.119–132; Sir Bertram Ramsay, 'The Evacuation of the Allied Armies from Dunkirk and Neighbouring Beaches', in: Supplement to the *London Gazette*, 17 July 1947, *passim*.
2. Saunders, *op. cit.,* p.121.
3. Ibid, p.125.
4. Ellis, *op. cit.*, p.182, Churchill *op. cit.*, p.127.
5. See Armengaud, *op. cit.*, p.215 (18–20 May) and Ellis *op. cit.*, p.178 (20 May).
6. The figures in the text are taken from Churchill, *op. cit.*, p.145. See statistical listing, p.166ff. (this book)
7. Ellis, *op. cit.*, p.186.
8. Churchill, *op. cit.*, pp.132–133: see also telegram No.3743, 28 May 1940, Admiral North to Admiralty. 'To French Admiralty – No.3743. 1. Use of port made impossible by Luftwaffe and artillery – Stop – Connection with land severed. Sea connection very uncertain. Retreat of all-important units by sea seems to me impracticable – Stop – 2. Means of lengthening the defence seems to me in

creating a firm bridgehead of adequate size so as to protect the beaches against artillery. 3. According to the Instruction with strong air and naval protection supply to fighting troops and evacuation of superfluous troop elements using port and beaches could be attempted.'

9. See p.147f.

10. Churchill, *op. cit.*, p.133.

11. Ellis, *op. cit.*, p.212.

12. For the protection of the evacuation from 26 to 27 May, the RAF deployed 16 fighter squadrons (from 0500 hrs until nightfall); initially 9–20 machines, later in greater numbers. See Ellis, *op. cit.*, pp.185–186.

13. Ellis, *op. cit.*, p.213; Four squadrons flew operations three times on this day. 13 RAF fighters were lost. (28 May 1940).

14. 19 RAF fighters were lost on this day.

15. Saunders, *op. cit.*, p,129.

16. On 27 May 1940 from 19 hrs.

17. 'The Prime Minister to the Minister for War, the Chief of the Imperial General Staff and General Ismay', 29 May 1940, Churchill, *op. cit.*, p.133.

18. 'The Prime Minister to General Spears (Paris) for Reynaud for forwarding to Weygand', 29 May 1940, Churchill, *op. cit.*, pp.133–134.

19. Churchill, *op. cit.*, p.133.

20. *Ibid.*

21. For the political developments during the Western campaign see Müller, *op. cit.*

22. On 30 May at a conference with the three Chiefs of Staff, the Ministers of the Armed Forces and the Chief of the Imperial General Staff, Churchill urged that without fail more French had to be evacuated. Churchill, *op. cit.*, pp.134–135.

23. Telegram No.563 Cab.D.N. (R.170) – 19 May 1940, 1930 hrs.

24. Telegram No. 3844D, 19 May 1940, 2110 hrs.

25. No.1081/3/F.T. 00011/ – 20 May 1940, 2100 hrs.

26. No.6766 (R187) – 21 May 1940, 0917 hrs.

27. See also telegram No.3743, Admiral North to Admiralty on 28 May 1940 in which is stated: '…Retreat…by sea seems to me impracticable…with strong air and naval protection supply to fighting troops and evacuation of superfluous troop elements using port and beaches could be attempted.'

28. Result of this conference of Auphan was a 'Protocol regarding the Planning of the French and British Naval Authorities for the Evacuation of the French and British Troops in the Dunkirk Area': 27 May 1940, Dover.

29. On 28 May the instruction had been issued to collect naval personnel and vessels at Cherbourg and Le Havre for a 'Flottille de Pas de Calais' under Admiral Landrieu.

30. Telegram No.3743 – 28 May 1940.

31. See also telegram No.7262, 29 May 1940 1620 hrs – (R329). See also Blanchard's Order No 36 to Army Group 1which stated: 'The evacuation of the French troops will take place as according to the arrival of the necessary ships at the beach west of the Zuydcoote Sanatorium inclusively.'

32. On 28 May individual French ships evacuated 1527 men, and on 29 May 5178 men.
33. Churchill *op. cit.*, p.134.
34. Ellis, *op. cit.*, pp.229–230, see also Saunders, *L'Evacuation par Dunkerque in: Revue d'Histoire de la Deuxième Guerre Mondiale*, No.10/11, p53, pp.119–134.
35. From 30 May the enemy was in contact with the defensive belt of the bridgehead. At Furnes the Germans made two attempts to break through, but were beaten off.
36. Gort was promised supply barges loaded with water, provisions and ammunition in quantities of one third of each.
37. The instruction was received by Gort at 1400 hrs (30 May 1940) as a response to his enquiry if he should hold Dunkirk for as long as the French commander there, Admiral Abrial, wanted, or if it was his assignment to evacuate the BEF as quickly as possible. (Ellis, *op.cit*, pp.229–230) In a telephone conversation with Gort at midnight on 30 May, the Prime Minister urged the most comprehensive evacuation of French troops.
38. At Bray Dunes and La Panne, British sappers built makeshift piers using automobiles pushed into the water.
39. Ellis, *op. cit.*, pp.231–232. The connection was maintained by lorry drivers and motorcycle riders.
40. British troops made several counter-attacks; in the course of the day the Germans made only localized gains of territory.
41. Brooke, *op. cit.* p.147. This decision resulted from the suggestion of General Brooke.
42. Before this there had been an exchange of letters between Abrial (30 May) and Gort (31 May) in which the latter had announced the appointment of Barker.
43. An explanation why suddenly Alexander commanded the last of the British troops and not Barker cannot be found in the known source material. Even the official British history is silent on this point.
44. Telegram No 3810 (R366) of 31 May 1940, 1730 hrs; Abrial to General Weygand: see also telegram No.7473 (R369) of same date, 2100 hrs.
45. Sources for this Supreme Allied War Council: Session protocol in Baudouin, *Neuf Mois au Gouvernement*, Paris 1948, pp.108–114: Report by Churchill, *op. cit.*, p.96ff; Reynaud, *La France a sauvé l'Europe*, p.250ff; M. Weygand, *op. cit.*, p.145: Spears *op.cit*, Vol 1., pp.292-319.
46. A French Admiralty telegram GMT 5202 (R363) sent at 1800 hrs (31 May 1940) informed Abrial of the decisions of the Supreme Allied War Council. (R363) GMT 5202D to Admiral Nord. 'The Supreme War Council has just adopted the following resolutions: 1. Hold a bridgehead around Dunkirk with the divisions under your command and those under the British High Command in order to make possible the embarkation of Allied troops. 2. As soon as you are certain that no troops beyond the bridgehead can read the embarkation points, the troops in the bridgehead are to withdraw and embark. British troops will remain there as rearguard for as long as possible. 3. When the total evacuation of land and naval forces from Dunkirk has been accomplished, the port will be made unusable by the British Admiralty. You will advise this at the appropriate time. 4. The

evacuation of Dunkirk follows on your order.' 1805/31.5, French Admiralty. Text of the telegram of the War Minister to Alexander in Ellis, *op. cit.* p.240.

47. See additionally telegram No. 10015 (R378) of 1 June 1940, 0830 hrs following the conversation with Alexander. As a result of this telegram, General Weygand sent the CIGS telegram No.7508 (R385): 'No.7508. I request with the greatest emphasis that General Alexander remain at the side of the French troops in order to terminate the evacuation, as the British Prime Minister assured the French Minister-President yesterday. 1203/1.6. Weygand.'

48. Which the telegram No.4593-4 (R.391) of 1 June 1940, 1734 hrs, shows.

49. Churchill, *op. cit.*, p.143.

50. Telegram No 4593 (R391), 1 June 1940, 1734 hrs – para 1.

51. See Sir Bertram Ramsay, 'The Evacuation of the Allied Armies from Dunkirk and Neighbouring Beaches' (henceforth, 'Ramsay, Despatch') in Supplement to the *London Gazette*, p.3309.

52. See the assessment in Ellis, *op. cit.*, p.240: 'General Alexander's view that the intermediate line could not be held was based on his knowledge that few British troops were left to hold it and on his ignorance of the number of French troops still available for defence. In the event, as will be seen, French troops fought for about two days and held off the German attacks while about 10,00 British and some 70,000 French troops were evacuated to England. General Alexander, therefore, underestimated the time for which the immediate position could be held, but he delayed the enemy's attack on that line by holding the forward position on the Bergues–Furnes Canal for twenty-four hours after Admiral Abrial had proposed its abandonment.'

53. The British complained at the failure of French leadership, the French for their part were annoyed that the British had left them in the lurch. See following telegrams No.4538 and 4539 (R.360) of 31 May 1940, 0814 hrs: 'It is important for you to know that evacuation of the BEF has been an operation long in the preparation which has gone ahead at the expense of the necessary (good) order for the defence.' No.7618 (R408), 2 June 1940., 1345 hrs: 'Contrary to what Mr Churchill himself demanded at the Supreme War Council, the French remained behind as the last to defend Dunkirk. Thanks to their resistance the British troops could embark.' No.3834 (R419), 2 June 1940., 1610 hrs: 'para (3): This evening all British officers will leave Dunkirk, but the help of British officers is indispensable on the night of 3rd–4th in order to organize the movements to the British ships.'

54. This was the day of heaviest aerial combat for the RAF: the Luftwaffe flew their attacks in unbroken waves. Apart from the sea patrols, the RAF protective units were 3 to 4 squadrons strong. These flew eight major operations. The total of RAF losses over Dunkirk during the evacuations was 177 aircraft according to Ellis, *op. cit.*, p.243.

55. Saunders, *op. cit.*, p.132

56. The last BEF units crossed this line at 0700 hrs.

57. Per Saunders, *op. cit.*, p.132, the evacuation fleet on this day consisted of 11 destroyers, 13 passenger ships, schuyts, tugs, etc. Churchill, *op.cit* p.140 has 14 minesweepers, and a total of 44 British and 40 French-Belgian ships. At 2320 hrs the SNO reported that all British BEF troops had been evacuated.

58. Ramsay, Despatch *op.cit.*, p.3310.

59. Telegram 552D (3 June 1940, 0315 hrs)

60. For the following see Armengaud, *op. cit.*, p.285ff.

61. On the night of 3 June the Royal Navy made an unsuccessful attempt to block Dunkirk harbour. Since this was done without the knowledge of the French admiral, it caused great resentment amongst the French.

62. Telegram 543D, 2 June 1940, 2230 hrs – see also telegram No.1192 (R413), 2 June 1940 1810 hrs.

63. See p.162 this book.

64. EOCA= Elements Organiques de Corps d'Armee = Corps troops.

65. On 3 June there were about 10,000 men in the Camp de Dunes waiting to be shipped out. Additionally around Dunkirk were 10,000 to 15,000 stragglers, deserters and other soldiers who had slipped through the controls. See Armengaud, *op. cit.*, p.362.

66. Embarkation terminals: Malo Beach: units of GA.1 in the Camp de Dunes, primarily remnants of 60th Division d'Infanterie. East Mole: EOCA 16, then 12th Division d'Infanterie Motorisée, last SFF troops. West Mole: (d'Embarquetage): 32nd 68th elements of 32nd Divisions d'Infanterie forming the second rearguard.

67. The 'Ordre Particulier No 78' of XVI Armee Corps regulated on 3 June (1500 hrs) the order of embarkation, allocated the embarkation places and set the time for the embarkation to begin.

68. Towards midnight thousands of stragglers and deserters stormed the East Mole causing a riot. This interfered substantially with the evacuation.

69. Armengaud, *op. cit.*, pp.353–354.

70. See pp.164–165 this book.

71. At 1030 hrs the evacuation fleet received orders to disband.

72. The French troops left behind in Dunkirk surrendered at 0900 hrs on 4 June.

8. The German Luftwaffe operations against *Dynamo*, 26 May–2 June

1. ObdL, Ic, No.10030/40 geh,. Situation Report No.264, appdx 4; KTB–VIII Flying Korps, 26 May 1940.

2. ObdL, Ic, No.10071/40 geh,. Situation Report No.265, see also KTB–VIII Flying Korps, 27 May 1940.

3. *Ibid*; Situation Report No.266-272 (4 June 1940); KTB–VIII Flying Korps 28 May to 2 June 1940; see also Kesselring, *Soldat bis zum letzten Tag*, p.77ff.

4. Gyldenfeldt's Notes, 26 May 1940.

5. Engel's Notes, 26 May 1940.

6. Engel's Notes, 27 May 1940. Emphasis of author.

7. KTB–VIII Flying Korps, 26 May–3 June 1940, 29 May 1940. Also in general: W. Baumbach, *Zu spät*, p.108f
8. KTB–VIII Flying Korps of 1 June 1940: emphasis by author. See also hereto: Galland, *Die Eresten und die Letzten*, p.80ff: additionally Jacobsen,, *Dokumente, op. cit.*,: KTB–A, Bock diary and Halder diary, 26 May–4 June 1940 (here are some individual indications).
9. Kesselring, *op. cit.*, p.78
10. G. W. Feuchter, , *Geschichte des Luftkrieges*, Bonn, 1954, p.144.
11. Report of the study group on the History of the Air War: *Der Einsatz der Luftwaffe in der ersten Phase des Westfeldzuges 1940*, 1956.
12. See p.167ff (Situation Report ObdL, Ic), information from Lt. General (ret'd) D. B. Schmidt (18 June 1954). *Hintergründe für den Einsatz der deutschen Luftwaffe bei Dünkirchen.*
13. See Situation Report No.272 (ObdL, Ic, No.1050/40 geh.) of 4 June 1940.
14. Bryant, *The Turn of the Tide*, p.116ff.
15. Ausarbeitung *op. cit.*, (see footnote 76 above); Schmidt, *op. cit.*, see particularly Ellis, *op. cit.*, pp.181ff, 192f, 212ff, 221, 235, 243; Roskill, *op. cit.*, p.218.
16. KTB–VIII Flying Korps, 25 May 1940.
17. Notes of 1d, AOK 4, 25 May 1940. As regards the German Navy in the Dunkirk action, apart from the sinking of two British destroyers on 29 May 1940, one by U-boat the other by S-boat (motor-torpedo boat), it was unable to become involved since it lacked the necessary seaborne forces. See Jacobsen, Fall Gelb, *op. cit.*, p.170ff.

VI. Summary

1. OKH, Army General Staff. Op.Abt.(1a) NO.350/40 g.Kdos, 31 May 1940. Aufmarschanweisung (Strategic operational instruction) Rot (see Jacobsen, *Dokumente zum Westfeldzug, 1940)x*
2. For Army Group C see Jacobsen, *Dokumente op.cit*: for Italy's entry into the war; *In Africa Settentrionale: La preparazione al conflitto l'avanzata su Sidi el Barrani*, Rome, 1955, pp.43ff, 76ff.
3. See Weygand, *Rappelé au service, op. cit.*, p.249ff; Müller *op.cit* p.39ff (and the literature quoted there).
4. See Klee and Wheatley, *op.cit*; G.-L. Weinberg, *Germany and the Soviet Union*, Leiden 1954 esp. p.106ff. W. Hubatsch says with justification (in: *Sachwörterbuch zur deutschen Geschichte*, Munich 1958, p.1373 – II. World War) that Hitler's decision for a 'Campaign against Russia' conjured up 'the catastrophe for Central Europe'.
5. Also Feuchter, *op.cit*, p.71ff.
6. See the sharp criticism of Goutard, *op.cit*, p.107ff.
7. Ellis *op. cit.*, p.350f; Butler, *op. cit.*, p.190, footnote 1; Fuller, Battles, *op. cit.* p.402.
8. See above all Rundstedt in a reply to Churchill's memoirs (March 1950); also Görlitz, *op.cit*, p131; Greiner *op.cit*,. p.103f; Lossberg *op. cit.*, p.81f; S. Westphal,

in: *The Fatal Decisions*, New York 1956, p.16; P. Kleist, *Auch Du warst dabei*, 1952, p.278 *et al.* Indications also in Taylor, *op. cit.*

9. See hereto p.120f; see also the rather pertinent statements by Taylor, *op. cit.*, p.385, footnote 88.

10. See also Meier-Welcker, *op.cit*, p.298f.

11. Jacobsen, *Fall Gelb*, *op.cit*, p.66. 112ff, 145ff.

12. *Ibid*, p.44ff.

13. See also Halder and Jodl diaries, 18 May 1940.

14. See also OKH instruction, 22 May 1940 (see p.77f): Taylor *op. cit.*, p.263.

15. Primarily; Hesse, *op. cit.*, p.243; Kleist, *op. cit.*, p.278; in a certain sense also Liddell Hart in: *Military Review*, *op. cit.*, p.62. This version is based predominantly on a statement by Blumentritt (see Liddell Hart, *Jetzt dürfen sie reden*) reporting Hitler's conversation with Army Group A at Führer-HQ in May 1940: it was on this occasion that Hitler is said to have expressed his thinking in this manner. But this may not have occurred in May 1940!

16. See p.52 and p.95; opposing the 'Golden Bridges' – thesis now also; Taylor, *op. cit.* p.263.

17. For Hitler's 'England' conception: *Akten zur Deutschen Auswärtigen Politik 1918-1945*, 1956, Vol VI, p.477ff (conference protocol, 23 May 1939); Vol VII, p.461ff (Halder diary); *Fall Gelb*, *op. cit.,,* p.15ff; 59FF, SKL War Diary 27 May 1940; Supplement to Instruction No.9 (OKW/WFA Abt.No. 330/40 26 May 1940). See also Klee, *op. cit.*, p.31ff.

18. Klee and Wheatley, *op.cit.*

19. Statement by Guderian *op. cit.*, p.107 requires correction: (…resistance of Calais… had no influence on the events at Dunkirk…').

20. Rundstedt in a written statement, March 1950.

21. So also memorandum by General (Inf., ret'd) Brennecke to this author 6 July 1958.

22. Report of the study group on the History of the Air War: *Der Einsatz der Luftwaffe in der ersten Phase des Westfeldzuges 1940*, 1956.

23. Churchill, *op.cit*, Vol 2, p.144ff.

24. Wilmot, *op.cit*, p.18; also Liddell Hard, *op. cit.*

25. Churchill, *op. cit.,*, p.170ff: Bryant, *op.cit*, p.183ff.

26. Equally, H. Gackenholz in an address to the Wehrkunde Section (March 1958).

Index